FICTION

FICTION

The
Art and Craft
of Writing
and Getting
Published

MICHAEL SEIDMAN

POMEGRANATE PRESS, LTD.
LOS ANGELES   LONDON

to the members of the board, the people who ask the questions that keep me searching for answers:

noteon, gwenjo, cherchair, heartoblue, sprtcs, tb40, celeste634, casee, whitwords, debwhit, dmrkozberg, sita12345, carolstig, mmurray3m, akiker, carito, lockhorn39, tlloftin, mstschramm, espahan, zinlady, haaland300, wtnlori, phylwriter, mmpzoe, nackyb, letsdolnch, mummylynn, dborys, notchbaby, rsckab, lhart, frankin817, poetsong, bobauthor, E3429, rrandisi, twisterb, thopeb.

Acknowledgments

S olitary writer or not, it's never done alone—there are so many people who help or have helped, who've brought us to this place, this time, this manuscript. Among those I have to thank:

My daughters, Erica and Lauren, and my wife, Elisa, for the time and space in which to work and for reminding me that the work had to be done.

Ted Solotaroff, Leona Nevler, Tom Doherty, Otto Penzler, and George Gibson, for the paychecks over the years and for the lessons they've taught me about the business of publishing.

Ed Lenk, Ralph Arnote, and Chris Carey, for letting me learn what it's like to sell a book into the marketplace.

David Bradley, Frederick Busch, Reg McKnight, and Harlan Ellison, for what they've shown me about writing, and also the hundreds of writers who have entrusted their work to me as I learned my art and craft.

My agent, Kimberley Cameron and my editor and publisher, Kathryn Leigh Scott, for their faith in the project.

The members of the Green River Writers, Louisville, Kentucky, for giving me a place to work when I needed one, and for their support over the years.

And all the others—editors, writers, publishers, art directors, sales managers, marketing and promotion managers, who've contributed to what I've learned; the misjudgments and mistakes are mine, not theirs.

Finally, the writers, no matter the level of their expertise, who have asked the questions that form the basis of this book. Without them . . .

table of contents

Introduction 11

PART ONE: Writing 17

I Have This Idea 19

Getting Started 27

Some Basic Decisions About How and What 35

Begin at the Beginning 53

Developing Characters 59

The Hero's Journey 67

Theme 79

Openings 87

Scenes 101

Description 107

Dialogue 119

Point of View 135

Style and What the Poet Said 151

Some Random Thoughts on Creativity 161

Revision 169

Always Beginning 179

PART TWO: Networking 187

Networking 189

PART THREE:
The Business of Publishing 205

An Introduction to Publishing 207

The Gentle Art of Submission 211

Beginning the Process 229

Negotiating A Contract:
Getting, Giving, Whys and Wherefores 249

Marketing: Art 271

Marketing: Publicity, Promotion and Advertising 279

Marketing: Sales 289

Pub Date and Beyond 307

Introduction

t he concept was a simple one: Prepare a book that levels the playing the field, that gives you the opportunity to compete equally for a slot on a publisher's list. That means offering you as much information as possible, in one place; information about writing and about publishing, about style, technique and business. And make no mistake about it: Unless your writing is meant only for your journal, this is about business.

In writing this volume, I've drawn on more than thirty years experience in publishing, as well as my experiences as a writer and speaker. The information is based not only on what I know because I've done it (which is the only way to really know), but from questions I've been asked at conferences and workshops, that have been sent to me for my *Ask the Editor* column (which appears in the Writer's Club on AOL and at the club's website, www.writersclub.com), and from the responses to my two previous books, *From Printout to Published* and *Living the Dream*. There is another source of inspiration as well: The exasperation and frustration I've felt as I culled through the hundred or so manuscripts and proposals I receive every week, seeing the mistakes and errors in judgment, whether they are in the writing or in the format of the submission; these failings can and often do result in a virtually instant dismissal of the material and if I can help you avoid that problem alone, I'll be more than satisfied.

You are a manufacturer of a raw product, something you want publishers to use in the preparation of what they sell. Your work has to meet certain tolerances, has to be able to withstand both definable and indefinable rigors. And you have to know the intricacies of the publishers' business, the publishing process, from what they're looking for to what they're going to do after they find it.

Your process begins with the writing and all that it entails, moves on to networking and finding the help you may need—and you will need it—and then to the search for an agent and a publisher. It doesn't end with that, though: you cannot sit back once the manuscript is acquired. For all the wonderfully romantic tales about the lonely artist in the garret, this is an extremely interactive business, and you are going to have to make the time to participate in those aspects of it.

You are going to have to make time for a lot of things: For the writing, for research (of story elements and of the publishing side), for rewriting, and for selling your work before and after publication.

If you're not willing to make that commitment, and if you're not willing to accept the responsibility that goes with it, well, you probably should consider doing something else because there are thousands, maybe tens of thousands, of others who are following the same dream. Just as there is a limited amount of running shelf space in the bookstores of America, there are just so many places available on any given publisher's list. You are in competition with every other writer—professional and amateur—sitting at a keyboard. As you contemplate that fact, keep this in mind: fifty thousand new books, on average, are published every year and first novels are released every month. It can be done, and you can do it . . . if you're ready to stop dreaming and start working.

⚙   ✎   ⚙

In addition to the facts, there's a certain amount of opinion and philosophy; you'll learn as your career progresses that opinions drive a lot of what goes on: Everyone has one (or many) and you'll hear them all at one time or another and you'll choose the ones that make the most sense to you, that fulfill your needs, just as you will develop your own philosophies about the art and craft of writing. While the phrase "follow your bliss" has become rather trite and tired over the last several years, there's still more than a little value to it.

Many years ago, my parents offered me two quotes: "Know Thyself" and "To Thine Own Self Be True." They were given to me as general admonitions; I've found that they've had particular impact and importance to me as a writer and so they're given to you, now, as something to keep in mind, especially as you consider the question I'm about to ask, one of two I place before writers on a regular basis.

Why do you write, why do you want to write? The easy answer, "Because I have to," doesn't satisfy me. Some creative drive has to be there, certainly, but we do, I think, need something more, perhaps an understanding of the obsession, and I've found that the better writers, the ones I want to read again and again, do bring something more to their work.

Flannery O'Connor said that she wrote because she could and because "I don't know what I think until I read what I say." Ned Rorem said that his work was his truth. Francine Du Plessix Gray said that she wrote "for revenge against reality." Alice Adams claimed to write "in order to make sense of what seemed and sounded senseless, all around us."

You may want to write because you enjoy entertaining people with your stories. It may be that you have something to say, something of importance to express. You may want to teach or proselytize. The reason is yours and yours alone; whatever it is, I want you to spend at least a little time—the shower's a good place for it—thinking about the question, discovering your answer and keeping it in mind as you work. It will help you form your writing, choose your form, and keep you true to yourself and your goals.

The primary focus of the pages that follow will be fiction. The discussion of writing will range from the evolution of a story idea through choosing a genre (if you want to choose one), mapping out the story, and then begin exploring the elements that make up the finished piece: language, dialogue, description, character evolution, and an assortment of tips, tricks and techniques and exercises (marked with "bullets" for easy location) that will help you find the answer to the second question I want writers to answer: Why should I—as an editor acquiring books for my list or as a reader spending my hard-earned money on a book in the store—choose your work rather than any of the thousands of other titles vying for my attention?

The answer, invariably, is because your work is better than anything else available to me and the goal is to make you a better storyteller.

Once you have the manuscript ready, it is time to start the networking that's become such a necessary part of the process. We'll look at conferences, conventions, workshops, peer group organizations: all the sources of information and contacts that will help you get that finished manuscript off your desk and into the hands of the people who are going to make the decisions that will make a difference to you.

Those people are the agents, first, and then the editors. We'll examine how to go about getting an agent, what to look for, what they can, can't, won't and don't do for you, and how and why they are necessary in today's market.

Finally, you'll spend a day in a publishing house and learn what the publishing process is: how decisions are made and what happens once they are, with a tour of every department and aspect of the industry of which you want to be a part. Reasonable expectations and realities—some of which are less than pretty; what can and might be done and what, if it happens, might be considered a gift; all the day-to-day details with which you, your agent, and your editor have to live will be explained and the reasons (or, at least, the reasoning) behind them will be there for you so that nothing will come as an unwelcome surprise or shock. It's nicer when the surprises are good, isn't it? You bet!

Included here you'll also find hints and tips about contract negotiation, in case you find yourself in the position of having to deal directly with an editor: you discover what can reasonably be asked for, what to give up in return for things you want, and what is out of the question unless you've hit it big . . . in which case, of course, you won't be dealing with the problem.

Being forewarned is being forearmed. Knowing what you're going to be facing, from the day you sit down to enter those first keystrokes until the day you hold the finished, bound book in your hands, will allow you to plan for the experiences you are about to absorb.

A last thought before we begin. No one can, in honesty, make any guarantees. There's no *magick*, no alchemical formula, that will take you from here to there with absolute certainty. There are, however, ways of giving you a better than even shot, of leveling that playing field so that you go out there as an equal.

It's my hope and my intent that, when you've come to the end of this book, you'll feel—at the very least—the equal of anyone else in the game.

Michael Seidman
New York, New York
January, 1999

PART ONE

Writing

I Have This Idea ...

*a*t the corner of Central Park South and Fifth Avenue in New York City, across the street from the Plaza Hotel, a guy named Nikki sets up business every day. He's a pretzel vendor. And we have an arrangement. I order a hot one, with mustard. If there's mustard on the napkin, too, I know to unfold it, there's an idea written inside.

I've lost count of the number of times someone has said, "I have this idea for a story. Someday when I get the time . . ." We'll ignore those folks; they're really not part of anything that we're involved with. But there's another comment that comes up with equal frequency: Where do you get yours? My answer is that thing about the pretzel vendor. Harlan Ellison gets his from a hot dog stand near the LaBrea tar pits. Every writer has an answer like that; you'll develop yours soon enough.

On the flip side, one of the questions I receive with frightening frequency for my Q&A column is: I want to write, but I don't know what to write about. Do you have any ideas . . .? (In one of the wildest variations on that theme, I once received a letter from a Princeton undergraduate during my tenure as editorial director of Zebra/Pinnacle—now Kensington—Books. The kid was getting ready for summer break and decided that a good way to make money would be to write a book. Since romantic fiction was absolutely dominating the racks, that's what he was going to write. Now, if I'd just send him some ideas, a couple of plot lines, and offer an advance, he'd get right to work. The letter wreaked havoc on my already faltering respect for the Ivy League.)

In truth, writers (and all creative artists) have more than enough ideas, which is why I'm always stunned when a writing magazine offers the readers an article on *Where to Get or How to Find Ideas*. Seems to me that if you're a writer, the problem is more one of how to choose which one to go with. Trying to pinpoint where they come from is another matter. Maybe they all exist together in some Platonic place in our collective consciousness, a set of "ideals" that allow us to recognize something for what it is.

They may also come from the fact that we are always thinking, always alert, always looking. We see things and react to them and then consider what we've seen and how that thing, whatever it was, acted on us. From that combination is born the idea for a story, a tale, something we want to share with the world-at-large.

One thing is, in my experience, crucial to the process of developing ideas: Don't look for them. When I was a recruit in the Army, back in 1961, one of the courses we took was called Trainfire. It involved long walks to the rifle range, lots of sweat, sore shoulders, and long evenings spent field stripping and cleaning our M-1 Garand rifles. Well, not every evening: there was also the night sniper course. Our Trainfire officer, a young lieutenant named Jim Morris, told us something that has stuck with me since that day: "Don't stare directly in front of you; you won't see anything . . . or you'll see things that aren't there. Either is deadly. What you do, gentlemen, is watch the horizon from the corner of your eye, use your peripheral vision; that's how you'll see the movement you have to be aware of."

Yeah, fine. He ended the sentence with a preposition; still, in the mid-'80s, Jim was sitting in my office at Tor Books, a manuscript I would eventually buy in hand. Later, the Disney movie, *Operation Dumbo Drop*, would be based on one of his short stories, so who cares about prepositions? What was important, and what we have to care about, is Jim's admonition and instruction about how to look if you want to see.

There's a variation of that, a comment from Shunryu Suzuki: "If your mind is empty, it is always ready for anything; it is open to everything. In the beginner's mind there are many possibilities; in the expert's mind there are few."

The good writer is a beginner, mind open, constantly absorbing. He is not searching consciously; rather, the subconscious is filing everything. In both S-matrix theory (a collection of probabilities for all possible reactions in given particle-scattering situations) and the *I Ching, the Book of Changes*, the emphasis is on the process, not the object. The process is a progression, and the process holds as true for writers and writing as it does for electrons or nations.

That phrase—"all possible reactions"—is important: An idea is a starting point. Where does it take you, what does putting one thing into action mean in terms of other things? The question isn't as abstract as it sounds: a story is built on a series of actions and reactions, a progression; that's an aspect we'll consider later. For now, the important thing is to remember that everything changes, everything moves, and it is no different with ideas.

 ✎ 

There's no denying that we all have fallow periods, times when nothing comes together. The easy explanation, and one writers fall back on with alacrity, is writer's block.

I'm in something of a minority position with my feelings about that. I don't think ideas dry up or go away, I don't think a creative person hits a wall, unless it is like the wall marathoners come up against at some point in a race and that, as I've experienced it, is more of a membrane than something solid: You can push through it.

More often than not, based on observation and experience, writer's block is laziness, weariness or fear. The laziness is easy to understand: it's so much easier to just watch television, surf the Web, or read (well, call it research, why don't we? That takes some of the edge off of it).

The weariness comes from dissatisfaction: The story just isn't reading right, doesn't sparkle; the feedback we're getting isn't properly reinforcing; and all those damned rejection slips. Why bother? The fear is a bit more complex. There's fear of failure; that stems from some of the same factors causing the weariness. There's fear of success: Lots of people are afraid of doing well, of having to live up to what they've done; as in *Wayne's World*, the idea "I'm not worthy" is too much with us.

Any or all of these mindsets—separately or together—feeding on each other, create a situation in which sitting alone, watching words that strike us at the moment as being meaningless and just *wrong*, is difficult if not impossible. So we stop . . . blocked.

I guess an analyst can deal with the psychological factors involved, help us work through them. I've come up with some exercises, though, that are fun (well, at least mostly enjoyable and painless) and easy and that can ease you back into a frame of mind that allows you to work.

✐ The first one takes a couple of minutes to set up, but it's something you should prepare now, against the day you might need it. Take a few sheets of lined paper (or, work at the word processor; there's something about just sitting and typing that helps free you) and create fifty or sixty-three word phrases: An article, a verb, a noun. So, you might have: "The cat purred, the man sat, a dog ran—" whatever combinations come to mind. Don't think about them too much in the construction, just put them together.

After you have enough of them, cut each phrase from the

paper and fold it, fortune cookies for the imagination. Put the pieces in an envelope and keep it all where you can find it when necessary.

Come that day, reach into the envelope, take out a strip, type (or write) the words you find there, and then just keep typing. Spend about a half hour at it: don't think about what you're writing, don't correct anything, cross anything out. You're not being judged; what you are doing is allowing yourself to string sentences together, what you're doing is writing, even if it isn't on the piece that's giving you trouble, or the one you can't start.

Don't be surprised if, somewhere in the middle of the session, a story idea begins to form or that a sentence leads to another and another that has nothing to do with where you began but definitely points you in the direction you want to go.

I tried this exercise first in a class being taught by Rex Burns, of the University of Colorado (and an Edgar Award-winning author). He used, "The dog ran . . ." and this is what I came up with:

> The dog ran through the camp; tomorrow or perhaps the next day she would be part of the feast celebrating Skunk's return from his vision quest. Walks Alone knew that; Skunk knew only that a vision hadn't come.
>
> He sagged against the thongs holding his body to the lodgepole he had carried to this place four days ago and felt the searing sun, both thirst and hunger baked out of him. The raven which had been keeping him company launched from its perch on the buffalo skull at the seeker's feet, its wings whirring and whistling in the still air, wheeling

I had been considering doing a sequel to my story, "The Dream that Follows Darkness," which had appeared in *Twilight Zone* magazine, and was having trouble finding the starting place; I'd never tried to do a follow-up. The magazine folded and the story, or the bits and pieces of it that are finished, live on only in my files.

But they're there, against the day I can use them. The important thing here is that the exercise got me going. (Another important thing: never throw anything away, it may come in useful at some other time.)

✍ A slight variation on the same theme is suggested by Lawrence Block; he used it in his Write-for-Your-Life classes. Instead of using the three word phrase, Larry recommends using complete sentences. There's a difference in how you will approach "the man sat" and "the man sat, hearing the creak of the old couch under his weight."

✍ A suggestion for both these exercises: rather than creating the starting words yourself, have someone else write or choose the sentences; if you do it, your mind will have already started to work on them. So, ask a writing partner or spouse or anyone to go through a book or two, pulling out sentences they liked (or disliked; you may enjoy the challenge of improving on what's been published) or phrases that you can use. When you need them, they'll be fresh . . . and you'll be ready to run with it.

Those are simple exercises; the next ones are a bit more complex and challenging, but can be lots of fun. Well, I enjoy them, and that's good enough for me.

✍ First up: Playing spy and using circumstantial evidence. This is an exercise I developed with middle school students when I was doing a workshop for them and the results were wonderful. What we did was go to a supermarket or a mall and watch people. Based on what they were buying, we began to project: What would they put in their cart next? Based on what they were buying, what could we reasonably say about who they were, what their families were like; it's remarkable, really, what you can learn about people that way. The stories the kids wrote during the next session were vibrant and creative; it helped get them away from the very autobiographical things they had been doing.

✍ Now, try the same thing at a bookstore; you may not come up with personality profiles, but you'll certainly learn a lot about readers' buying habits and that information certainly won't be wasted for you.

There are a couple of bonuses to this exercise: The development of three-dimensional characters is extremely important; creating (or stealing) lives, based on what you are observing, helps you, the writer, to create more fully rounded people for your stories (matters we'll be discussing later). At the same time, of course, it stretches your imagination and forces you to be creative during those fallow periods.

And there's this: the exercises force you to observe. Among the failings that can bring a manuscript back to you is a sense on the part of the editor reading it that the writer has no idea whatsoever of what is going on in the world. Characters act as they need to for a story, not the way people do, and thus they come across as contrived, unnatural; they move in the spaces created for them not as you or I really do, but unvisualized. Their language (spoken language as well as body language) in those manuscripts, is "made up"; not created in the sense that a writer creates all, but without any echo of the conversations that advance our lives. Since dialogue is going to be used to advance your story, it has to fall naturally on the ear. Spending some time watching people will help you take the images you have as your characters and, like Michelangelo, chip away everything that isn't David.

The last exercises will be gone into in a later chapter, but they deserve passing mention here. They are visualization exercises, ways of releasing your mind and allowing it to work on writing problems (*where is this scene going, anyway?*) and let you project the action (as on a movie screen or in dreams) so that you can transcribe it. They'll combine autohypnotic and meditation techniques that I've learned and use; I don't doubt that you have your own experience with forms of these exercises; if you know them already, use them as writing tools—they're as important as your keyboard or your pen.

Socrates is credited with saying that the first step in knowledge is to know that we don't know. Our ideas come from being aware of what is going on and wanting to know more about it; knowing what's going on doesn't mean understanding it, and all the great novels share two things branching from a common root: A desire to know more, to answer a question, to discover and, second, timelessness. The questions we have are always with us. Every generation rediscovers the questions and seeks the answers . . . even if, as parents, we shake our heads and wonder why the kids just won't listen.

What you see, and the questions posed are what, ultimately, you write about. As long as you remember that you're always beginning, you'll be fine.

And so will your story.

Getting
Started

Okay, you've got your idea, have a grasp on what you want to do? Does that mean you're ready to begin? Maybe. I've found that there are still a few decisions to be made.

Because I have—for more years than I have fingers to count them on—been associated with category fiction (as an editor, at any rate) it's become painfully obvious that far too many writers take a rather helter-skelter approach to what they're doing. Bending to the whim of every fad that comes along, racing after every trend, they produce work that has a vague relationship to what they're hoping to accomplish, but all too often misses the point of the category. It is, really, the same reason the majority of new businesses fail: A lack of research, of understanding what it is the public wants or needs. Another reason businesses fail is because of underfunding.

In the case of writers, there are several publics to be served: there are the agents, who want to place your work; there are the editors, who need your product so that they'll have something to sell; and there are the readers, the most volatile group of all, the one to which we're all beholden. Unfortunately, speaking to seven friends and two guys down at the diner doesn't really function well as market research: We can *never*—any of us—count on them to buy books.

No truly effective method has ever been developed that will tell us what the reader wants. Generally, we use bestseller lists (national and local) to give us some idea of what interests people, but they're subject to so many flukes and chaotic twists that no one really wants to bank on them; we use them as guidelines.

Which brings us back to getting started . . . somewhere. The effective genre writers are those who read the genre. It seems obvious, but the obvious and what happens aren't always that closely related. Without fail, at one writer's conference or another, someone will approach an editor or agent and ask, "What's selling? What are you looking for?" (There's a word that should be appended to that second question: *today.*)

Now, it doesn't seem to matter what these people have been writing, or what they read, or what they like, particularly; if we say something, they answer: "Oh, I can do that." Odds are, though, that they can't, and I base those odds on seeing the work they produce. If you don't read mysteries, you are not—usually—going to be able to produce one that will appeal to anyone in the food chain. It's like that kid from Princeton I mentioned earlier: it isn't simply a matter of reading one and then going ahead and doing it, or of having someone spoon-feed you the parameters; it has to be part of you, and even your success in one area is no guarantee that you'll be able to do it in another.

Another question to ponder: do you even want to write in a category? Most people who do, do so for one of two reasons: first, they're hooked on the genre, a given necessity or, second, it is perceived as an easier and more lucrative route to follow. After all, with the number of category titles released each month—in both hardcover and paperback—there is an obviously (and, I'd warn, relatively) voracious market. With more potential outlets for the novel, it seems to make sense that a writer stands a better chance of selling. Uh-huh, and don't forget that the competition for those slots is more hectic because there are more people trying to get in the door.

(At a conference in Virginia, a woman asked which was selling better, fiction or non-fiction. Then—and today, as I type these words—non-fiction seemed to be dominating. She was going to decide what to write based on my answer. Being a cranky sort, I asked instead how she was going to make her decision: selling better or less competitive? My friends then dragged me away from the microphone. I have to admire her confidence but still have to wonder: has she sold anything yet?)

Research, then, is going to be a key factor in your decision, just as research for content is going to be vital once the process begins. As for the underfunding, there's a lot to be said for those who advise that you don't give up your day job, at least not yet. The average writer (and that includes all of us: essayists, short story writers, novelists, magazine freelancers . . . all who call themselves writers) may earn about $7,500 a year from his efforts.

You're entering a quicksilver marketplace generally. Magazines come and go, publishers are swallowed by others, distinctions between houses blur. Once upon a time, it was possible for a reader (and for editors and writers) to know that a book from such-and-such a house meant that it would fit certain literary, qualitative criteria; now, with certain exceptions not only have the publishers become homogenized, so has the fiction they publish (Farrar, Straus, & Giroux still means something; what does E.P. Dutton mean?). *Most* books we find could be published by anyone; I don't think that bodes well for the industry or for us, but it is something we have to be aware of because it will either broaden our chances or narrow them painfully. Keep in mind, though, that some editors and publishers are fighting the trend and creating niches, carving out little hidden places in the wall because they either believe in writers who write for story or because they know that they can't compete with some of the bulldozer conglomerates either in terms of advances or rack and shelf space.

For the writer, that means doing something that short story and articles writers have been doing all along: reading the product.

It really isn't enough to know that a publisher does a category; you have to read the books they release and determine whether your writing is suitable to a particular list. A simple example: As the mystery editor at Walker and Company, I receive about a hundred submissions a week (manuscripts—even though we don't accept unsolicited manuscript submissions—proposals, query letters) and a good ninety percent of them can be rejected out-of-hand because they don't meet our requirements. Our list consists of 70,000 word, series-oriented, play fair mysteries. (That's easy to discern; the editorial tastes that I bring to the schedule are more subtle, though they should be obvious after careful reading.)

That's a thought that'll crop up a lot in these pages; it represents another choice you have to make, whether you want to be an individual or a clone, whether you want your book to be noticed because it is different or because it is the same as everything else on the shelf. And given that I bother to mention it, my choice is clear: Do you want to be a writer that sets the hallmark and have others trying to do the impossible—writing in your style—or are you satisfied if your work is found firmly in the tradition of someone else's?

Given that description of my list, why would anyone send me a 150,000 word thriller? Why would they send a book that is clearly a one-off, a title meant to stand alone? Why would they send horror, or romantic suspense, or whatever it is that I'm not doing? I don't know; I just put a form rejection note in the SASE and make it go away.

How do you go about doing the necessary market research? Well, while you're in the bookstores doing that customer-watching exercise, look at the books on the shelves. Check the publishers' logos and see what we're doing and then buy the books (well, as many as you can), and read them. Get a feel for the content: are they written at an eighth grade level or for a more literate audience? How does the publisher seem to treat things like sex, violence, and mature subject matter? Does the publisher do books with international settings? Do they do books with historical content? What do they seem to represent, even in a world of read-a-likes? Editors reveal tastes, biases, prejudices, the gamut of emotional and intellectual response to all aspects of whatever it is you're doing, and you have to know those things. Mistakes are costly.

Another approach, and one with reward down the line: Become friendly with an independent bookseller. Hang out in the store, buy books there, talk to the owner/manager/clerk—to whomever you have access. Don't let them feel they're being used or interrogated (one of the reasons you're going to make purchases). Ask them about business, about what they see: to a great extent, the bookstores dictate a lot of what is getting published, they are the places in which trends are first discovered and they let the publishers know through returns, through a lack of support for new titles, and by telling the sales reps, flat out, "that stuff just don't fly no more."

I'm not going to do anything dumb here and tell you how to go about establishing a relationship; that ball's in your court. But if you do it well, the dealer may let you look at the publishers' catalogues in his file, allowing you to know what's coming up. (The catalogues are probably also available at local libraries—and librarians are among the most helpful people around—and you can always call or write to a publisher requesting them.)

Remember: the books you see on the new release shelves were probably acquired at least a year earlier, maybe as much as two years. Because publishing is, by and large, a very reactive business, what is being acquired today could be different, even within a category. Several years ago, the mystery shelves would have been dominated by novels about female private eyes; they've fallen off a bit as the market leveled and tastes changed. One of the problems of a less than proactive publishing industry is that when something is perceived as working, everyone rushes to fill their lists with whatever that something is. Quality invariably suffers. And the readers let us know by leaving the books on the shelves. There may be fifty ways to leave a lover, but a book left on the shelf becomes a return, and returns don't help anyone . . . but for the fact that they tell us something isn't finding favor.

In view of that time warp, you'll want to do some other things to try to keep on top of what the editors are looking for on any given day. (And it is volatile enough that needs can change from day to day.) *Writer's Digest* and *The Writer*, two of the leading magazines in the field, both publish market reports on a monthly basis and both publish books—*The Writer's Market* and *The Writer's Handbook*—as well as genre-specific guides. Again, the risk is that by the time you read them, the information could be outdated. My personal favorite, *The Gila Queen's Guide to Markets*, is a monthly magazine that does a pretty good job of keeping things updated.

Every major genre has a peer group organization that allows associate memberships; you don't need to have published to join and learn. If you've decided to pursue a writing career in a category, join the group. In addition to market information, you'll find tips in the newsletters, group-sponsored workshops and conferences, and general information that can prove of value.

Each category also supports a number of magazines (some firmly in place while others seem to come and go) that also have news and gossip from within the genre community: the movements of editors, trends as seen the by the publishers of the magazine, new title information (along with critical comments: "Oh, no, not another vampire on the plantation novel." Or, "Finally, a vampire on the plantation novel"). I'm not suggesting that you take any of the information as gospel; just that you be aware of it and use it as you see fit.

Conferences and conventions are important parts of a writer's life, and we'll look at them closely a bit later. For now, remember that it is at these gatherings that editors and agents are on display, ready and willing (until exhaustion sets in) to answer questions and tender advice. They range from small, local gatherings put together by a writer's group to international events. They take place throughout the year, in every region of the country, and if you can get to a couple, you'll never regret the experience.

If you can link up with a critique group or workshop in your neighborhood, you not only get the support (to my mind sometimes too enthusiastic) of fellow writers, but the insights they've gained through the submission process. Most groups have published writers as members, and they are more than happy to share information based not on hearsay (of which there is far too much), but experience.

Finally, in addition to the magazines and guidebooks, there are two other essentials. They're both very expensive, but the members of a writer's group can pool resources to obtain them; failing that, they're both available at all libraries.

The first is *Literary Market Place*, or *LMP*: It is a directory to every book and publishing related person and organization imaginable. It lists all the publishers, the editors (well, not all of them, but the majority), agents, newspapers and magazines, freelancers, organizations, prizes and awards. It is, ultimately, indispensable.

Second is *Publishers Weekly*: It's filled with ads addressed to booksellers, reviews of upcoming titles (about three months in advance of release date), articles on the state of the business, on categories and forms of writing, general essays, interviews, people . . . *PW* is the bible of the book business. The primary market is the bookseller, and there will also be articles pertaining to that aspect of the industry. Knowing what they're facing, knowing what publishers are saying (whether it is the truth or not; ads are, after all, hyperbole designed to entice purchase), and getting a sense of how certain books are being envisioned before publication (and comparing those feelings with what happens after the book is released) is alternately enlightening and frightening, always interesting, and—all of it taken together—vital if you're going to approach writing as a business. For our purposes, it is.

There's another resource available; unfortunately, it's impossible to speak about with any sense of certainty because it is changing regularly; that's the Internet. I'm not one of those who thinks that a writer has to be on-line; we've managed for centuries without it. However, as a used-wisely tool, there's a world of information at your fingertips. There's also a lot of misinformation, and a lot of opinion that may not be based on anything more solid than one person's experience in one place.

Publishers have websites that can be used for ordering and that often contain catalogue and other information that may prove useful. The major on-line services all have chat rooms and bulletin boards and some even have classes, aimed at the writer. (I run a bulletin board on AOL that evolved from columns that I do for the Writer's Club, and have been known to stop in and visit a chat room now and then. I don't do that often because I've found them rather less cost effective, in terms of time spent, than I'd like, but that's a personal thing.)

If you're already involved with the Web, you know what's there, in fact and in potential. If you're not, after the first, bleary-eyed week of discovering how far a link can take you, you'll settle in and start using it, rather than playing with it. It's so easy to forget about the writing while the "research" is going on; so, if you want to start playing, do it between projects.

Now, the next step before we step off the ledge and begin writing. . .

Some Basic Decisions about How and What

Where do we begin? There are some decisions that have to be made here, and the first is: What is it we're writing? You might even want to give some consideration to this conundrum: Do we begin by choosing a genre or form, or do we begin by writing and worrying about the market afterward?

Most people, when they're beginning, do so by pinpointing the audience, first, so it seems to make a certain amount of logical sense for us to discuss the different forms of adult fiction.

There are several easily identifiable genres, as we use the term: mystery, science fiction, fantasy, romance, horror, western, and variations on the theme—suspense, space opera, anthropological, sword & sorcery, historical, shapechangers and novels of the American frontier are respective subsets of the mainstay categories. If you're writing what you've been reading and loving all along, you know what's up in each; if you're exploring (and we'll keep reiterating the risks of that; taking risks is fine as long as you know the penalties) some basic guidelines will be necessary, and they'll be following along, shortly.

When you get right down to it, every form of writing is a genre, bounded by certain iconographies that are identifiable and expected by the readers: a *New Yorker* short story is not the same as one that will appear in *Cosmopolitan*; there are different approaches, just as there are between a cozy mystery and a hard-boiled one. Published guidelines may be inherently the same, but an understanding evolving from reading, reading and more reading is what will help make the differences clear. With that thought in mind, we'll look at the categories as they've become defined by the Association of American Publishers, tradition, and the publishers themselves.

When I first started buying books on a regular basis, I'd go into the bookstore (it was right next to Carnegie Hall and specialized in paperbacks) and run my eyes along the spines until I found an author's name I knew or had heard, a title that struck my fancy, or something else that caused me to pick up the book and begin the process that led to a purchase. Back then, in the mid to late '50s, there was nothing on the spine of the book to indicate what it was in the genre sense; there may have been some grouping in some stores, but it was done by the owner of the shop. As a reader, I was able to recognize certain titles and specific authors as being mystery or science fiction (those were the categories I read, then); otherwise, everything was simply a novel. Ah, for the good old days.

Today, the spine of every paperback is "slugged" to give both the person doing the shelving and the reader an immediate knowledge (still, if it says mystery, does that mean cozy, hard boiled, police procedural?) of what the book is. From there, it was an easy step down to labeling the shelves: We can go into the bookstore, go right to the section that represents our interests, make our choices, and leave. Too many of us do that, I think, thus missing out on a lot of fine reading; we don't even see the other books except as a flash of color as we walk by them.

Most of those books we're passing up are slugged Fiction. That's the broad mainstream of writing, all those books that don't fit (or are purposefully not put) into a genre slot. They may be category books that have transcended genre or they may be books written with the broadest possible audience in mind; they may be written rather simply and straightforwardly or with more complexity; they can be carefully plotted or loosely told tales; realistic, surreal, picaresque: the variations are as many as are the ideas and needs of the writers. Some will be (or become) classified as literary novels, post-modern, metafiction, magic realism. The field of literary criticism creates new tags and movements as the need arises. What is important for you to know is this: If you can conceive of it, there is a place for it.

For lots of cultural and sociological reasons, people will deny that they read a particular category: Romances are only for . . . Only lonely kids read science fiction . . . Those same people make bestsellers out of books like *The Bridges of Madison County* or *Jurassic Park*. A large percentage of the novels written by Joyce Carol Oates are, nominally, mysteries (and more blatantly so when she writes as Rosamond Smith), and it approaches the absurd to say that Patricia Cornwell doesn't write mysteries, period. Something about those writers makes them appeal outside of the more limited genre market: it can be storytelling, it can be timelessness, it can be good luck (hey, you can't discount the impact of Dame Fortune).

Oates was never sold as a genre writer, Cornwell was. Like others who have broken out, the success of her Scarpetta series didn't begin with marketing; it began with critical response and word of mouth, the two most effective selling tools available to us and both completely dependent upon outside forces; no one can create them for you, they just happen. Once the ball starts rolling, momentum keeps it going, forever or until the readers—fickle souls—change their minds. Her success, and that of other writers who have moved from category to mainstream, is the golden ring on the genre merry-go-round.

Mainstream also makes up the bulk of what has come to be known as midlist fiction: it's expected to do better than the categories (with the possible exception of romance, which—at least in paperback—is the dominating force in the fiction market today), but at the same time, there's no bottom line demand that they become bestsellers; if they sell, in hardcover, between 15,000 and 25,000 copies, the publisher is satisfied. Of course, the possibility that it will cross that line, the way *Snow Falling on Cedars* or *Cold Mountain* did, is always in mind and, if word of mouth is good—or if Oprah Winfrey decides that the book is right for her—anything can happen.

So, as a writer, the focus on the wider audience has much to recommend it. There are some drawbacks, though: the competition is stiffer, the odds of being found in the middle of all the new fiction are not with you, and—today—midlist is considered to be in trouble. Because there are so many books competing for what has become, much to our misfortune, limited reading time, your manuscript has to stand out in one way or another: brilliant writing, powerful storytelling, or clear appeal (with potential for more) to the marketplace. We'll look at the various financial and other problems facing midlist writers when we talk about the publishing process (that's where the decision gets made, really; your idea of what you may have produced doesn't really have all that much to do with what the editors and publishers decide); for now it's enough to know that mainstream fiction is fiction that anyone might want to read.

Literary fiction is, well . . . I don't know that anyone has bothered to come up with a working definition, at least not in terms of what publishers do. One writer, Donna Kozberg, related this story, which serves us with some insights. While speaking to the teacher she worked with while pursuing an MFA several years ago, the question of literary fiction came up. The professor's comment: that's what you write while you're in your MFA program; once you grow up, you just write.

I don't know any professional writer who sits down with the conscious thought of writing "literature." It's something that happens, a result of how the writer sees the world, the risks she's willing to take, or an experiment in storytelling that she wants to try. If it works, and if it sells to a publisher, and if critics take notice of it once it is released, that's wonderful. The market is, unsurprisingly, small and, if there is any truth to the theory that reading is an elitist activity (because only that undefined elite has the time to read, and read carefully), that's where you'll find your audience. Literary experimentation can be successful. David Foster Wallace's *Infinite Jest* is one recent example of an experimental novel that became a bestseller. (How many of the purchasers finished reading it, however, is another question.)

Today, more than literary, I think the issue has become one of literacy. In a publishing atmosphere in which writers are advising those trying to break in to limit themselves to chapters of no more than ten pages (because of the sound byte mentality and the limited attention span that goes with it) and to never use words of more than three syllables, the thoughts of using language to its fullest, of telling stories that are not completely linear, of using dialogue that doesn't drive the plot but, rather, aids in character evolution, are being discarded in favor of a simplicity (and simple-mindedness) that leaves people stunned when confronted by a novel of ideas. They call it, as bestseller Clive Cussler has, "literary crap." Others, a bit more forgiving, call it art, but say it with a sad shake of the head.

I tend to call it fiction, and say it has its place along with every other form of storytelling that allows the writer to do what storytellers have done since that first huddle around the campfire: entertain the tribe with tales, with the myths of the people, that serve, at the same time, to explain just what's going on around them.

The manner in which you decide to tell your tale should depend only on this: it is the way that makes you comfortable, puts you at ease. Writing is hard work; there's no reason to make it more difficult for yourself by trying to write what you think the broadest market is demanding. Since there are no guarantees that can be offered for your success under any conditions, you might as well be true to yourself as you move from once upon a time to the end.

✑   ✑   ✑

Category, genre, pulp or, as the late John Gardner called it in *The Art of Fiction*, "drugstore fiction," is where it all began. The tales of the knights were called *roman*; novels, romances, and all those categorized books today are lineal descendants of those tales. (A case can also be made for them having their roots in the Bible, and Otto Penzler, bookseller, publisher and critic, has said that *Grimm's Fairy Tales* also deserve some credit.)

The Grail hunt, which is at the heart of the tales of chivalry, is present in all contemporary fiction, and most obviously in the genres: each of them has a search for something—love, justice, peace—at its core. The big difference is that the knights never did bring the Grail back to the King's court; in successful category fiction, it is always found. The readers demand it, and we do it.

The knights' search—and struggle against overwhelming odds—took them into fantastical landscapes, filled with dragons (I love Tolkien's comment: it never pays to leave a dragon out of your considerations, especially if you happen to live near one) and other monsters. Now consider the traditional genre novel: the hero or heroine is placed in a setting most of us never see, be it the surface of a distant planet, the mean streets of a naked city, the antebellum South, or the buffalo-darkened plains of a frontier about to be conquered. These are, for most of us, fantastical landscapes as remote as any blasted plain in the Fisher King's domain.

In the course of the hero's search, he will do battle against monsters real or imagined and it is a fight that lasts throughout the story; death (or worse) awaits at every turn of the page. The quest, whatever it is, and whether expressed or understood, drives the action, is the story; from the pen of a better storyteller, there may even be a moral or lesson, never stated, simply, suddenly made clear.

Homer was the Charles Frazier of his day (actually, that should probably be put the other way round: *Cold Mountain* owes more than a little to *The Odyssey*); Shakespeare the Tom Clancy of his . . . and maybe the Joan Collins, too. (These aren't qualitative judgments, just parallels in terms of public acceptance and importance.) We really don't know which of today's popular writers is going to be studied, much less remembered, a hundred years from now; one thing is certain, though: if we don't do it well, we can pretty much count on not being part of some future canon of world literature.

And that's important to remember, always: most of those classic authors we study were not sitting at their desks thinking that they were creating something timeless: they wanted to entertain their audiences, make a few pence, and enjoy themselves. We remember them because they told their stories well, study them because they did something "different" in their categories (Milton's rhyme scheme, for instance, in *Paradise Lost*), and can read them with appreciation today because what they were writing wasn't fixed in a period so firmly that later generations can't understand the situations or care about the characters. *Pygmalion*, *Romeo and Juliet*, *Great Expectations*, and other works have been adapted to modern dress and lost little or nothing in the process.

Do you remember the song, "Is That All There Is?" as sung by Peggy Lee? Maybe not, but the title tells you everything you need to know about what's coming next. We're told that the children of the '60s grew up worrying about The Bomb; today's Baby Boomers are worried about whether Social Security will be there for them when they're ready for it; we watched a war from beginning to end on CNN—everywhere we turn, it seems, we're confronted with terror, trial and travail writ large.

Writers of popular fiction, of category fiction, look at the question, is that all there is? and say, No. While much mainstream fiction follows the classic lines of tragedy, genre fiction always end positively and that is, in no small part, the reason people read it. It doesn't matter whether we read mysteries (which seem to sell better in times of national distress, especially economic), a romance, a science-fiction adventure, we can be certain that the author will leave us reassured. The perp will be captured, love will out, the earth will be saved.

In that sense, all genre fiction is the same story; no matter which category you choose, in addition to whatever guidelines and formulæ are in place, you have an obligation to your reader to offer that bright spot, that reassurance. I have, over the years, edited genre novels that have toyed with that rule and while many of them received excellent reviews, there's always been a negative rumble in the background. In one case, *Blind Side*, by Dave Klein, my brother-in-law called me and said that while he'd continue to read Dave's non-fiction (he's a sports writer), he'd never again read one of his novels because it left him feeling hopeless. (If the book had been released as fiction, rather than suspense, no one would have commented on the tragic ending; one of the leading reasons people claim not to read contemporary, mainstream fiction, is because they don't want to risk that disappointment.)

The popularity of categories is always changing: there may be a glut on the market, as happened with horror, or the core readership may have vanished, as happened with the traditional western. There's also a theory that these things are cyclical; give something a seven year rest and it will come back. (You aren't going to wait around for it, though; can't trust those theories.)

There are how-to guidebooks available for writing in any genre, so I won't go into it in detail here; if you're thinking of writing in a particular category, editors are going to take it for granted that you read in it, understand it, are in a real sense, part of it. But, as an overview:

Mystery

The mystery novel is what the mystery novel is: different things to different people. For most, it means a playfair puzzle: a sleuth (amateur, private eye, law enforcement officer) attempts to solve a crime worth solving (usually a murder). The clues are presented fairly, so that the reader has an equal opportunity with the detective to arrive at the solution: it is a game between the author and us; the point of the game is misdirection. Just as when we watch a magician, we want to think that we know how the illusion is done but are disappointed when we're right, we want the mystery novelist to let us think we've figured out whodunit, and then discover we're wrong. That's a strict constructionist's definition. But crime fiction (a more appropriate label for the genre), is more inclusive.

John leCarré's espionage novels, the thrillers of Robert Ludlum, John Grisham's courtroom melodramas . . . they all fall under the general rubric of mystery. There are crimes, or the threat of crimes, and the story is about solving the mystery or preventing the crime. The big difference, to my mind, is this: in a mystery, we never know more than the sleuth; in suspense, we usually know as much as the antagonist. Mysteries *qua* mysteries have a limited point of view—that of the detective; the suspense novel has a much broader perspective.

Unarguably, the most popular form in mystery fiction is the amateur detective. The character has no particular forensic training and generally uses his or her knowledge of people, and an ability to see things that others miss, to arrive at the solution. Usually, these novels tend to be non-violent, non-graphic, at worst rated PG.

The private eye novel, most often written in the first person, is considered grittier, harder edged, hard-boiled, following on Raymond Chandler's thought that Dashiell Hammett put crime back on the mean streets, where it is really happening. (The debate as to which is more realistic is on-going and will never end.)

As the name indicates, the police procedural deals with law enforcement at work. The research necessary is demanding: one of the reasons Ed McBain turned New York City on its side and renamed it Isola was to avoid issues of "reality": whether dealing with Miranda warnings, getting warrants for a wiretap, or the hierarchy of a precinct, if you're going to write procedurals and set them in actual places, you have to know how the agency you're following really works. (My vote, by the way, for the most realistic form of crime novel, goes to the procedural. It is also the least popular, generally: one of the reasons people read crime fiction is to avoid the realities of the newspaper headlines and to reaffirm for themselves the proposition, as P.D. James puts it, that we live in a rational universe. That is another debate, entirely.)

In the last few years, the historical mystery has become extremely popular, and they can be set in periods as widely varied as pharaonic Egypt, ancient Greece and Rome, the Victorian period, or any other era that interests an imaginative writer. Historical accuracy is called for (no fingerprints allowed in the *agora*); also necessary is a sense of which times are of interest to the readers. That's a tough call for the writer and publisher both, and the risks involved may make you want to think twice about trying it. If the book's good enough, we'd like to think that it won't matter, but given, for instance, the lack of interest in the 1940s, I don't think any publisher would run to try a series set during the war years. At the same time, just because a series set in ancient Rome is working, it doesn't mean that another one in the same era will be successful.

This still leaves a lot of room for a writer to play in: *Snow Falling on Cedars*, for example, does have strong mystery elements, and found lots of fans among mystery readers (who then argued about whether it was "really a mystery"); and those mystery writers who have "transcended genre," like Sue Grafton or Robert B. Parker or Patricia Cornwall, see their new novels released as "fiction," but still have a readership base in the genre.

As with any category, lines are often blurred: many mystery publishers also publish romantic suspense, a novel in which a woman (generally) is placed in jeopardy, and eventually gets out of it while also finding love. To my mind, these books aren't crime novels (and they're most often not mysteries: the solution isn't arrived at through deduction, but by happenstance) because the emphasis is on the romantic relationship. And that brings us, naturally, to:

Romance

This is the most popular category in terms of readership: the last figures I saw indicate that close to forty-nine percent of new paperback releases are classified as "romance." (It is also a genre that seems to be primarily paperback; though there are some hardcovers published, they are treated as women's fiction, a broad area that includes any book deemed to have women as its major market. That doesn't mean that men won't read Wally Lamb's *I've Come Undone*; only that they're not expected to.)

As with most categories, there are subsets: the Regency romance, the gothic, the historical, the contemporary, the western, romantic suspense . . . each has its adherents and fans, and variations on the theme crop up with regularity. If the gothic falls off in popularity (as it has today), it's replaced by reincarnation romances or angelic romances or . . . . The adjectives pretty much explain what the subject matter is.

Just about every mass market publisher has slots for romance on its list; they also have pretty strict guidelines; if it's an area you're interested in, it's vital that you get in touch with the publishers and find out exactly what they're looking for, not only because of the rigidity, but because the market, and therefore the needs, change rapidly.

And there's this: because the market does reinvent itself so regularly, and because the readers often seem to be buying the books by the pound, the publishers are always looking for new authors. At the same time, supply and demand plays another role: competition at every level is stiff—whether we're talking about shelf space or space on the list, everyone is battling for position. For you, as a writer, it means that advances may be lower than you'd like, and sales might be as well—there are, simply, too many books. (And that isn't a problem only in this genre; when something is perceived to be working, publishers overindulge.)

Romance authors, as is the case elsewhere, can and do break out. Danielle Steel and Rosemary Rogers are the two I always think of who have moved into hardcover and gone mainstream; women who wouldn't think of reading a romance novel (well, that's what they say; every category has its closeted readership) will read them.

An observation: because there are so many people vying for a fixed number of slots, I've noticed scores of romance writers attending conferences these days, studying other categories, either to move over completely or to find a way to weave two genres together. While challenging, that latter approach helps to create a new subgenre in one place or another. So, again: an opportunity to lead a parade.

Westerns

No real parade here, I'm afraid. As a category, the traditional western is about as gone as the Old West itself. Based, as much category fiction is, on a myth, no one is certain whether it is revisionist history (and we can argue whether the history is really being revised or finally being told honestly) or a change in the moral temper that has brought an end to the myth. Even library purchases (which have been a staple of the genre for years) have fallen off; one theory is that the core readership has died away . . . literally.

All is not lost, though: there seems to be a growing interest in larger novels of the West, "real" stories that follow the themes of books like *Northwest Passage*: historical novels, featuring strong men and women, taming the frontier. As with the category western, the period of most interest seems to be those years between the end of the Civil War and the turn of the century, an era of great expansion and adventure. Historical accuracy (as accurate as we can be, anyway) is important, here, and so is this thought: as a category, this is something that's being reborn; whether it's going to take root for any length of time is uncertain. As with anything you're going to write, keep a close eye on the shelves, on publishers' catalogues, and on the market guides. Just because something is seen as moribund today doesn't mean that it will be tomorrow, any more than today's popularity guarantees longevity.

Horror

This is another genre that seemed to dominate and then fell on hard times. The reason, to my mind, is simple: greed. Seeing something work, publishers and writers rushed to fill a vacuum. Having done that, we just kept stuffing new releases into a space that had no more room. Often, we released titles because we needed to, because we'd committed a slot to a new book and settled for the best thing in the pile, rather than demanding the best book possible. The readers, as always, let us know that we'd failed.

There are two main directions in the category: the supernatural (which, at its heart, is about good versus evil and stems from a Judeo-Christian ethic) and psychological horror, which is broad enough to include Dean Koontz on one side and Thomas Harris on the other; *Silence of the Lambs*, which I read as a crime novel, won a best novel award from the Horror Writers of America but was ignored completely by the Mystery Writers of America.

Today, Stephen King and Dean Koontz (who is increasingly considered a suspense writer—but it doesn't matter because both of them are marketed as fiction) seem to be the dominating forces and most publishers have stopped their horror programs. There are still some revisionist vampire books (those that have moved away from the standards and rules set by Bram Stoker in *Dracula*) being released, but they're few and far between.

As with anything else in this business, though, someday someone is going to follow her heart, write something in the genre that's so exciting and fresh that an editor is going to be forced to take notice—and the risk—and publish it. And the next cycle begins.

Fantasy and Science Fiction

Fantasy continues to be popular, and why not: it is one of the purest forms of escape imaginable. It ranges from the sword-and-sorcery tales of Conan to gentler worlds of faerie. Integral to it is the rigid physics the author creates: having built a world of magic, you have to be certain that your world operates according to the rules you've established . . . consistently.

Science fiction grew out of adventure tales of bug-eyed monsters and quickly evolved into one of the standard genres, sophisticated, witty, thoughtful . . . and often prescient: there was a news story not too long ago about NASA's plan to launch a rocket driven by an ion drive; the scientists working on it were inspired by an episode of the original *Star Trek* series.

As always, there are variations and they take turns being at the forefront: hard science-fiction, concentrating on hardware and mechanics and adventure—the place where it seems to have begun—remains strong, but so-called anthropological science fiction, stories more concerned with contact and the interplay between us and them, grows always stronger.

The writer is required not only to know the necessary science but, as with fantasy, be able to create and maintain the rules of the worlds being created, and make them real. It's a challenge that not all are up to meeting.

As with romance, most paperback houses seem to have imprints devoted to the genre; the editors are experts, fans who've grown up reading the fiction. For me, that's one of the best parts about the category: that expertise creates standards that are firmly in place and help maintain quality.

Series

I've broken this out separately, because it is an aspect of genre fiction that deserves special note. In mystery, science-fiction, and fantasy, series—ongoing characters, fixed (and sometimes shared) locales, especially in the more fantastical categories—are a staple. If you're going to write in those categories, it isn't enough to have one idea, one adventure for your character: think ahead at least two or three books into the future, and be certain that these are people you're interested in spending several years with, that they interest you enough that you're going to want to keep exploiting their lives. Not only is your publisher going to be looking for that, but so are your readers, and it's one of the best ways for a writer to build a reader base.

That doesn't mean that the one off, the stand alone, won't work in those categories, just that it may be more difficult to get a hearing, and with so many others knocking at the same door, well, you get the idea.

For all the restrictions category fiction places on writers—the traditions, the readers' expectations (translated into those of the editors), the iconography—we have some wonderful opportunities to experiment within a chosen genre. It's not always easy: publishing is about profits and risk takers are few.

Characters are no longer always white, always heterosexual, always unchallenged. Someone took a chance and did it well, somewhere an editor said, "Okay," and the readers enjoyed what was done and came back for more. And something else disappeared, either quickly or slowly.

I didn't go into the needs of each category in depth because, as mentioned, there are books devoted to all of them, books that offer to show you everything from the plotting to the placement of clues to the structure of a love scene. I will make a suggestion, though, one you'll hear again later in a slightly different form. Don't only read the books aimed at you; as a romance writer you may not have to know how to place clues cleverly . . . but it won't hurt. As a science fiction writer, sensuous scenes could prove valuable. Writing is writing.

✐   ✐   ✐

I want to take just a minute now to talk about the short story. At a conference I attended in Oregon a few years ago, a bestselling writer talked about how her family laughed when she sat down to write her first novel because she hadn't even written a short story. The thought seemed to be that she should try to write something short, first.

Yes and no. What this writer clearly does not understand is that the short story is far more demanding. You have to be able to say everything, and give the reader the full experience of the events, in a few words. It teaches you to be concise, to focus on what's important in the story. It is one of, if not the, greatest tools for learning what writing is about. I've lost count of the number of times I've rejected a manuscript with the thought that it would have made a great short story. Bad novels, though, are easier to write than short stories. Or good novels.

It wasn't too long ago that writers honed their art and craft in that form; there were hundreds of magazines that used fiction on a regular basis. Today, the pulps are a dim memory, with only a (relatively) few category-oriented magazines left; most of the newsstand magazines that use fiction have cut back on the number of stories they take, and working in the genre is not lucrative. (Sure,

Playboy will often pay as much for a short story as some book publishers pay for novels; on the other hand, they seem to be publishing one story a month these days, and most of them are from well-known established writers.)

It is, without question, my favorite form, and when you read Raymond Carver or Andre Dubus, you get as much in ten pages as most authors can give you in a hundred. Learning how to do things like that yourself, especially if you're going to concentrate on the novel, will do nothing but make you a better writer. And that's what you want to be.

So, let's begin.

Begin at the beginning....

a good story is about something: it has characters who cause things to happen and react to what has happened and it has a theme—an underlying idea or question. It's in the exploration of those two elements that the seed of the novel is sown. You nurture it with scenes, description, narrative, and dialogue, as well as your use of language. You trim and weed so that it grows clean and strong.

Before you plant anything, though, you have to get the soil ready, and for our purposes that preparation is outlining. I'm not talking about the outline or synopsis that will accompany your submission, once you're done; think of this one as the trellis upon which your story is going to grow. (Stop flinching; it isn't that painful; you've been carrying the outline for that outline in your head for a while now, haven't you?)

Lots of writers, amateur and professional, dislike this stage. One of the reasons is laziness. An effective outline takes time, and too many of us think that that time is wasted, that we should be writing, instead: "Hey, you just said I've been carrying the outline around with me, I know the story, so why bother?"

You should bother because that image in your mind lacks substance and detail; you're making quantum jumps: some homeless people are disappearing from a park in New York, there's an arrogant teenaged girl and her father who will lose his job, and the troubles they face, and someone who is responsible for the disappearances, and they all come together. The story's about the price of gentrification. And that, in fifty words or less, is the outline I had *in mind*, when I sat down to write my story, "What Chelsea Said." The other important factor, and this is a spoiler, something that gives away the punch line of the story, so you may want to skip the lines set off below:

> this all happened because of a bitter comment made to a friend, writer Charles Grant. I said something about feeding the homeless to the hungry, and ten minutes later he said, there's a story in that line. I didn't remember what I'd said; it really was a throwaway line. His wife, Kathryn Ptacek, was trying to put together a cannibalism anthology and he thought it would be a good idea for me to try expanding my modest proposal into something longer. I began with this in mind: I couldn't use the line as the title, and a homeless woman we'd seen regularly for the last couple of years, was no longer around.

If I sat down to write the story without thinking it through further, without at least giving myself some guide, I don't think it would have sold. So, I began by considering what I had so far, and decided first, that since the story was about one particular individual's collision with certain realities (I always begin with character and tell the story from there), I had to know him, and those around him; thus, character sketches.

Then, the events: who would be introduced first, who would be doing what to whom, and what would the reactions be? My character is a good man suddenly out of his depth; would he act or react? The theme allowed me to do something I don't do often:

create a character who isn't proactive; a venture into existential-ism. Still, I wanted to have some idea of how Koenig, and his daughter, Chelsea, and the rest of the cast, would be spending their time. That knowledge would keep the characters true to them-selves and would also allow me to get to the end; I had a limited number of words to work with and, while street life in New York is rich with potential, I couldn't let it all into the story. If I started falling in love with scenes that didn't advance the story, I was going to be in deep trouble.

The outline I finally came up with, one that worked for me, looked like this:

1. Introduce Koenig (loving, caring and without a clue) and Chelsea (spoiled rotten); allude to missing person (but don't mention that she's missing).
2. Introduce Lavery—the Walker: frightening but harmless, mental patient capable of caring for himself. Walking along Broadway, looking in dumpsters, offering to get coffee.
3. Introduce Franchi—people knew that in him the milk of human kindness had curdled into nothing. Scene set in diner he owns. Turn down woman asking for donations to church soup kitchen.
4. Lavery and Franchi; plant idea of what to do about the homeless.
5. Intersperse scenes with Koenig, alone and with Chelsea. His observations in contrast to Franchi's. While action begins today and proceeds, Koenig's scenes will cover a period of years, from Chelsea's birth to mid-teens. Koenig's deterioration and Chelsea's increased self-absorption.
6. Koenig turning into Lavery.
7. Set up for punch line.

It probably took thirty minutes to put it all together; it's not very detailed, but it gave me what I needed to keep on track. (I've left out some items, because—like the spoiler—they'd give too much away. If you read the spoiler, you know what doesn't appear in the outline; if you haven't, you can still read the story.)

Back in 1988, when Yellowstone was burning, Rex Burns (I mentioned him earlier; he's the man who taught me the three-word-exercise) and I were driving to a conference in the Gallatin National Forest, in Montana. As we bounced along the rutted road, we saw a sign that read, Natural Bridge and Falls, Next Right. Well, we had some time, we looked at each other, and we took that next right. There was another sign, then: Danger, Stay on Path Natural Bridge collapsed. We looked at the jumble of rock, turned around, went back to the car and continued on our way.

As important as anything else we might think about here: the outline I show above isn't particularly restrictive, it doesn't force me into anything. The argument against outlines that I hear most often is that they are confining: if I write it down, I'm stuck doing it a particular way and what if the characters start demanding a different direction.

But that's only the case if you look at an outline as a blueprint; take out an I-beam, and the structure isn't stable. I consider the outline a map, a way of getting from here to there. Sure, most of the time I might want the quickest route, just get on I-95 and put the pedal to the metal. But, and it's an important but, if I see a sign up ahead that tells me there's something I've never seen before and might like, I can get off the highway, explore the new place, and then either keep looking or turn around. If the bridge has fallen, all that's lost is a little time. Because writing isn't a race, that lost time doesn't matter.

(Seeing that jumble of stone in the canyon did actually make a difference; it let me know that there were things to see in this country before I worried about seeing other places. But that's another story.)

Here's an example of an outline, done in a narrative form

(because the form doesn't matter) that isn't holding up to the end. It's for a novella on which I'm working, titled *Slow Dancing to Loud Music*:

> Jonathan and Rachel, two people who have no business being together, meet, sparks fly, a relationship begins. After parting, they begin to correspond, talk on the phone all the time. (Shift between what he is seeing and doing and what she is; home lives). They arrange to meet; describe the trips to the rendezvous, what happens. Part again. (She wants to call things off; the decision lasts about twenty four hours.) Jonathan's reactions. Several more meetings, increased tension, love scenes. Scenes apart, continued phone calls and letters. Ending: Ambiguous; together in place they first met, looking at each other.

About sixty pages into the piece, I realized that the ending was a lie; these characters would never settle for that ambiguous ending, even if it does create a satisfying denouement: they—and the reader—are left with a romantic hope. It was the ending I wanted— from a marketing sensibility—but not the *right* one. I discovered it because I moved away from the outline in one scene, just to see what would happen.

So, I made some minor adjustments and the novella has become an exploration of decreasing intimacy. There are other themes woven throughout, questions of whether it is better to experience and know, or imagine and remain safe, for instance; but those don't have to be spelled out in my outline because they are what the story is about, they're clear in mind. The plot is something else, and we'll consider that in the section on theme.

That the metaphoric excursion on the side road cropped up in the middle of one of the scenes I thought I knew so well was fortuitous; it strengthened the novella, made it, for the characters and for me, as the writer, more meaningful, more important. It took the story from what I see now as banality—it wasn't any different than hundreds of other love stories—and gave it a twist which may not be original, but which, at the very least, has not been overdone. (There are some other things that make it different; you'll get to read some of it later.)

The first outline, the one for "What Chelsea Said," is a variation of the formal, Roman outline that my generation learned in grammar school; I still use that for non-fiction. For fiction, these days anyway, I either do a straight narrative, just a couple of paragraphs to give myself a skeleton, or for a more complex work, I'll use index cards, jotting notes for particular scenes and keeping them in order. (I also put character descriptions on index cards; fortunately, none of them are carved in stone; just pen on paper.) I don't worry about transitions or any of the detail work; that comes with the writing.

Neither of the outlines would help you write my story; looking at them now they are, for you, meaningless at best ; at worst, they'll make you shake your head and wonder if I know what I'm talking about. And that's fine; those outlines are for me; you'll find the approach that works best for you through trial and error.

Lots of top professionals don't use outlines: Stephen King thinks they take something that should be plastic and malleable and flowing, and turns them into something else. Then again, King doesn't really have to send his editor anything more than a title page to get a new contract. Unless you're that well established, you're going to have to show the decision makers something, and doing the outline for your novel gives you that something, and since you're going to have to let us know what your characters are going to be doing, anyway, you might as well get used to doing outlines now . . . at least until you can dictate the rules.

And speaking of characters . . .

Developing Characters

Philip Roth puts it perfectly: "Beginning a book is unpleasant. I'm entirely uncertain about the character and the predicament, and a character in a predicament is what I have to begin with."

It seems so obvious when it's stated that way, but the obvious is not something people are looking at; maybe it's like not seeing the forest for the trees. Maybe, and more likely, it's because too much of today's fiction is based on plot or—and this is so frightening it is enough to make me consider another line of work—from a high concept approach. A writer friend in from England was given this advice: "When you present your work to an editor or agent, make it high concept, you know, *Moby-Dick* meets *Gone With the Wind*. That's the way you have to think." The concept of high concept comes down to us from the movie business; they can keep it.

Because every season brings a couple of articles about books that have begun that way, people trying to break in scramble to come up with their own high concepts. And when the manuscript arrives, there's all this action, but no characters; the people in the story seem to have been created for the sole purpose of carrying the storyline. It is vital that you make me, as an editor and as a reader, care about your characters, make the novel the characters' story. If you create them to fill the needs of the tale, they have no dimension, they don't matter. And if they don't matter, their conflicts don't matter. Nothing matters, except returning the manuscript to you quickly.

The situation is at its worst in the various pop fiction categories. A writer decides to start a mystery series; he's got some wonderful ideas for crimes and clues, knows the ins and outs of forensics and procedure. Well, okay. But who's going to solve the crimes? Oh, okay, well, let's see, amateur sleuths are doing pretty well these days, so I'll make her an amateur, maybe a real estate agent, because they can go all over town. Hmm, she'd better have a buddy, someone she can talk to because that will also allow me to have conversations where the clues can be discussed so I can be sure all the clues are in place and also the friend can be around in case something happens . . .

Time and again, in every category, I see manuscripts and books that have clearly been cobbled together this way. That results in novels and characters that are interchangeable. There may be some small differences between detectives, between the evils, between the women inheriting plantations or companies, between the sorcerers, but one can be placed in another's novel without losing a step. That's what will keep their creators, and the books, small, keep them from moving up in sales and reader attention and, most important to you, in advances offered.

Start with a character, though, and find the conflict that that character is likely to face, and make the character change, visibly, because of what's happening, and you'll have a much better chance to create a novel that people will talk about and a character they might want to visit with again. (And if it isn't a series, readers will still trust you to allow them to become voyeurs following the lives of people they can identify and maybe even identify with.)

The shopping exercise we tried earlier is a good place to begin.

Think about the people you see and decide what kinds of problems they might be facing, what conflicts exist in their lives. Are they desperately broke? Are they worried about what's going to happen to them because they're of an age when losing a job means becoming dependent?

If you want to write a mystery, begin by creating your detective. Who should she be? What's in her background that allows her to do what you're going to be forcing her to do? How are you going to keep the contrivance fresh—of having an amateur be thrown into a murder on a regular basis? What makes her different; what keeps her from being renamed Jane Marple (beyond copyright considerations)? At some point, your sleuth is going to have to get a confession or, at the very least, motivate someone into talking to her.

What is it that's going to accomplish that?

Why should I read about her, instead of any of the other detectives on my desk; why should any editor, any reader, choose to spend a part of his life with your character?

Every story is about a problem and the resolution to that problem; even in genre fiction, where the problem is inherent in the structure, the better writers are certain to create other difficulties for their characters or, at least, their hero. The end of the book is not finding the solution to the problem or conflict, *the end is in the effect of that discovery on the protagonist.* She must be different at the end, changed, more aware . . . something, anything; if she isn't, what was the point of the conflict, what difference did it make? And if it didn't make a difference, why did you bother to tell me about it?

Let's make it simple: how has your problem—becoming a writer who has turned an avocation and hobby and creative drive into a money-making proposition—affected your life? What accommodations have you and your family had to make? How are you different now, because of what you're doing? Do you see things around you from a different perspective? Is everyone you pass on the street taking part in some kind of mental casting call that you're holding? Have people started to notice that, even in the middle of a conversation, you seem to be drifting away (because someone said something that kicked something into place, and now a story is running away in your head)? Those changes, and the ways in which you deal with them, and what the ways result in in their turn, is far more interesting than hearing about the hours spent at the desk; we all have problems, goals, dreams. Our interest as readers is in learning how other people deal with theirs and finding the lesson in that for ourselves: Could I make the sacrifice he's made? Is there a way that's less costly to me, personally? Would my kids put up with being kicked out of the house so that I can work in peace and if not, what will I do?

The most successful fiction is not linear, a one-dimensional line connecting non-dimensional points; it is very much three-dimensional and to a great extent rather more like a nest or basket, lots of pieces woven together so that the piece is, in the end, capable of standing on its own. That extra depth comes from the characters and what you do with them. You can't do anything with them until you know who they are, and you can't know who they are until you create their biographies.

I asked a writer I used to edit something about the background of her heroine. She said that she couldn't be bothered knowing who the character's third grade teacher was; and one of the problems with the series (and the reason she isn't writing these days) is that the character didn't have a background. It was made up as the writer went along: *uh-oh, better give her some martial arts training if she's going to have to fight her way out of this fix.* Thinking on your feet is a trait worth developing; but the job is easier if you know what you're doing before hand.

Those background details are often urgent: if the reader can't understand the motivation for an action (we're not discussing sociopaths here, just plain folks), credibility wavers. Do we know enough to accept that this character would throw a punch or offer lips up for a kiss? You get that point made—subtly or with a heavy hand—by either knowing the past and sharing it with the reader, or as part of the depiction of the character's evolution; the changes wrought by events.

At a mystery writing conference recently, one of the authors was talking about how his p.i.—a traditional loner—would be joining a very upscale private security agency. The reason was simple: the author was getting tired of the stories he was telling (something that happens to series writers regularly) and this would allow the stage to open, to give the character more to do. Unfortunately, there was no thought given to how the change in the detective's situation was going to change his life. How would he react to a regular income? Given the new class of clients, and the new milieu in which he'd be working, would his investigative techniques have to change? How will he develop new informants? What about the high-tech equipment with which this, until now, ham-fisted individual would have to work? Would he remember his failure with one society matron in a previous novel and come up with a new approach when he has to tangle with another one in the future?

As we talked, it was clear that none of these issues had been thought about and it was also clear that as far as the writer was concerned, it didn't matter. After five previous books in the series, during which the sleuth had been carefully developed, background firmly in place, the author was saying he didn't care; if the author doesn't, why should the reader?

In an essay titled, "How should one read a book?", Virginia Woolf wrote: "Do not dictate to your author; become him." Once upon a time, readers would willingly meet the author on the author's terms: "This is what I've written, you may read it or not." Today, especially in the bulk of popular fiction, the situation has been turned on its head. The reader says "This is what I want," and the writer complies. Characters now rarely age (at least not in real time), there is no character evolution (evidence, through action, that the character has changed), just characterization, a static sketch drawn in broad strokes (because the reader is coming back to read about a person he's met before; if the character has changed . . .), and few writers take the chances necessary for the growth of their own writing, forget about the growth of characters.

The few who do take the risk push the boundaries, ignore the limits. James Sallis, in his Lew Griffin series, is one who does. Trying to synopsize the work is a fool's errand; reading *The Long-legged Fly*, *Moth*, *Black Hornet*, and *Eye of the Cricket* in order will give you everything you need to know. (After an article of mine on character evolution was published in a writer's magazine, a reader wrote an angry letter, wondering why I didn't quote scenes from the books I was mentioning; after all, my readers were busy and didn't have time to read all those books. Think about it.)

Short story writer Andre Dubus, and a British historical novelist, Brian Unsworth (especially in *Stone Virgin*), are two others who've learned the trick of making characters grow and be meaningful to the reader. Try 'em, you'll like 'em.

⇨   ✎   ⇨

As with outlines, just because you start with a character doesn't mean that, finally, the story will be about that character. My Spur Award-nominated "The Dream That Follows Darkness" began as a ghost story and the story I thought I wanted to tell was hers. What finally appeared (in *Twilight Zone* magazine) is probably best classified as a reincarnation romance as magic realism, and while the ghost has a miniscule role in events, it became the story of David and Peg.

That could happen easily enough because I'd created both of them early on, knew them (even David's third grade teacher), and had them facing conflicts (a love triangle within a love triangle within . . .) that I was going to enjoy exploring. Everything they did was "in character," and remained that way; while there were unexpected events—I hope they were unexpected, anyway—the characters' actions never made the reader say, "No, they wouldn't act that way," even as I was asking the audience to accept as real things that must be only of the imagination. Or are they?

There's a wonderful way of outlining your characters (well, at the very least, your central character, your hero) that also works nicely as an additional outline for your novel.

We'll go to it now.

The Hero's Journey

according to the dictionary (well, one of them) a hero is 1) a mythological or legendary figure endowed with great strength, courage, or ability, favored by the gods and often believed to be of divine or partly divine descent; 2) a man of courage and nobility famed for his military achievements; an illustrious warrior; 3) a man admired for his achievements and noble qualities and considered a model or ideal; and, finally, 4) the principal male character in a novel, story, etc.; or the central figure in an event, action or period.

Our main concern is with the fourth definition, and I'm spending a lot of time on character because they are so important to fiction. That seems like a gimme, but—as I've said before and as I'll undoubtedly repeat—too many manuscripts and, for my taste, too many published books, make the action the central issue.

As a nation, we really don't have a mythology, not a living one that's handed down from generation to generation. John Henry, that steel-drivin' man, and Paul Bunyan along with his great blue ox, Babe, are fading memories now, and we have nothing to replace them. So, we make a hero of Pete Rose, of Madonna or, more reasonably, Davy Crockett. But as soon as we do that, we start tearing them down. Charles Barkley said it flat out, "I'm not a role model, I'm a basketball player." As we cast about for a hero, we seem more than willing to ignore a word that's central to those first definitions: nobility. Maybe that's why we wind up spending as much time looking for the feet of clay as we do looking for a hero.

The mythological hero as we know him was handed down to us by storytellers, by myth-makers; as a fiction writer, that's one of your roles as the shaman of today's tribe. It's up to you to present the readers with a central character who is a hero, someone to inspire the reader, to represent a goal and ideal.

In the late 1940s, Irving Stone wrote a novel about the opening of the American West titled *Men to Match My Mountains*. Think about that: Look at the Rockies and think about the kinds of people, men, women, and children, it took to conquer (or at least fight to a draw) with the purple mountains' majesty. Where are the characters in today's fiction to match those mountains? That's the kind of hero I'm talking about, the kind of character. Consider the aspects of heroism as defined above and find ways to imbue the central character in your drama with as many of them as you can. Do it absolutely right, and you may be the one to create the kind of hero that people will remember and talk about for years to come; just get close, and you'll offer us a character that will capture the attention of editors and readers, create word of mouth, and help carry your book from the shelves to the bedside table.

It falls to the writer of popular fiction to build these characters because of the nature and purpose of the stories you tell: providing escape, a way to throw off the cares of the day; don't just make your hero the central figure in an event, make her illustrious and a functioning ideal. Accomplishing that is what we're going to examine now.

There's another word we should consider, right now. Plot. I don't consider plot *what* happens; to me, it's the order in which things happen: it's that meshing of the gears of action and charac-

ter interaction. To make story and plot come together successfully, your characters must be motivated, not manipulated; they must
drive the action, make things happen.

Joseph Campbell has written about the hero of a thousand
faces, showing how the mythic characters of all cultures are just different aspects of the one archetype of all myth. One school of contemporary psychology posits that we model our lives (and so should
model the lives of our characters)—unconsciously or subcon-
sciously—on mythological figures. People have Promethean personalities or Dianic or whatever. Whether you accept the Jungian
interpretation or not, you should accept this: Readers, especially
those of series fiction, are drawn first to the character. They will,
when a series begins, come into a bookstore and ask for the new
Robicheaux; it is only after the books are firmly established that
they begin asking for the new (James Lee) Burke. The detective
became myth; the reader wanted more of his adventures. (That's
one of the reasons, for good or ill—I don't like it, but that's one
man's opinion—some characters become so entrenched that after
the death of the creator, other authors may begin using them in
their own works.)

The genetic code of the hero has been mapped for us by writers since Homer; using it to build your character helps you create
one that will drive the story. All you have to do after that is make
sure the story is worthy of the character you've created.

Incidentally, I used the word "mapped" for a specific reason:
the map is not the territory, it's only a representation. Like the outlines we've already discussed, the eight steps we're going to look at
now are just guidelines, in the broadest sense of the term: use them
as you need them, don't be rigid. Series begin to bore both the
reader and the author because the hero is simply there (and as
some have said about certain places, there's just no there there),
repeating endlessly the same actions and moves. It's a lot like a
chess game played against someone who not only uses the same

opening match after match, but doesn't seem to care about any of the variations; it doesn't take long before you need a new opponent, someone who will challenge you.

Most readers of category fiction want (expect, demand) the comfort of familiarity in both story and character, and you probably don't want to disappoint them, but the next to the last thing you want to do is bore your reader. The last thing you want to do is bore your editor.

This is one of the maps. It begins once upon a time, at the beginning.

Birth

Unless it makes a difference (your hero was born with a caul, for instance), birth doesn't mean the day he slipped into a doctor's hands. What we're talking about here is being born to the action that will follow. Batman is a good example.

Bruce Wayne was born at some point in history; The Batman —the original noir character and the later simplified one both—was born on the evening that his parents were killed. That event gives rise to a series of actions and to the birth of the character/hero who will perform those actions.

Nothing, we're told, is constant but change, and the birth is the first of the changes, the first in a series of impacts between character and action. It helps define the hero, to shape him as he begins to move the story: the decision to become a crimefighter (in this case) means that the character will have to do certain things, doing them means other things happen. And you have created the first of the conflicts and resolutions, of scenes and sequels, that are so important to effective storytelling.

Equally important, you've shown the reader this birth, not simply told them that Bruce Wayne always wanted to be a hero.

With your hero established . . .

Initiation

Have you ever picked up a novel, started following a character's adventure, had an image of who and what the character could and would do, and then have something happen that was "out of character?"

Now, we may very well want characters who can do everything, be all things to all people . . . there's always a place for someone like that in fiction. But, and it is an important but, those abilities have to be established, and if they're hard-won, all the better. (Don't perfect people, those who can seemingly do anything, just get your blood boiling? It's one of the reasons I despise the TV series *The Pretender*.)

The mythic hero has to undergo a period of initiation, of learning, of developing the skills necessary for the tasks you're going to set for her. And this sets another layer of motivation: because she wants to do something, she has to ready herself. King Arthur studied with Merlin for years before taking his seat at the Round Table; in fantasy and adventure tales, the lessons she learns will be obvious ones. That doesn't keep us from using the same approach in other fiction.

An integral part of your story about a woman growing up to take over a business will be the ways in which she learns how to run it; taking someone from the farm and throwing them into a boardroom doesn't work by itself; we should see her managing the business side of the farm and then, through trial and error, using what she knows about business and applying it to something different. How'd she get there? Well, maybe she married a businessman and then either inherited the company or won it from him in a divorce suit or has to take over when he has a stroke . . . that depends on the story you're telling.

It's obviously easier to have this evolution occur over the course of a series, but it's still something writers keep forgetting: the character isn't the same tomorrow as she was yesterday; if she is, nothing has happened. Period. But it can be utilized in stand alone fiction; your choice will be as to how much of it you want to show.

It is during this period of learning that the character is making decisions that will set the events of the story and the plot elements you're going to use. You have the opportunity to foreshadow and to establish the ground rules, the rigid physics of your created world: how and why will your hero react in certain ways to particular occurrences. Too often we seem to forget that a character is a depiction of a person, and people react to things because of who they are, what they know through experience . . . or refusing to gain experience. Nothing happens in a vacuum, nothing happens simply because you, as the author, want it to, or need it to; that's another contrivance unless the happenings are based on a yesterday in the character's life.

By creating a realistic, fully-rounded past, you're establishing the psychological, sociological and historical motivations that serve to maintain the reader's willing suspension of disbelief. Again, the amount of "training" you depict will be dictated by various factors . . . genre, length of the work, pacing. It may be enough to simply throw in a few lines or a scene describing her being forced to learn to defend herself from her brother, the bully, to establish that she can fight, that she's wary or distrusting, that she can take care of herself.

If you've shown it to the reader early on, planted it in the reader's mind, *if you've made the reader experience it along with the character*, we will go with the flow of the story. And you've accomplished something else: some foreshadowing, setting us up, creating expectation . . . that's suspense and that keeps us turning the pages.

Have you ever read a book, or watched a movie, and sat in disbelief, shaking your head, because the character rushes into a room where the storyline's particular bogeyman happens to be hiding? For the character to remain sympathetic, something different has to happen at that juncture . . . and it's as important a growth stage as any other.

Withdrawal

At some point in the story, your mythic hero should sit back for a moment, look the situation over and decide that the action called for is just plain crazy . . . and choose not to do it; he should withdraw.

Pulling back is an action and like all actions it results in a very clear, equal and opposite reaction. By not being in a particular place at a particular time, we are causing something to happen, though it may not be the expected one: a shot won't be fired, a potential love interest not met, a deal left unfinished. And that, in turn, results in something else happening, which in turn leads to another twist, another conflict.

It also leads to another important consideration, one which gets debated every now and then. Should a hero have a wart, an imperfection? I think so: I don't want them to be perfect, because if they are, there's no way I can take them seriously; I can't aspire to be them (one of the functions, remember, of the role) because I know I'm not perfect. By giving the hero that moment's doubt, that scene of fear and indecision and introspection, we make him just human enough that the reader has some small hope of being able to see that character reflected in his own mirror.

Just because the hero has withdrawn doesn't mean the story has stopped; things continue to happen because of that moment. A situation may become clearer, a crisis worsen. Events, their momentum unchecked, speed up. Now the hero must do something.

Quest

We've talked about the Grail hunt nature of popular fiction and when you get right down to it, a search of some kind is at the heart of every story. Sometimes it's obvious: wealth, love, justice; sometimes it's a bit more philosophical: what is my place in the scheme of things? What's the meaning of life?

The quest is at the center of everything, the focus: this is what your novel is about, the question you set out to answer . . . for yourself and for the reader. From this point on, the hero is forcing matters; pushing, prodding, being a presence, acting with a goal in mind. Everything she does advances the story, sets up the next conflict, makes things happen. When you're out hunting for something, you have to go to where that something is; you have to search, and searching usually means getting in the way of someone who doesn't want you to reach the goal. Everything that happens is a pebble thrown into the pond that is your story, sending ripples in every direction . . .

Things are happening, and they're happening because your hero is standing right in the middle of everything, making them happen. The conflicts are there at every turn, the challenge is set. And your hero will continue growing to meet it.

The Underworld

A story is a series of beginnings and endings and your hero is at the start of another growth spurt. She's been born, studied, backed away and finally accepted her role in her life. Each stage represents a change; each change, each experience, brings new knowledge, new vision, as she sees what's possible. She can walk down the cobwebbed stairs to the basement because she knows exactly what she can do.

You've been creating a series of escalating conflicts, but those are battles, you still need to win the war, the threats are more fearsome: everything you can throw against your hero to stop her is in place. This is the point in the story when the hostile corporate takeover is about to happen, when the lover leaves, the failing grade on the Bar exam arrives: whatever you're teaching us through the life of your hero, whatever lesson you may have, whatever your book is about, is *about* to happen.

Your hero is in a metaphoric fight for her life. And since I've set the scene in the underworld, is there any question as to who the antagonist is?

Meeting the Devil

There are times when the antagonist is clear: a killer, the rival, the politician, the censor. (The editor.) There is always an enemy, someone to stand in the way of your hero achieving his goal. No matter who or what, this stage represents the hero's final conflict.

Everything you've had the hero learn now comes into play. Because we've watched that learning process, we know that he's equal to the task; we're counting on him winning, almost taking it for granted, but we still want to see how it happens.

Because you've made me suspend disbelief, everything is "real": you've taken the chaos of a sheet of blank paper and created a world that I can enter; because every event was driven by your hero's decisions about how to act, and not by the kind of random factor that does exist but is inexplicable, the reader cares and is cheering the hero on.

To a sea-change.

Rebirth

This is the penultimate stage: Having been tried by fire, the hero emerges victorious. The conflicts are finished, the final resolution awaiting statement; the last scene, depiction.

Everything changes us. If your hero isn't somehow different, a new person, what was the point of the story? What do I, as the reader, gain from having read it? That doesn't mean that you can't write a novel that will sell (and even sell well) if all that's been achieved is stasis. It does mean that the book will be ephemeral; it'll just pass through, take up some shelf space for a while, and disappear unremembered. That may be enough for you. Think about it.

Rebirth is enlightenment; your hero, having learned, serves to guide your reader to the same insights. All the conflicts, including those that may have seemed chaotic, random, now make sense. Your story is told.

Transformation

As good as your hero was, having undergone the tests you set for him and survived them, he is better still. He's also ready to begin again, bringing everything he's learned and experienced to the next phase. It's all a circle and it's time to begin again.

All the conflicts in your fiction are the result of human action and interaction; the story is about people and how events change them. All of the characters are affected, but not all of them are heroes; their actions and reactions are meaningful, but secondary to those of the hero.

The story is finished; the acknowledgement of the transformation is the final resolution. By making certain that the reader can see this, and recognize your hero, letting the reader share in the events that make him a hero assures not only that you've given us someone memorable, but ensures that your story will evolve in the right way, driven by the character. Each of the growth periods, the changes, the events that shape the hero are major pivotal points in the fiction, notes to help you create the how that make up your plot and guideposts to the what that keep your story on track.

Most important, you will have brought together the three things an editor is looking for—character, story, and plot—and done it in a way that's withstood the test of time and literary criticism.

There's a final thought to be shared here: most fiction doesn't come close to fulfilling this outline, this ideal. Obviously, looking at the racks and shelves, it doesn't matter. But if you can improve your work by trying to draw a hero in this way, if it helps make your work stand out, be positively different, if you can make it happen, it's worth the effort. And if you can't, it's worth the effort. And if you can't understand that, you're in the wrong business.

Theme

So, tell me what your book's about."

He leaned forward, too close. "Well, it's a mystery, a detective story, about a p.i. who gets hired to . . ." I lean back, listening, but not hearing anything. I've heard this before, five minutes ago, five days; I'll hear it again ten minutes from now. I reach back and snag my jacket from the table behind me, slipping into it while nodding pleasantly, smiling. Texans and air conditioning.

". . . so then, as the investigation heats up, Jim has to try to get help from the cops because—"

"Yeah, but what's the book about, what's the why of it?" I light another cigarette; the fifth? sixth? since the meeting started. "Want one?"

"Oh, thanks. I didn't know you could smoke here." He tosses his match into the overflowing ashtray. "Well," he says, squinting as a bead of perspiration rolls into the corner of his eye, "it's about this investigation . . ."

The interview goes on for ten minutes this way; the writer telling me about the action in the story, me leaning back, asking him again and again, "What's it about?" Around us, people in the room are growing silent and nervous; the woman in the black turtleneck who'd been waxing eloquent at lunch about how anyone can write about anything and how all the rules are beside the point, shifts and looks up. "He told you," she whispers, but even over the rattle of the air conditioner, everyone can hear her.

"No, he didn't. He told me what happens, not what it's about, not why."

The scene is drawn from life; I spend a lot of time in rooms with writers, listening to them pitch their books. They're nervous; they've been coached on what to do during this meeting, but I'm not playing by the rules. I want to know what the book's about, but not what happens; I want to know why I'd want to read their manuscripts, instead of any of the others that will be offered to me over the three days that I'm here. They aren't questions most of the people I meet think about very often. They should. So should you.

I'm sure you've heard journalists talking about a story being put together from who, what, when, where, and why. (A journalist friend in Louisville adds *to what effect* as the kicker; I think she's absolutely right.) Using that formula as another form of a writing outline is worth considering.

Who is the character.

What is the storyline.

When is part of the setting.

Where is the rest of the setting.

Why and To what effect is what the book is about:
the theme.

Lajos Egri, in his indispensable *The Art of Dramat!c Wr!t!ing*, begins by discussing premise, the point that drives the story. While his book was written for playwrights, his point (on premise and just about everything else he discusses) is equally applicable to the work we're doing. We have to have a why (why are these things happening) and the To what effect (what difference has it all made). As the journalist pointed out to me, if that last isn't answered, the story winds up on the inside, as filler next to the used car ads; if it is answered, it'll be on the front page, above the fold.

The premise, or theme, can be anything; it's part of the initial conflict that gets your story going. Lots of writers explore the same theme every time out; lately it's been called the world view, and there are those who won't read a book if they don't like the author's. Their loss; if readers can't accept the fact that things aren't black and white, but grey, they probably should find another way to fill their time.

Theme may be tied into motivation (and motive, in certain tales); it may only make itself clear as you start telling your story and you see changes taking place: It's a key aspect to the idea that the characters are taking over the story. You may have set out to "prove" one idea—obsessional love causes disaster—and then, with that infamous mind of their own, the story people decide to explore some other premise. Fine, go with it.

Every piece of fiction worth reading is attempting to answer a question, and as we saw earlier, that question isn't whodunit or will someone find love; the questions that matter are about why it was done or why that particular love. It isn't enough that it was done because of jealousy; you have to explore the roots of jealousy and look at the price of that emotion; what is it you want to say about it? It isn't enough that she's rich, good-looking, smart and witty: what is it about the other person in the affair that makes those things important?

Knowing your characters, having some premise in mind when you begin, and then letting the characters explore it for you *and along with the reader* is absolutely crucial in the creation of a story of lasting value. Whether we, as readers, recognize the theme immediately, can voice it, isn't all that important: the insight comes later, when we may face a given situation. I fell in love with the writing of Andre Dubus, as I mentioned earlier; it was only later, after thinking about several of the stories, that I realized that what he was writing about was redemption.

Egri sees the theme of *Romeo and Juliet* as "Great love defies even death." I may see it as "The price of love is too high." Is the theme of *West Side Story*, which is the same play, either of those? Or is it, as the lyric says, "stick to your own kind?" I don't know that it matters; it may be a subject of interest only to analysts and critics, once the writing is done. The theme is the author's personal voyage and what counts is that you have something to explore.

I will admit that my challenge to the young writer was, in terms of what he wanted—permission to submit his novel to me for acquisition—beside the point. You won't state the theme in a cover letter or query, you won't talk about your book in those terms, and an editor will rarely read the manuscript with thoughts of theme in mind. There are exceptions: Turner Publishing began with a contest; the submitted novels were to explore the issue of creating a better world; the judges were looking for that to be clearly stated.

I do what I did, and continue to do it, because good writing is not simply about telling a story about some created event; that's reportage. Every category has itself as its theme; the difference between the writer who remains at the bottom of the list and the one who begins to rise through the ranks is that the latter uses the form, while the former is used by it: I have to do this, that, or the other thing, as long as they're present, the book will sell.

Let's try a scenario. We'll put someone on a street in New York; the narrator: "I."

I'm standing in front of an apartment house, smoking an evening cigar on a winter's day that holds more than a hint of spring.

Someone comes out of the building: a young man with carefully tousled hair, he's wearing baggy Dockers, a heavy, woolen pullover sweater with a designer logo, tan work boots. As he climbs the steps to the sidewalk, he flips open a cellular phone, dials a number, and starts talking.

What's he saying? "I just spoke to Joey, they'll meet us up on Broadway . . . yeah, I guess they're back together . . . what? Oh . . ."

Banal gossip; it goes on for about ten minutes, until the person he's talking to appears on the far corner. They wave and put away their cell phones. I've been watching all along, invisible, because everyone in the building is so used to seeing me out front, smoking a cigar or a pipe, that I've become part of the background.

We can make certain assumptions: about the narrator who goes out each evening to smoke (and then create reasons he's doing it; it's not just because of the weather—people are used to seeing him there). The young man has a certain amount of money, certainly: the clothes define a lifestyle that he's probably living: he can afford to stay on a cell phone for what most of us might find a prohibitive amount of time . . . as could his friend. (We haven't given the friend a gender; what suits you?)

But there are also questions: Why didn't he just stay in his apartment and use the phone there? Showing off? The call isn't important, it's just trivialities.

If the character means enough to me, this guy whose life I might be stealing for a story, I can cast him in any number of roles: he could be a murder victim or a killer; a lover, an FBI agent, an extraterrestrial studying mankind. Whatever I choose, based on the genre I want to use, my suppositions about the kind of person who would be doing what he's doing with that cell phone will become my premise, my theme, because that's what it was about him that drew my attention: if he'd just walked out and waited, I wouldn't have noticed him. My premise might be that people without lives have lots of toys to fill their time. Whatever role he has in the story, his toys and the fact that he finds gossip so fulfilling and rewarding that he has to talk about it even during those ten minutes of waiting (making certain, at the same time, that everyone who passes sees him talking on the phone as if he is so important and busy that he can't just enjoy the evening for itself) is going to be what the story is about—if there is a story.

At the same time, maybe the story is about the narrator; it's another valid option. "I" go out to smoke and, while I'm there, I'm busy watching people, paying attention to them, eavesdropping, cataloguing. Am I an author in search of six characters? Am I a police officer, by training given to careful observation and trained well enough to make myself unobtrusive? Character issues settled, and a story form chosen, the premise might be that invisibility is the way to get through life; it might be that people without lives of their own try to live through others. Again, whatever aspect of the character and situation strikes me (as the writer) as interesting will become the theme. At the end of the story, the question will have been answered to the best of my ability at the moment.

The TV series "Seinfeld" is famous for being about "nothing." But that's not really true; it is about something—if you're cynical, the premise might be that you can live a vacuous life very happily; if you're more forgiving, the theme might be that good friends are always there to help each other. A premise isn't an absolute; it is an idea, something around which to drape a drama.

There's another side to the issue and it gets mentioned frequently in discussions between commercial and literary writers. The pop novelists say that their only goal is to entertain and accuse the others of being pretentious and preachy, more involved with ideas than story. That thought is what makes some lines from John Irving's recent *A Widow for One Year* so entertaining. Irving's certainly commercial, and he's popular; he also experiments in ways that seem more in keeping with literary traditions. Anyway, in the novel, his central character, Ruth, is a writer. Asked where she gets her ideas, she says, "My novels aren't ideas—I don't have any ideas. I begin with the characters."

At another point she says, "It's a novel. It's not 'about' anything.
It's a good story."

I'm not going to argue here with either Irving or Ruth beyond
reiterating my feeling that while theme is only part of your story, it
is a keystone. That's why I push writers to answer the question. I
want to know if the story is about anything.

For all his denials, Irving's are. Is yours?

Openings

have you ever stood quietly in the corner of a bookstore, and watched people choosing the titles to take home with them? Or, maybe even more to the point, have you ever analyzed the way in which you buy books?

Most of the people I've seen do it in much the same way. They pick the book up, read the cover or flap copy, open the volume, read the first page, and make a decision. It's the same thing even if they've come in with a particular book in mind: having found it on the shelves, they read the first page.

Now, there are editors who claim to read every word of every manuscript that lands on their desks. (Yeah, and pigs can fly.) Sure, maybe in the first days of their first job they do it that way. But the first editor for whom I worked, the very wise Theodore Solotaroff, put it to me this way, while looking at a stack of manuscripts that was increasing geometrically: "Michael, there's a prurient interest that will drag you to the end of every one of those manuscripts if you let it. And if you let it, you might as well look for another line of work because you'll never be able to do this the right way.

"You have to trust yourself, your judgment. You know what it takes."

So: You have exactly that long to grab my interest, the same amount of time the reader is giving you in the bookstore. That's why so many writers' conferences have Great Openings contests; that's why, when we ask for partial manuscripts to be submitted, we ask for the first three chapters. That's why, when doing one-on-ones at a conference, we expect you to bring the first pages. Because if they don't work, if they don't grab the reader immediately, your brilliantly conceived scene on page twenty-five is absolutely and forever beside the point.

There are two decisions you have to make as you begin: where and how; where does your story begin and how should you present it to the reader? Remember, it's those words that are going to enthrall her, make her go from one paragraph to the next to the next page and on to the end.

Blind Homer set a wonderful standard in *The Odyssey*: he began *in media res*, in the middle of things; Book One begins with the gods talking and Athena saying, "But my heart breaks for Odysseus,/that seasoned veteran cursed by fate so long—/far from his loved ones still, he suffers torments/ off on a wave-washed island rising at the center of the seas/. . . Atlas' daughter it is who holds Odysseus captive . . ." (Robert Fagles, tr. Viking, ©1996).

As the story continues, we discover how Odysseus became a captive of Calypso and then pick up the adventures until his return to Ithaca. The opening lines contain some backstory (for those who hadn't heard *The Iliad*), lets the reader know what's been happening since the end of the Trojan War, and leaves questions: how did he get here and what's going to happen? Because we want to know, we keep reading.

Frederick Busch, in his 1997 novel, *Girls* (Harmony Books), uses the technique as well as anyone and better than most:

We started clearing the field with shovels and buckets and of course our cupped, gloved hands. The idea was to not break any frozen parts of her away. Then, when we had a broad hole in the top of the snow that covered the field and we were a foot or two of snow above where she might have been set down to wait for spring, we started using poles. Some of us used rake handles and the long hafts of shovels. One used a five-foot iron pry bar. He was a big man, and the bar weighed twenty-five pounds, anyway, but he used it gently, I remember, like a doctor with his hands in someone's wound. We came together to try to find her and we did what we needed to, and then we seemed to sep-arate as quickly as we could.

At Mrs. Tanner's funeral, they sang "Shall We Gather at the River," and I sang, too. It was like that in the field. Everyone gathered, and it was something to see. Then we all came apart. Fanny went where she needed to, and Rosalie Piri did, and Archie Halpern. I did, too. Most of them, I think, remained within a few miles of the field.

The dog and I live where it doesn't snow . . .

As the novel is constructed, this is a flashback, the relating of an incident from deep within the heart of the story; the rest of the novel will bring us not only to that scene, but to where the dog and the narrator now live.

Consider the information we're given. (And while you're at it, look at the language, the simile of the big man using the pry bar "like a doctor with his hands in someone's wound": the size of the man, the hardness and weight of the metal, and the delicacy of the action. It enhances the mood, the effect of what's being done on the participants who "go where they have to go.") We know there's been a tragedy of some kind, we know that the people involved have suffered terribly; we're left with questions, with wanting to know because the author has started by giving us, at least in part, the answer to one of the journalist's points: To what effect. What made the narrator want to go where there is no snow?

Another contemporary example of beginning in the middle of things comes from Jeffrey Eugenides' first novel, *The Virgin Suicides* (Farrar, Straus and Giroux, 1993):

> On the morning the last Lisbon daughter took her turn at suicide—it was Mary this time, and sleeping pills, like Therese—the two paramedics arrived at the house knowing exactly where the knife drawer was, and the gas oven, and the beam in the basement from which it was possible to tie a rope. They got out of the EMS truck, as usual moving much too slowly in our opinion, and the fat one said under his breath, "This ain't TV, folks, this is how fast we go." He was carrying the heavy respirator and cardiac unit past the bushes that had grown monstrous and over the erupting lawn, tame and immaculate thirteen months earlier when the trouble began.

How many sisters have committed suicide . . . or tried; we don't know that Mary was successful in her attempt. Why? What's been happening in the Lisbon household for the last thirteen months? Obviously, we're going to find out, Eugenides isn't going to set something like that up without explaining it.

At the same time, he's set a tone: the "fat one" speaks (and he's carrying the "heavy respirator"; there's a parallel set up between the man and the machine that plays quietly in the back of the mind before we move on); then the opposites: the tame lawn and the monstrous bushes.

Between the question and the writing itself, the authors have hooked us.

There's nothing wrong with starting a story where it begins, where the events we're going to examine, start . . . *for the contemporaneous action*, starting with the character's *now*, and proceeding from there. That also means that, sometimes, you'll have to use a flashback. Unfortunately, because either they were overused or poorly done, conventional wisdom is that one shouldn't employ the technique. One of the reasons given is that it stops the forward flow of the story (there's misuse, in a nutshell); the other is that it makes things more difficult for the reader, who has to shift frames of reference. Just between the two of us, I think you can forget about that one. If a person is a reader, they're capable of going where you lead.

David Guterson does it in the best-selling *Snow Falling on Cedars* (Harcourt Brace & Company, 1994):

> The accused man, Kabuo Miyamoto, sat proudly upright with a rigid grace, his palms placed softly on the defendant's table—the posture of a man who has detached himself insofar as this is possible at his own trial. Some in the gallery would later say that his stillness suggested a disdain for the proceedings; others felt certain it veiled a fear of the verdict that was to come. Whichever it was, Kabuo showed nothing—not even a flicker of the eyes. He was dressed in a white shirt worn buttoned to the throat and gray, neatly pressed trousers. His figure, especially the neck and shoulders, communicated the impression of irrefutable physical strength and of precise, even imperial bearing. Kabuo's features were smooth and angular; his hair had been cropped close to his skull in a manner that made its musculature prominent. In the face of the charge that had been leveled against him he sat with his dark eyes trained straight ahead and did not appear moved at all.

The novel is—at least at one level—about a murder trial; we learn that in the next paragraph. But the trial has roots that go deep into the past. That means the backstory, important to several of the central characters in the drama about to unfold, has to be brought into play, given to the reader at the proper time.

It's far too complex to try and reproduce examples of how the author accomplishes this, but I'd recommend reading *Snow Falling on Cedars* to learn how to do it not only seamlessly, but in a way that keeps the story going forward: all the information makes a difference, makes the characters who they are today. It is done so naturally that you don't even realize the time shift until you're into it. Guterson could have started the story in the days just preceding World War II and then come forward; but the novel wouldn't have been as effective that way; it would have been just as wrong for him to begin with another technique that is finding increasing favor these days.

I'd say that at least seven out of ten of the manuscripts I receive as submissions or for critique begin with a prologue. They're often ambiguous: no one is referred to by name (lots of "he" and "she" and "the man"), the setting is left undescribed or, at least, nondescript, and the action is blood-curdling or frightening or threatening. And, it would seem, the events took place some time in the past.

Now, we know why this is being done, right? Some occurrence, barely remembered, is going to surface during today's story. But we're being kept in suspense: since we don't know which character is being watched (some clever writers do the prologue in first or third person and the rest of the novel in the other voice), we don't know, as we keep reading, who it was that suffered. There'd be nothing wrong with this is as a technique were it not for the fact that it's so overused that it loses it's impact. Moreover, the majority of these prologues are either dealing with child abuse, witnessing an act of violence, or present an action scene (most common in thrillers, espionage stories, and adventure tales) and I, as a reader, shrug. Been there, done that, don't see any reason to go back. For me, the writer has tipped his hand too soon.

There's also this to consider: if everything an editor sees coming across his desk looks the same, how's he supposed to find the novel that's different? There really are only so many ways in which to show a childhood trauma, and any novel that seems to be simply repeating the past should go to the bottom of the pile. So, if you want to use the prologue, if that's the only way you see to get that backstory incident into the novel, help yourself by finding something different to do.

Helen Dunmore, in the absolutely remarkable *Talking to the Dead* (Little, Brown, 1996) does it this way:

The newer graves lie full in the sun, beyond the shadow of the church and yew tree. Two of them are covered in plastic-wrapped flowers and raw earth; these graves won't have stones for a while yet, because they must wait for the earth to settle.

There are a lot of things you need to learn when someone dies, and you have to learn fast, from people who are paid to teach you. They come up with hushed, serious faces and they must wait. It's their job. There were two of them standing there, noting down the requirements. One glanced at the other, and they gleamed with satisfaction at phrasing it all so well. But they were much too professional to smile.

And then the food. After a funeral you have to eat, to prove you're still alive. There are foods that are suitable, and foods that are not. The suitable ones turn out to be ham, or cold chicken. Quiche is very popular, and Australian wines. I can remember staring at a big glazed ham, its rind scored into squares and glistening with syrup. I thought of how it would be sliced and fed to us after your burial. Someone was asking me if I would like fresh pineapple to garnish the ham, or tinned.

"Will you want the coffin open, or closed?"

"Some people," one of them whispered, "some people find it a great comfort actually to have *seen*. Not to have to *imagine*. It can be a great comfort."

"A great comfort," I say aloud now, taking the words
out like stones from my pocket, tossing them into the
quiet air.

It's beautiful here, where you are . . .

Who's speaking? Being spoken to? Are the two people in the ceme-
tery there to speak with the narrator, or is she remembering?
Dunmore has given us hints, has engaged our senses (food, at it
turns out, plays an enormous role in this highly sensuous novel),
has made you want to go on. At the same time, she's offered a bit
of the past and disquieted us at the same time: "'A great comfort,' I
say aloud now . . ." Clearly, comfort is something the speaker has-
n't found. And we have a prologue that doesn't attempt to manipu-
late the reader into caring based on a situation.

Dunmore and Busch share one thing in their very different
opening scenes: they've presented us with a character, have gotten
us immediately involved in the lives of the people they'll be telling
us about on an emotional and personal level. But people are not,
necessarily, the only "characters" in a novel. Locale, weather, situations—they all play a role. Here's the opening page of Alice
Hoffman's bestseller, *Turtle Moon* (G. P. Putnam's Sons, 1992):

The last major crime in the town of Verity was in 1958,
when one of the Platts shot his brother in an argument
over a Chevy Nomad they had bought together on time.
Usually it's so quiet you can hear the strangler figs dropping their fruit on the hoods of parked cars, leaving behind
pulp and tiny black seeds. Since Verity is the most humid
spot in eastern Florida, local people know enough to drink
their coffee iced in the morning. The air all around the
town limits is so thick that sometimes a soul cannot rise
and instead attaches itself to a stranger, landing right
between the shoulder blades with a thud that carries no
more weight than a hummingbird.

Charles Verity, who founded the town, after killing off
as many native people as he could, is said to have discovered this the hard way.

The first thing we notice is the dramatically different storytelling
style; Hoffman is almost oral in her approach and we get a sense of
someone on a porch, filling us in on local events. What's important?
That the last murder was in 1958 . . . hinting at the possibility that
one may have just taken place . . . or foreshadowing that one is about
to? Undoubtedly. But, she uses that line to start telling us about the
town. (The chapter goes on to tell us a little about Charles Verity
and his times and trials.)

We are also gently introduced to some local magic (Hoffman is
one of the leading American magic realists, so that comes as no surprise), when we're told about the souls not being able to rise
through the thick air: both an image of the humidity and a warning
that all things may not be as they appear to be in Verity.

Again, a word choice is important: it's not just figs that are
falling, it's "strangler" figs. Granted, we know that a fig isn't going
to jump off a tree and throttle us, but the use of the word, coming
immediately after mentioning the Platt killing, places emphasis on
a lurking danger, creates a mood, sets a tone.

We also know that the weather, the conditions in and around
Verity are going to be major players in whatever follows; if nothing
else, they are going to be root causes in the way people think and
look at each other. We've been prepared for this (even if it isn't part
of our usual process) and so are helped in suspending disbelief.

(Oh, just a thought, here: none of the books quoted from to
this point are mystery novels, at least not in the sense that we use
and know the word as writers and publishers. And yet . . .)

I think that any reader of at least average intelligence would
be drawn in by any of those scenes; not one is action, bang-bang,
hit the ground running, though. That's something to keep in mind

the next time you run across an article on hooking the reader, one that begins by saying, "You've got to get them into the story fast" and generally implying that that means some kind of action scene; after all, the scenes we've just examined are all almost static, ruminative. Just goes to show ya.

Because Hoffman has given us a very informal tone, I want to offer something else for your consideration. This is the first paragraph of J.R. Pearson's riotous *Off for the Sweet Hereafter* (Simon & Schuster, 1986):

That was the summer we lost the bald Jeeter who was not even mostly Jeeter anymore but was probably mostly Throckmorton or anyway was probably considered mostly Throckmorton which was an appreciable step up from being considered mostly Jeeter since Jeeters hadn't ever been anything much while Throckmortons had in fact been something once previously before the money got gone and the prestige fell away leaving merely the bluster and the taint and the general Throckmorton aroma all of which taken together hardly made for a legacy worth getting stirred up over but any one of which taken singly still outstripped the entire bulk of advancements ever attempted and realized by Jeeters who had scratched around in the dirt but were not much accomplished at farming and who had speculated in herds of cattle but were not much accomplished at speculating either and who at last had turned their energies to the construction of a henhouse which commenced ramshackle and got worse but became nonetheless the chief Jeeter advancement along with the hens and the little speckled brown eggs and the localized ammonia cloud which was itself most probably the primary Jeeter success though no particular Jeeter or group of Jeeters together actually contributed to it or could prevent it either so when the bald Jeeter, with the fat Jeeter as her maid of honor, exchanged vows with Braxton Porter Throckmorton III in the sanctuary of the Methodist church on Saturday June the twelfth, 1942, and afterwards set up house in Neely proper she got away from the hens and the henhouse and out from under the ammonia cloud which was most likely beginning to expand in June of 1942 since it set in to expanding most every June and swelled straight through August and on into September, especially this past August and especially this past September when it was bearing down on the town limits and posing some threat to the icehouse which was regular and ordinary for the season, particularly in August and particularly in September, so we were having what had come to be our usual summer straight up to the moment Mr. Derwood Bridger laid his ladder against the Throckmorton clapboard and climbed to the upper story where he pressed his nose to the bedroom windowscreen and shaded his eyes and called and hollered and shrieked at the bald Jeeter until he was satisfied that she was gone from us for good.

Now: Pearson's certainly obeyed the "rule" about keeping paragraphs to no more than eight sentences. However, that injunction against sentences of more than twelve or fourteen words seems to have been ignored. And it doesn't matter, does it? Pearson has put us most definitely in a place (it doesn't take much thought to know that this is a "southern" novel); he's set the tone for the novel (comic; relaxed and informal); and, if a reader likes a tale, a yarn, well, clearly that's what's being held in hand.

Both the Hoffman and the Pearson share that storytelling tone, both set it immediately, both have made place central. So does Arundhati Roy in her bestseller, *The God of Small Things* (HarperCollins, 1997):

> May in Ayemenem is a hot, brooding month. The days are long and humid. The river shrinks and black crows gorge on bright mangoes in still, dustgreen trees. Red bananas ripen. Jackfruits burst. Dissolute bluebottles hum vacuously in the fruity air. Then they stun themselves against clear windowpanes and die, fatly baffled in the sun.
>
> The nights are clear but suffused with sloth and sullen expectation.
>
> But by early June the south-west monsoon breaks and there are three months of wind and water with short spells of sharp, glittering sunshine that thrilled children snatch to play with.

Sounds a lot like Verity, Florida—but this is India. We know what this place feels like, and we know the effects of those conditions on people. But there's another reason to read the paragraphs carefully: look at the way Roy has engaged the senses: the jackfruits bursting carry sound; the fruity air goes right to the sense of smell; the humidity speaks to our sense of touch. By using that technique, by putting us right in the scene by giving us the information we usually process to define things, Roy (who won the 1997 Booker Prize for this novel) has broken the wall that exists between reader and text and brought us into the story. Hooked us. Made us want to go on.

Making us go on is all the opening has to do. It does not have to tell us what kind of book we're reading, doesn't have to define all the action (there's all sorts of foreshadowing in the samples we've looked at; none of them were genre titles per se, though there were love stories, crime stories, slightly fantastic stories); they can set a tone, a voice, let us know where in space (and maybe in time; a reference to some known event will place a book nicely) we're going.

What none of the writers did was try to put everything into the opening paragraphs. It happens that way all too often; a writer attempting to set a scene, a character, and an occurrence will make the opening top-heavy, sinking what comes later under the weight of too many words, too many adjectives and adverbs. Even the most complex of the openings we looked at were, in the end, rather simple and straightforward, giving you just as much as you needed to know—and leaving something to be said in the next paragraphs.

Every day brings a new selection of openings from which to choose to learn; the ones I used all came from books that I browsed in a store and decided to buy and read. None were a disappointment. I purposefully didn't use category fiction to draw the examples from because there's a point to be made: you, as the writer, can do it the way you want to without losing a step on the competition. Here's the way to prove it:

You know the story you want to tell, have the core well in hand by this point. Try rewriting your opening from various points of view, with different approaches. Create a scene that might be pivotal and that will, normally, appear in the middle of your story; then, put it up front. Remember, your reader doesn't know what's been happening, but you can't tell them everything. Give just enough and then segué into the story. Don't use hackneyed phrases: "How did we get to that point?" Instead, make an action shift. In *Girls*, Busch goes from the scene we looked at into a phone conversation that ends with a question and the question allows the narrator to begin at the beginning.

Or you might begin by using the setting to create a mood and then use the mood: if you begin with a dark and stormy night, streets reflecting the constantly changing traffic lights, switch from that point to the narrator waiting to cross a street, stepping back as a car drives through a puddle. The character reacts (how will help define the character, if you want to play with it) and continues on to act out her part in the novel.

Write the pages without any preconceptions, feel free to just put one word after another, letting it build. As Anne LaMott puts it so succinctly and perfectly in *Bird by Bird*: there's nothing wrong with a shitty first draft.

And try several approaches, not just one: see what you can do with setting, with character, with voice; play with starting your story in different places, rather than the obvious ones.

Leave a question in your reader's mind, a question that may define your theme or your storyline; whatever it is, it is the search for the answer that hooks the audience.

What you may end up with is a different kind of opening, one that will set your novel apart, that will tell the editor (and the reader) immediately why they should buy your book instead of any of the others waiting to be picked.

Scenes

1ife proceeds through a series of actions, large or small. (Usually, they're small, but most lives aren't particularly dramatic—except to those living them, which might make an interesting premise for a novel.)

Your novel is going to be put together the same way; even if you use flashbacks, and unless you're trying something experimental, it will be more or less linear. You will be answering the six "W" questions by depicting things that happen and the effects that they have.

The really nice thing about that structure, for you right now, is that it allows you to think in "local" terms, rather than universals. You write your book one word at a time, one sentence, one paragraph, building a story through a series of revelations. All you have to do is put one on top of the other until you're done. And believe me, it's a lot easier thinking in terms of *well, today I'll write the scene in which Jonathan meets Rachel*, rather than *I've got to get Jonathan and Rachel together so that Bill will find them and* . . . You know you have to do that, yes, but you don't have to think about it today; you can't put the capstone on a structure until you get to the top.

You know already that events are moved by cause and effect,

motivation and response, and they're tied as tightly as anything you can imagine. Dwight Swain put it this way: "Cause becomes *motivating stimulus* . . . effect, *character reaction*. A motivating stimulus is anything outside your focal character to which he reacts; character reaction is anything he does as a consequence."

Look back at the opening of *Girls*. Something has happened to the narrator; he's reacted. The scene of the digging is a motivating stimulus, one of many in a richly textured novel; there were other stimuli that got him to that place. That, at its most basic, is the blueprint for any novel you will ever read or write. And all you have to do is write each one, one at a time.

Let's say you have a character who wants to know everything he can and he's learned that the only way to know is by experience. He's told that if he goes in a certain direction, he'll find something. However, gaining the knowledge is dangerous, deadly, in fact. Thinking about it, he comes upon a way to protect himself from the worst of the danger, and gain the knowledge that he wants.

So he sets out. There's motivation: the character has been established as one who wants to experience everything. (Or needs specific knowledge.) That's one scene: having him learn that the knowledge is available. He reacts: by discovering how to protect himself; a second scene. He prepares and sets out; the third scene. Fourth scene: we follow him into the action, see the danger and how he survives. Finally, with the knowledge, he moves on, making use of it.

That sequence is found in *The Odyssey*, as Ulysses ties himself to the mast of his ship so that he can hear the Sirens; it's also in every James Bond novel, every love story in which one or the other of the lead characters is warned away from the other . . . it's everywhere. (And if you look at it closely, it's also the Hero's journey writ small.)

Every cause has an effect, placed together the scenes become an act(ion). And the beauty of it is that you don't have to think in terms of all the action—one at a time is enough; as you write, you'll be placing the things you need next on stage so that when you begin that next one, everything is already there.

Now you've got two choices. Action causes reaction, characters reacting cause conflict and conflicts are a crucial part of the combination that make up a readable novel. It might satisfy some need buried deep in a reader to have a story that begins on a high note and continues from there at a nice level pace, everything coming to the hero(ine) as needed, life flowing smoothly. It would, if nothing else, be a completely and truly escapist novel, wouldn't it? And it would fail miserably, wouldn't it? I mean, talk about your fairy tales! Simply, if nothing gets in the way of your central characters as they try to achieve their goals, you don't have a story.

So . . . you can go immediately into the next bit of action, creating confrontation. That has a certain appeal: the pace never flags, the reader doesn't have a chance to stop because something is always happening. During the heyday of the men's adventure novel (which are, really, the male equivalent of the romance novel in intent, if not in longevity), that's how the books were put together: every chapter ended with a cliffhanger and the next began with the fall from the cliff. The drawback there is that the reader is left with the impression that the characters never think: they are *reactive* rather than *proactive* . . . dogs being wagged by the tail of the action.

There are times when, in life (and a novel is a depiction of a life) things do happen that way, and if you use it occasionally in your story it won't cause a problem. More often, though, you're going to want to create a sequel to the scene that serves as a transition. It gives your character the chance to think about what's going to happen next, to consider what has to be done, to recognize and acknowledge events and to make a decision about what's going to be done next.

And it helps keep the tension alive because the reader is left, on the one page, with the image of the character dangling from that metaphoric cliff, while on the other, we're participating in another set of events.

And that leads, inexorably, to the next scene.

Think of it as a roller coaster—one of those old-fashioned ones, like Coney Island's Cyclone. You begin slowly, taking the reader up that first incline. Tension begins to build: we know that once we get to the top, we're in for the ride of our lives, but right now, as we begin, all we see is sky and all we feel is the pressure as we're pushed back into our seats.

Then there's the rush down, breathless, with momentum carrying us halfway up the next rise, then a slowing, then a rush . . . I've seen fiction diagrammed in terms of hills and valleys and it's apt. Whatever goes up has to come down . . .eventually. If you're of a mind to, you can also think in terms of storms: the calm before, the quiet eye in the middle, the blue sky at the end. What you want are a series of linked climaxes, each preparing the way for the next.

What you're doing as you pace yourself that way is creating expectation, but making the reader wait for it to be fulfilled. We hear a lot about reader expectation; if you follow that roller coaster scheme, using quiet scenes that seem to be about something other than the plotting at hand, you add an extra layer of tension, one that seems to play between you and your audience. When they don't know what to expect beyond the unexpected, you have them in the palm of your hand.

Now, look at your outline (and keep looking later, when you revise): study the scenes you've decided to use—undoubtedly, they'll be sequences you're going to use to keep the storyline moving forward. Do they offer the reader a sense of time and place? Does the reader know who's on stage? Do we know why they're on stage? (We don't have to, but you do.) Does the *character* know why she's on stage? What is happening? Is it motivated, or is it there because you need it to be? (Not the best approach; readers will put up with a little contrivance now and then, but not a steady diet of it.) Are the characters' actions realistic, at least in terms of the story? (We're back, once again, to the character in jeopardy going down to the basement in the deserted house in the storm, the scene that makes us laugh in movies; why, I wonder, do so many writers and readers accept it in fiction?) Is there a conflict, someone or something keeping the central character from achieving her goal? Are you creating a series of climaxes? Once you have the technique down, you'll be able to create a sequence of scenes, each with a small ending, that will lead to a cumulative climax.

How are you getting from one scene to the next? Is there a transition, one in which causes for later actions are being created?

So far, then, so good. If not, try this:

✍ Write the scene that immediately precedes an important revelation in your novel. Let's say you're looking at having two people who will be lovers meet. How do you get them together? Even if you've decided on a some-enchanted-evening approach, strangers across a crowded room, you want the reader to know something about them, about their separate states of mind. So, write a scene in which he is arriving. Do you want him open to events, or closed? What's his state of mind? Remember: *the reader doesn't know this is going to happen*, but we've been following the character during some crisis, perhaps, the resolution of which might dictate the mood.

Establish that mood, and try doing it by showing, not telling: let us see the character standing outside, chain-smoking, taking a nip from a flask, just staring at the door, turning away, seeing a shadow against the drawn curtains, turning back. Each of those actions will indicate something about the character, his attitudes. Finally, he knocks at the door. End of scene.

✍ Or this one: At some point in every mystery novel, a body is discovered. It really isn't enough to have that first person at the crime scene just stumble across the corpse. (And give some serious thought to what the person's reactions are going to be; having had more than my share of that kind of experience, I can assure you that you don't just calmly run to call the police. The first time it happened to me, I looked for a place to leave the dinner I'd eaten shortly before.)

Again, set the mood. Out dogwalking, thinking about her date later that evening. Distraught because the date was broken? Certainly, the last thing she's thinking about is what only you know is going to happen. As before, write so as to put the reader into the character's head. And then she turns the corner.

These scenes are, in and of themselves, simple enough, but they have to serve several purposes: One, they will add to and forward character evolution. Two, they involve the reader with the character, establishing our relationship with, and reaction to, him. You don't want the reader disliking the character, unless that feeling is going to be used somehow, perhaps to change our minds later as we watch him grow. Third, you're compelling the reader to go on: whatever is happening is interesting enough, in and of itself, to make us concentrate on the scene and not try to think ahead. You're preparing us, by lulling us. The dog walk turns into the shock of finding a body, the entrance to the party is the beginning of a new stage in the character's life.

What you're doing is establishing your control over the reader and over your material. Of course, we know that the control over material may be short-lived: characters have been known to take over. That's fine—something you've done earlier caused it (they really don't have minds of their own)—but once it happens, you have to make the decision as to how to use it. Now you're on the roller coaster, too.

Description

there's a line I'll never forget, read in some otherwise for-gotten novel:

A black shirt, black pants, and black boots hugged a broad-shouldered body.

Right: in a published novel. It makes me wonder, sometimes, why any of us bother. (How did those boots get up to his shoulders, anyway?) I admit, you do want to make your work memorable, but is that what you want it remembered for?

Several friends—editors and writers—were at a summer conference in Maine and one evening we sat around the faculty lounge, a Miles Davis disk on the CD player, his trumpet coun-terpointed now and again by the sound of thunder rolling across the campus. We were as comfortable as we could get on the inexpensive furniture (during the year, the lounge was the fourth floor common room in a students' dormitory), leaning forward for another beer or to simply peel the backs of our thighs from the vinyl chairs. David chose to sit on the window sill. He was get-ting wet, but he wasn't under the cloud from the various cigars, pipes and cigarettes that were fireflying around the room; his clothes wouldn't reek as badly as what the rest of us were wear-ing. The discussion focused on helping our students at the

,orkshop overcome one of the major weaknesses we'd seen so far in our readings: description.

It's a problem I was all too familiar with: just the week before I'd been talking to an editorial assistant about a manuscript he wanted to acquire, and when I asked him to describe the hero, he was at a loss for words. The author had been, also.

Look back at those scenes you were working on. How clearly described were they? How well did they engage the senses of the reader? When we go someplace new, when we meet someone, we use all of our senses. And your job, as a writer, is to create sensuous scenes.

Skim back a couple of paragraphs, to my description of the activity in the lounge. You may not know the color of the furniture or the walls; you don't know how many people were in the room or who they were. But look at what you do know: the heat and humidity are obvious; most of the people were probably wearing shorts (which is why the backs of their thighs were sticking to the furniture). There are sounds—thunder, conversation, the trumpet jazz of Miles Davis. The room is dark, or darkened: the lit ends of the cigarettes are "fireflying"—a construction I might not let you get away with, but this is my book. The sense of smell is involved: that's why I mixed cigars and pipes and cigarettes, and added the reeking clothes. By mentioning the cloud and making you "look" at David on the window sill, I've brought in sight. Even touch is there: at some point we've all had that sticky feeling in humid weather. Combined, they make the room more real, bring you into it more than if I'd talked about colors or numbers or the kind of rug: those are unessential details and they're the type that most writers seem to concentrate on. Anyone actually coming into that room on that night, though, would have experienced it as I described it, and that was what was important.

Or look at the "scene" that begins the chapter on Theme. Without going into great detail, I've been able to create not only an ambiance, but also given you a sense of the character, "I." Just by saying, for instance, "Texans and air conditioning," I've set a place and given an idea of season . . . and of the character's attitudes about where he is.

   ✍ So, here's your first exercise to help build vivid description. I first saw it used by Boston law professor turned p.i. writer Jeremiah Healy in a bar in Philadelphia. As soon as we walked in, before we'd ordered, Jerry took out a pad, and began writing. Looking over his shoulder, I saw five items listed: the wine bar against the right side wall, the horseshoe bar in the center of the room, the bottles of small-batch bourbons lining the bar, the vines on the walls and the firepole in the middle of the room. These were the items that he'd use if he used the bar in a scene. (It also allowed him to make a decent case for the time spent there to be interpreted as research.)

   I saw other things, but I was seeing them after I became aware of the fact that I was looking for things to notice. But the room was no longer new to me; now I was looking for various details.

   If you're going to do this—and I don't know why you wouldn't—remember: write down the first five things you notice when you go into a place *for the first time*; subsequent visits, just like my looking around later, never give the same impression. And if you're going to use wherever you are as a setting, those are the five things you mention first: they are the things your character will sense and they will begin to define the space for the reader. Notice: the things your character will *sense,* the things you *notice*. A place, a person, a thing, is rarely just a visual experience. Yet if you look at a description you've written, or look at what appears in most books and stories, you will find, among other sins, the only one of the five senses that gets real attention is sight. Granted, there are times when it might be difficult to include touch or taste, but . . .

   I've been told (by my wife, who knows about these things) that a woman's sense of smell is much more acute than a man's; my reading bears that out: women tend to include the sense of smell much more often in a description—at least those who are paying attention do. So, it's here as a reminder to everyone.

If you look back at Jerry's notes on the bar, for instance, you'll see that every one of his notes had to do with a visual, with the placement of things.

But is the impact of a busy bar or room only what's physically in there? Here are a few lines from the opening scene of my novella, *Slow Dancing to Loud Music*:

> Smoke, and the music so loud: it must be, you feel the vibration through the tile floor of the men's room. Your stomach rebels after a day starting in last night's promise, ending here, alone. Who was last night?

The first thing the character notices is the smoke and the music, and the music is a physical presence. There's nothing about what's in the room, who is in the room (in fact, as the piece now stands— it's still in first draft—there is never any more description of the place), nothing but the smoke and the sound. Anyone who's walked into a party in a bar or a fraternity house, or even into the lounge in a hotel on a Saturday night, will recognize the place immediately. Each will have different reactions: I know people who think that's what a party is supposed to be like; I may have, once, too. But I was younger then, and so is my character. His sense of the room is in keeping with his condition.

Here's some more, a few paragraphs later:

> You walked around the edges of the room, edging toward the bar, edging toward the edge of the bar and the keen scent of sippin' whiskey. Jackie waved to you, all silky hair and long legs, from across the dance floor; you nodded, waved, thinking of talking and of hiding in words that wouldn't be heard. But first you go to the men's room so you can begin again. You don't look in the mirror.

Now in a corner, you sit, watchful, wanting to dance, watching shades move to the bourbon-mellow sounds of Willie Nelson. Rachel is elsewhere, elsewhen. You watch the movements, the possibilities without risk; patterns emerge, merge, shuffle of feet to an insistent beat. You light a cigarette.

You drink; dancing is a matter of mood; mood a matter of whatever is going on tempered by the warmth of drowning drinks. It wouldn't be fun, you knew that before you pushed the door open; it would be too crowded, too hot, too noisy (but you can lose yourself in noise) and airless and too goddamned bad you think.

"You," (his name is Jonathan) is not happy where he is or at best has mixed feelings about the place. What are the things he's noticing? There's the scent of sippin' whiskey, there's a bar, there's Jackie . . . and what do we know about Jackie?

Well, what she's wearing is beside the point, obviously, and so is the color of her eyes. In that kind of (implied) crowd, with all the smoke, all that can be seen is her hair and her legs; there's no way to know whether her eyes are blue or brown or anything else. (We don't know the color of her hair, either, though I'd guess most readers will see blonde; it has something to do with "silky." Donald E. Westlake once described a character as having "hair colored hair." Works for me.)

What else do we have: a reemphasizing of the discomfort levels: hot, airless, noisy. What is being described is only what's needed for the mood that's being created. Even the music is being handled in a particular way: generally, the music would probably be considered by the reader to be metal or rock; here, though, we have the "bourbon-mellow sounds of Willie Nelson." (Another level of the sense of hearing and a hint—to those who enjoy sippin' whiskey—of taste.) This is a quieter kind of music, a ballad most likely. But it's turned up so high, so amplified, that the vibrations are felt through the men's room floor. (Which introduces the sense of touch.)

The scene has served several functions: We've put a character in a place (it is purposefully ambiguous; thematically, it could be—and should be—considered Everywhere). Given Jonathan's mood and feelings, we sense, at least, that some kind of confrontation is going to take place. Now, admittedly, I'm taking something for granted here; counting on my reader being experienced enough to have seen something akin to this situation and being able to read between the lines and to understand that the combination of drinking, angst and ennui—*It wouldn't be fun, you knew that before you pushed the door open; it would be too crowded, too hot, too noisy (but you can lose yourself in noise) and airless and too godamned bad you think*—foreshadows something, even if we don't know what. But we have a hint—*Rachel is elsewhere, elsewhen.*

We're also getting the initial sketch of the character; the scene is used to give the reader some idea of Jonathan establishing, at least in part, the way he thinks, the way he feels about certain things, about his drinking and smoking. It's all being established without breaking the forward motion of the story to stop and tell the reader this, that, and the other thing, while at the same time engaging all the senses.

And finally, to this, the last paragraph of this set piece:

Yes, you say as Jackie looks down at you, mouthing "Jonathan" or saying it; in the noise it is all the same, hand extended, offering her body for you to worship on the dance floor, and she steps into the circle of your arms, belly to belly, groin to groin, moving slowly, sexless and intimating sex. She is safety and you shuffle to the sound, speaking banalities, then silent in timeless movement. You imagine holding Rachel, still missing between

where you were and where you are; see her in your arms
and someone else's, see her as a pattern of stars and feel
your partner slide into another step with another person
and find a bourbon up, coke back and a cigarette.

It is now, two and half manuscript pages into the story, that we get
Jonathan's name, but we've already heard Rachel's a number of
times; she is, right now, more important than he is, even though she
isn't (as far as we know) there. Everything is being introduced as it
needs to be.

Which is the point I want to make now. Take a look at your
manuscript or, more's the pity, at a published novel. Turn to a page
of description, a passage in which a character or a room is being
introduced to the reader. See what's been done? In the vast majority of cases, the action stopped and you're reading about a room,
being given everything that's there: the furnishings, the flowers on
the table, the wood the table's made of (do you really know, walking into a room, what kind of wood was used?), something about
the rug, something about the paintings on the wall, the number of
lamps . . . all too often these scenes read like pages out of an interior decorating magazine.

Look back at my undetailed description of Jackie. She's a
minor character, you've read everything about her that you're
going to ever know. But, in most of the manuscripts I receive,
she would be treated to a much fuller treatment: hair color, eye
color, maybe fleshtones. I'd know the color of her clothes, and
probably get some kind of brand identification, just to make it
more "real"; but if I don't know Donna Karan from Anne Klein
(and I don't), what difference will it make? As far as I know,
they're both overpriced, and that's about it. If Jackie were
important, I might have mentioned that she looked like a page
out of the L.L. Bean catalogue, or an issue of *Vogue*, because that
would serve to tell us something about her.

The only thing important, though, is given to the reader in that last paragraph: that in Jonathan's perception her dancing is sexless and intimates sex, and she offers her body for Jonathan to worship. (Yes, it says as much about him as about her, but that's the point, isn't it?)

Also to the point: I used a couple of brand names above; more and more, it seems, descriptions of places are being couched in terms of what are expected to be easily recognizable brands: a Sony television, a Dell computer, Ikea furnishings. It does work as a shorthand of sorts, but seems most useful as a way of indicating financial or class status. Used occasionally, I don't argue about it too much; a steady diet of it, however, becomes wearing. And since we don't get paid by the manufacturers for using the product names—unlike movie studios that don't have to pay for the items they use on the set as long as they give credit . . .

✍ Try this: describe a room (and after that, a person) through action, incorporating the elements as they might be logically experienced by someone seeing them for the first time. Remember, if you're describing a man, women are much more likely to notice eye color than a man is—unless there's something dramatic about them; a guy's probably more likely to notice a black eye than the fact that they're gray. In fact, women are much more likely to be aware of just about everything than men are (excepting trained observers: law enforcement people, spies . . . writers). I mention all of this just in case you're doing a little cross-gender writing.

Back to the exercise: we tend to notice four or five things first, when we enter a room. Those items are defining and they're the ones that should be offered to the reader right off the bat; everything else comes in as needed, and as the character would come into contact with them. If, for instance, you have lots of pictures and other *objets d'art* on your walls, it's likely that someone coming into the room would notice the number, the color, but not the details, not what a painting depicts, not what the framed plaque says. She might see the bookshelves, see a matched set of leather-bound volumes, but wouldn't know what they are. Do they make a difference, are they going to be part of your story or in some way add to understanding of your character? If the answer's yes, have her walk to the shelves and lift one of the books. You've accomplished several things by doing that: You've told us something about the person who owns the books (The books we display say a lot about us, don't they?) and something about the person who just entered. It may be about her powers of observation, or it may be about her interests. If that leatherbound book is *The Oxford Dictionary of Quotation* and she just shrugs and puts it back, we get one message. If she opens it and leafs through, we get another. Does she turn away from the shelves after examining the volume, or does she look at the other books, touching them, or lifting one?

You should, by this point, realize something else about everything you write as part of a novel: every scene serves more than one purpose. You've constructed a scene because you want to establish the primary conflict; the scene, though, is not only about that. Whether you're explicit or subtle, you're planting ideas in the reader's mind about other things: character, frame of mind, frames of reference. If, as an editor and as a reader (because I must be both), I sense that a scene is there only to advance the storyline, that there's nothing more to it beyond getting me ready for the next turn of events, I've discovered that my eye begins to slide down the lines, looking for the place where things begin to happen again.

That always happens when I get to a paragraph or two that are simply blocks of narrative description. One writer with whom I've worked laughed when I pointed out that he'd introduce a character by saying that he was heavy-set and had black hair, and then continue with the action. Sure, he avoided the long interruption, but I insist that it would be more effective if we got those two absolutely unnecessary bits of information (because they make no difference) through some kind of action: the chair creaks under his weight as he sits down, he brushes some strands of black hair off the pages on his desk. It's still unnecessary information, but at least it's in some context; he wouldn't have stopped me even for a moment or caused my eye to skip.

I know, you're thinking of Jackie and her short description. Why did I even need that information? Because as I used it (and if I was successful), it is reflective of Jonathan's point of view—it's what he's seeing, what he's aware of, what matters to him. If Rachel were the observer in that scene, the clothes and something about Jackie's figure (she is, potentially, a rival in Rachel's eyes; in Jonathan's, she's just someone who is there and who doesn't matter). There's a world of difference between that and a narrator saying: "Her narrow, but pleasant face lit up. 'Billy Sadler?' she asked. She was a slightly built woman with short dark hair, deep, almost coal black eyes, and a very good, if small figure. She looked to be in her mid to late thirties." It tells us nothing about Sadler, adds nothing to the story; it's just there.

Another habit writers are falling into these days: using brand-name people as reference points to describe their character. I realized the error of that approach one afternoon when I was writing about New York City, and described the West Side as Sophia Loren and the East Side as Phoebe Cates. That only works if everyone who reads it thinks of Cates as she was in some made-for-TV movie that had been playing that week. Right now, I can't conjure an image of Cates (yesterday or today); what would my reader have been left with. Sophia Loren is relatively safer: she's a genuine icon who should last (just like the West Side). If you can't think of a way of describing your character on his or her own merits, and fall back on a comparison of this kind, be sure that there's a timelessness to whomever you choose. (A friend of mine tells me he's too young to remember Sophia Loren. Oh, well.)

That isn't to say, at all, that details are unimportant; what counts is finding the right ones. I'm sure you've seen the scene in which a director looks at the movie set through a finder. What he's doing is "framing the scene," making sure the important things are captured on film. And he's finding the item that's going to get a close-up: the Venetian glass figurine on the wall shelf that will create an echo of *The Glass Menagerie*, the overflowing ashtray . . . the detail that carries weight. You can do the same thing.

✍ If you have a camera with a good telephoto lens, view the room you're in through it, first at its widest angle and then zooming in. When you have the tight view, what's the thing you see that's important? That's the item you mention. And if you don't have a camera, just use the tube from a roll of toilet paper or paper towel. It's the same thing we did as kids, using those tubes as telescopes; by blocking things out, they did, almost, bring things into clearer focus, didn't they?

✍ Write the same scene (using two characters) from the point of view of each one. Do they see the surroundings in the same way? How do they react to what the other may be saying or doing? And is the other aware of the differences? Why or why not? Does that awareness present itself in some way when you're writing from the other character's viewpoint?

✍ A final exercise. It's time consuming (but if you're in a hurry, you're doing it wrong), challenging, and will stretch your abilities to their maximum, as well as teaching you to use all of your senses. (By the way, the next time you're at the library or the bookstore, I'd suggest you pick up a copy of Diane Ackerman's *A Natural History of the Senses*. Not only is it a pleasure to read, the lessons are invaluable.)

Create a scene, it doesn't matter what it is. But, do it six times. For each of the first five, use one sense and one sense only: sight, sound, taste, touch, smell. (I remember a quiz show from the late '40s or early '50s in which the contestants had to identify selected items that way, using just one sense. I think it was called "The Sixth Sense"; something to do with intuition.) In the sixth writing, use the strongest images from the first five—and if you can't use all five, don't worry about it. When the scene is done, it must read naturally, not like a catalogue of sensory impressions received.

If you can do that regularly in your writing—not every scene, be judicious—you'll be creating scenes that remain with the reader long after the book has gone back on the shelf. You are writing about specific people in specific places (the ambiguity of my story notwithstanding) and you need to have your reader know them as well as you do. But details are like spices: they have to be used delicately, so that the flavors come together as a medley—those are the meals that are remembered.

Dialogue

Once upon a time, someone decided that words like "said" and "asked" were dull, and that there had to be a way of spicing up a novel by using other words. And thus was born the Said Book, a collection of words to be used instead of the dull and perfectly appropriate "said." Unfortunately, writers bought into the proposition, and ever since then we've been seeing sentences like: "Have a seat," she invited. Can I tell you how much I hate constructions like that? A whole lot, I retorted. (In this case, "have a seat" *is* an invitation, why did we have to have the tag?)

I hate them so much that, back in the early '90s, when I received a manuscript that had been acquired before I took the job, and discovered that virtually every line of dialogue carried something like that—the author thought he was being funny—I literally struck every one, even the one or two that might have worked and been appropriate. The author complained, actually threatening to sue; he would have lost, but it wasn't worth the effort it would take to defend. So, I reinstated all of them and called the author's agents and let them know that the author's option book was hereby rejected. That's how much I hate them. Not to mention authors who threaten to sue.

Said is an invisible word; the reader's eye skips over it. It's also unnecessary, once dialogue has been established. He said, she said, and after that, all you need is what is said; if the reader can't keep track of who's speaking, nothing you do is going to help. (We are assuming, as dangerous as that is, that your characters don't all speak in the same voice, that they sound different. If they don't, you have major problems to contend with. Of course, if you've got three or four characters in the scene, using names or other references is recommended.)

The same can be said of replied or asked. It cannot be said of *hissed, pouted, sneered, observed* or any of the hundreds of other words that are being used these days. I've read far too many novels in which every line of dialogue is followed by one of those Said Bookisms, and the result is that I start laughing and then I throw the book away; they are comedies, after all. Every word carries weight, baggage, meaning; when you use those words as a way of explicating your dialogue, you're calling attention to the word and away from what was said. It's only the briefest loss of attention, but when it happens again and again and again, the cumulative effect is destructive.

One of my favorites, these days, is *interjected*, as in: "Well, let's take a look at our options," Johnson interjected. The statement isn't an interruption, which is the sense in which most of the writers are using it; nor is there anything abrupt or parenthetical about it (and believe me, I know all about things being added parenthetically). Even if we go to a definition of interjection, it doesn't wash: it's not an exclamation. There are ways of indicating interrupted dialogue—and interjections—and we'll look at them in a while, when we talk about some of the accepted ways of letting a reader know what's going on without spelling it out.

Dialogue tags are another problem: "Get out of here," she hissed, angrily. We'll begin with the fact that it's impossible to hiss a sentence that isn't stuffed with esses and cees and zees. That's carried in the primary definition of the word "hiss."   The thought that, *well, everyone understands what I mean* is not an excuse.   Mark Twain said that the difference between the right word and the almost right word is like the difference between lightning and a lightning bug.   Hissed is, more often than not, simply the wrong word.

"She said, angrily."   Why did you have to tell me how the sentence was delivered?   Could it be because the words themselves and whatever actions you had surrounding them, didn't carry their weight?   If the reader can't tell, from the dialogue itself, and from what the characters are doing, what the emotions are, I'd say that you're telling, not showing; that the dialogue is wrong; and that you, as the writer, recognize the problem and rather than trying to correct it, are putting a Band-Aid on a major wound.   And I'm not convinced that she hissed it angrily.   If I don't believe you about that, how much suspension of disbelief do you think I'm going to carry to the next page?

One of the first lessons poets learn is to forget adverbs.   The advice should not be lost on novelists, either.

⟴   ✎   ⟴

If a scene is supposed to do more than one thing, what can we say about dialogue?   Try this on for size: it's the most important tool in your writing arsenal, and as with any weapon, misuse can be deadly.

It is through the conversations between your characters that conflicts will begin and may be resolved; they are the way you are going to tell your reader what he has to know, and you'll be doing it through the words of your characters, not through your own intrusions and long passages of exposition and narrative—in that sense it is a way of showing, not telling: we see the events you want us to see through the eyes and responses of the characters.

Dialogue is a way of updating the reader, bringing her up to speed on events that may have taken place offstage (because, as in real life, things are happening to each of us, even if we aren't participating . . . you remember, "no man is an island" and all that); it is a way of developing or easing tension, developing character (there's that again), adding flavor, foreshadowing, describing, and advancing your story.

If we accept the fact that even a moderately attentive reader "hears" your voice, the storyteller's voice, while reading, just imagine what will happen if they can't "hear" the conversations your characters are having. All it takes is a few pages of boring, unrealistic blocks of dialogue, and you can kiss him goodbye.

Dialogue, in a novel, begins with why something is being said, then moves to content and manner. While we all spend a lot of time talking, most of our conversations don't stand up to the rigid physics of fiction. That's one of the writing traps eavesdropping sets up for us. We've all done it: Sat in a diner or on a bus, doesn't matter where, and listened to a conversation (something about what was being said caught our interest; why it did is a subject for psychiatrists), wrote down the highlights as soon as we could and then used that dialogue in our own writing: Hey, this is real life.

But it isn't real fiction. While the conversation intrigued you, what does it have to do with the novel, with the story, with the characters? Every word in your novel has to serve the needs of your story, and that includes dialogue. And just because "it happened that way" happens to be true, it doesn't mean it works in a fictive sense.

And there's this: most conversations are boring, of interest only to the speakers; the conversations in your novel have to interest the reader. That means that whatever's being said adds something to the reading experience: information that makes a difference in how things are going to happen or be understood and that helps us to understand the characters or adds dimension to them.

Everyone should eavesdrop; it's part of observation and it can be useful. With a little practice, you'll be able to listen to three or four conversations at once, picking out the lines that might make a difference; I do it at parties and conferences, to a certain extent listening for something of interest, but most often just to hear the cadences and rhythms, absorbing the patterns of speech, not only for use in dialogue, but as part of the natural poetry of prose; if you can make someone feel that they've just gotten up after talking with you personally (when all they've done is read your book), you can deem yourself a success.

I'm not only looking for regional differences, dialects and the like; I'm listening for nuances and subtleties: it's in the words, but it's also in the rise and fall of a voice, in the mannerisms—facial and hand gestures, body language—and the way emphases fall. (Almost automatically, the reader will place a different emphasis on "it's" and "it is.") What is it I'm hearing and seeing, and how can I translate that to the written word, translate it so I never have to use an adverb as a dialogue tag?

More fun is hearing the one line that's going to be a springboard. I was listening to a couple of women talking in a hotel lobby in Denver, and one said, "They all look alike, don't they?" I haven't given you any reference points: tone of voice, anything about the rest of the conversation, any idea of what the "they" is . . . by this time you're ready to do your own research. But if and when I use that line, or another that is born of it, the woman's tone—which is what carried the line to my attention—is going to be a part of the scene; it will tell you so much about her, I think, that you'll think you know her.

Dialogue, then, isn't just the words that are spoken; it's how they're said that often carries the meaning and that brings us back to dialogue tags; by choosing words carefully and letting the characters express them—not simply say them—we bring our story people to life.

What's the purpose of the dialogue in your story, how are you going to use it?

Here's an example of doing it right, taken from Jeremiah Healy's *Blunt Darts* (Walker and Company, 1984):

> "Hitchhiking," said Val as she squeaked open the Styrofoam chest. "John, I'm sorry, but I'm starving. Can we start just a little bit early?" I didn't like her voice when it wheedled.

Several things: Squeaked, which might refer to Val's voice, is used to describe the sound of the chest opening, but it reinforces the final "wheedled." The narrator tells us that she wheedled, which serves the additional purpose of telling us a little more about him: the things he notices, a like or dislike. If Healy'd gone the more common route, "'Can we start just a little bit early?' she wheedled," the sentence wouldn't be as effective; it would have left John Francis Cuddy, the protagonist, out of the event.

He also put an action in the middle of the dialogue: it's a visual aid, and it keep the characters from being simply talking heads. People don't usually sit still and talk—there are movements, conscious or unconscious— that we all make during conversation; using them to bring some life to a scene isn't a bad idea, at all.

In the same novel, Healy uses dialogue to establish his character, to give us everything we need to know in order to begin becoming involved with Cuddy. The approach is so simple and straightforward, I'm surprised I don't see it more often: an interview, in this case in an unemployment office. In a couple of pages of dialogue we have an idea of Cuddy's background: education, military service, employment record, as well as his attitudes, his outlook, the essentials of the man.

This is how it reads:

> "Name?"
> "Cuddy, John Francis."
> "Address?"
> "74 Charles Street."

"In Boston?"

"In Boston."

"Social Security number?"

"040-93-7071."

"Date of birth?"

I told her.

"She looked up at me, squeezed out a smile. "You look younger."

"It's a mark of my immaturity," I said. She made a sour face and returned to the form.

"Occupation?"

"Investigator."

"Previous employer?"

"Empire Insurance Company." I wondered whether Empire had to fill out a form that referred to me as "Previous Employee."

"Reason for leaving previous employment?"

"I have a letter." I took the letter from my inside coat pocket and handed it to her. Opening and reading it slowed her down. I looked around the big, clattering room at the thirty or so other metal desks. Each had a woman filling out a form and an applicant answering the same questions. Most of the applicants were men. I wondered why we applicants couldn't fill out at least the first few lines by ourselves.

The man seated at the desk next to me sneezed. Brittlely old and black, he looked as though he should have been applying for Social Security instead of unemployment. He wiped his nose with a clean handkerchief that had a hole in one corner. When he was finished he folded it so that the hole didn't show.

"Mr. Cuddy, if you'll pay attention to me, we'll finish this procedure much more quickly."

I turned my head to face her again. "That's all right," I said. "I've got time."

She fixed me with the sour look again and tapped her index finger on the paper before her. "This letter from your previous employer is beautifully drafted, Mr. Cuddy, probably by a company lawyer. It nicely provides every fact the regulations require. Accordingly, I have no choice but to recommend you for benefits. I must say, however, that seeing a man of your obvious abilities here instead of out in the world earning his way makes me sick."

"I didn't think you were looking too well. Would you like me to complete the rest of the form myself?"

"No!" she snapped. I thought I heard the man next to me stifle a chuckle. She and I operated as a more efficient team after that.

"Education?"

"High School, then Holy Cross. One year of night law school."

"Military service?"

"Military police, discharged a captain in nineteen sixty-eight."

"Employer prior to Empire Insurance Company."

"Just the army."

She looked up at me again. "Do you mean you worked for Empire since nineteen sixty-eight?"

"Since nineteen sixty-nine. I traveled around the country for a while after the service."

She shook her head, and we completed the rest of the form. I signed it and got a brochure explaining my benefits and rights. I also received a little chit that entitled me to stand in a slow-moving line ten or twelve people deep in front of a window like a bank teller's.

We could have gotten all that information through flashback and backstory, but it would have slowed things down because it would have taken longer, and it wouldn't have been as interesting, because Cuddy's asides and thoughts—which go to his humor and state of mind—wouldn't have been quite as effectively presented if it were simply narrative.

Is the scene "real?" Well, if you've ever had to go to a government office and fill out forms while dealing with officious bureaucrats, you know just how real it is. The reality is helped by the details (remember: Healy's the man who writes things down when he enters a place for the first time); the old, black man with the handkerchief with the hole; the "clattering room," which brings sound into the scene; other details might be added but in this instance they may have distracted from the dialogue, which is what was important.

As in the brief lines quoted earlier, in the scene with Val, Healy breaks up the dialogue with bits of business, actions. It's always important, and it is even more important if your characters are speaking in paragraphs, rather than two or three sentences. While it's true that most of the time we do tend to speak in spurts, there are instances when a speaker is explaining something, or taking a strong stand on an issue, delivering a speech as much as simply talking; at times such as those, including the actions is even more important.

You might have one character interrupt (for clarification or argument or to heckle); you can have someone push a chair back or sneeze . . . whatever is appropriate to the scene, anything to interrupt the stasis of speech and add movement.

And speaking of interruptions, they are indicated by the use of an "em-dash":

"So, there I was, ready to kiss her, and—"

"Ah, c'mon, I heard this already."

You do not have to say anything about someone interrupting, jumping in, cutting in, interjecting, or any other tags. The dash (indicated by two hyphens, if you wish), followed by new dialogue tells the reader everything; we understand it without being told.

Sometimes, we pause when we're speaking: to gather thoughts, to deal with a sudden memory that a word might create; whatever the reason, the pause is indicated by an ellipsis, with no other punctuation, unless it comes at the end of a sentence, when it is followed by a period. Like so:

"He didn't want to hit me . . . it was an accident, really."

"He didn't want to hit me . . . ."

Again, the reader will understand exactly what's happening, so no further explanation is necessary. You can follow a pause with an action:

"He didn't want to hit me . . ." Susan pulled at a loose thread in the upholstery, eyes concentrating on the job.

Is Susan lying, is that why she's broken eye contact? Is she so ashamed that she has to look away? Is she just shy? The rest of the dialogue, whatever surrounds that scene, is going to reveal the answers to that.

Another aspect of dialogue, the thoughts of a character, should be considered here. So . . .

You *never* have to use the words "she thought." And you must never use "she thought to herself." How else does one think? Nor are the thoughts put in quotation marks; they're used to show the spoken words; now and then for emphasis, calling attention to the word in the text as being used in an uncommon manner. But never for thoughts.

How do you show thoughts, then? They might be indicated through the use of italics in the course of the text: Susan was gone; *how could I not have noticed before this?* However, as long as you, as the writer, have maintained a character's point of view in the scene—without either you or another character coming forward—you really don't have to do anything. The reader will understand that: *Joey looked at the naked hangers rattling in the closet. When did she have time to pack? There was no one to answer him,* means that Joey was asking the question of himself, that it was a thought.

Yes, a certain amount of care is necessary, but that caregiving is one of your primary functions as a writer, anyway.

Also revealing is dialect, idiom, regionalisms, and other speech patterns. Dialect is difficult to maintain unless it is part of the way you speak naturally. At the 1998 Novels in Progress Workshop, conducted by Louisville, Kentucky's Green River Writers, an agent complained about one manuscript, saying that she doubted the author could maintain "that voice." (It's akin to Pearson's in *Off for the Sweet Hereafter.*) However: it isn't going to be a problem because the author, a Southern woman, speaks that way naturally; what would be more difficult for her to maintain is a more formal, less idiomatic narrative style.

The biggest pitfalls open when dialect is indicated by intentional misspellings, attempts to create a sound phonetically. It makes the sentences very difficult to read because the reader is constantly trying to "interpret" what is being seen on the page. The use of idioms and local speech patterns and regionalisms goes a long way toward relieving that, while still leaving all the flavor. (Peppering the text with an occasional phonetic isn't all bad; the final decision will come down to discussions you'll have with your editor.)

Dealing with dialogue (and narrative) in contemporary fiction is relatively easy: it parallels the way we speak, taking into consideration the various societal and cultural influences, class distinctions and mores that lie at the heart of the way we live. A small word of warning, though: don't use other fiction as the research tool: if you're going to write about people in a mining camp in West Virginia, go there and listen to them. (I don't know why you'd want to write about them without knowing them, anyway, but I see all manner of settings cross my desk and have learned that there ain't no accountin' for what folks'll do. Well, maybe there is: perceived popularity and commercial potential of a subject. Because American natives—more accurate than Native Americans, to my mind—were a popular subject a few years ago, lots of people were creating Indian characters with absolutely no real sense of the People. Everything seemed lifted from the book that was popular the year before.)

The language of a novel, both the dialogue and the narrative, will also be affected by the genre you've chosen. Historical fiction, fantasy, social history (stories of the immigrant experience, as an example) require a knowledge not only of the demands of that genre, but of the "sound" of a period.

American historicals—both as part of the romance genre and the more generally directed tales—call upon the writer to know the syntax of the period, the words that were in vogue and that hadn't come into the language yet, as well as words that have since disappeared. Reading novels of the period (and essays and newspapers) will offer much of what you need there.

One of the dangers, especially when dealing with the Indian nations, is the propensity to make them sound like characters out of a bad movie or, on the other hand, like Oxford graduates. The reality is that when speaking among themselves, the language was colloquial: if you're recording a conversation between two Lakotah warriors, make them sound like your white characters. It may not be accurate in the sense of the words inherent in Lakotah, but it is spot on in terms of how they'd sound to each other. It is when they're speaking English that the dialogue becomes a bit stilted; that's because they don't have "our" words in their vocabulary. Turn of the century oral histories are a good source of information and insight.

The same holds true of family sagas: the French, German, Russian, middle European and other immigrant populations did not speak English with native fluency—that fell to their children. Their language was a mix of their own language and English and, if they lived in certain areas, probably included words from still other tongues. Some of those words, from the Yiddish and German and Italian, have worked their way into our spoken language; those words are ideal for your use. They require no translation or explanation and add flavor without overwhelming the finished product.

Fantasy fiction—sword & sorcery, Arthurian, faerie—has as an accepted conceit the use of an almost courtly English. I don't know that it's mandatory (I neither read nor write in the genre), but if that's what you do, you already know what the sound is, and where it is appropriate. If the genre means nothing to you, you have no business writing it (and that goes for any genre).

It should be kept in mind, however, that unless the concept for your novel demands that it sound like Sir Thomas Malory's rendering of the Arthurian legend, don't force that syntax onto it. I see it sometimes in the historical mysteries that are sent to me: the author has recreated a sound that is supposed to be accurate for the time; not only do anachronisms tend to creep in, but it becomes so difficult to read—at least for me—that I just give up. That's one of the reasons Lynda S. Robinson's Lord Meren series, set in pharaonic Egypt, are so appealing to me: she chose to keep the language colloquial and idiomatic, and it falls on the contemporary ear comfortably while never letting us forget the time and place portrayed.

Another excellent example of dealing with the thrilling sounds of yesterday can be found in A. S. Byatt's *Babel Tower*. In the telling of this contemporary novel, Byatt includes the text of another novel, a fantasy, set yesterwhen. There's never any doubt as to the otherness of that setting; at the same time, the reader is never jolted by the language of either narrative or dialogue. It's as natural as that of the main story.

Sustaining a voice, re-creating a dialect in such a way that a reader both understands it and is willing to stick with it, are very special skills. If you have that talent, exploit it; but if there's anything that strikes you as false, you can usually drop the attempt without hurting the work. And if you have to have people "talking funny" in order to create and maintain the world you're depicting, the problems go far beyond dialogue, problems you should probably look at immediately. Remember: anything that isn't "normal" in the mind of your reader causes problems for you. And for your editor. And for your sales.

Most fiction doesn't need anything but everyday speech. That's the kind that uses contractions (and I'm one of those weird folks who doesn't have a problem with contractions in narrative, either), that uses regionalisms and slang and idioms, and that falls easily on the ear. Listen to the people around you speak. Pay attention to what they say and how they say it, because they're also the people who are going to be reading your book.

What it comes down to is this: If your reader doesn't want to listen to your characters speak, anything they . . . or you . . . have to say, will be lost. And that's both the battle and the war.

There are a couple of wonderful dialogue exercises that will both sharpen the conversational skills of your characters, and teach you how to use the words that are being said to convey just about everything that needs to said.

✍ The first requires you to tell a story (well, a scene with a beginning, middle, and end) in dialogue only. Nothing appears on the page but for the words contained within the quotation marks. Any actions have to be related through the speakers' words. You can use the ellipsis and em-dash, of course, and italics for emphasis (but sparingly). Try to use words that convey all the meanings inherent in what's being said; if someone is supposed to be speaking angrily, let the reader know that through the statement, not by having the other character in the scene say, "Why are you angry?" (There's nothing wrong with the question if the speaker *wants* to know *why*; everything is wrong if the sentence is there to let the reader know someone is angry.)

You'll notice that this is not limited to any particular number of speakers; I've had students successfully use as many as four characters: They're clearly capable of delineating character with a few sharp strokes. But even with only two in the scene, the voices have to be distinct so that the reader never becomes confused, is never forced into looking back and then counting through the sentences thinking he said, she said, he said . . .

✍ The second exercise allows you to use some narrative. It's a conversation between two people, one of whom is not being entirely truthful, honest or revealing. Whatever is being hidden cannot be expressed, nor can you fall back on things like, Joey (or I) knew she was lying. In essence, just as you know—through body language, pauses, and common sense—when someone isn't being entirely forthcoming, and can often arrive at the truth (remember how our mothers always knew?) through asking the right questions, or our own body language, your character must arrive at the answers the same way: through showing, not telling.

✍ To take the challenge one step further, try doing the dialogues in both first and third person; in the second exercise, when switching to first person, do it twice, giving both characters the chance to be "I"; as with the description exercise, it'll do wonders for your ability to characterize.

If you do these exercises seriously, you'll never run into problems with dialogue . . . he said.

Point of View

a s I sit down to write this chapter, there's a debate on the DorothyL mystery discussion list (for the Luddites: lists of this kind, about every area of interest, abound on the Internet; if you don't know, the technology will just bore you) about point of view, and the one clear thing is that people seem to want one point of view . . . unless they don't mind shifting points of view. But if a straw vote were to be taken, a rather more limited approach seems to be favorable.

All of which gets terribly confusing or, at least, disconcerting and leads to another of those popular conference discussions that begins: Is it permissible to change point of view, i.e., the character through whom action is being revealed, the one in whose mind we are?

Yes.

How many points of view am I allowed?

As many as you find necessary.

How do I indicate a change in point of view?

By changing it, usually, though there are some indicators you can use. The most popular one is the line break, generally indicated by a couple of centered asterisks or whatever other dingbat you feel like using. No one cares; the publisher's designer and/or house style will dictate what it looks like, finally.

(How many times have you had that conversation or over-heard it? That's what I thought. That's why I left out all the quotation marks; figured to hold your interest that way, at least a little. And, funny thing: you were still able to understand what was going on. Literacy is a terrible thing to waste.)

Conventional wisdom is that you stay in one point of view, and if you must change it, you wait for the next chapter, or the next paragraph, at the very least. Consider this, then, in light of that wisdom. It's taken from Brian Unsworth's *Mooncranker's Gift*. Farnaby is sitting in the dark, remembering an incident that took place about ten years earlier:

> One of the few bits of tracking she actually set under way: a grizzly in the heart of the bushes, in the depths of the cave formed by their ancient ramifications. A lurking, vindictive bear. Their bodies in the passage through the glossy dusty leaves thunderous in the absence of all other sound. Their breathing was loud when they finally reached the heart of the bush, in the cave formed by the outward arch of branches. Here they were able to kneel . . .

Unsworth has gone from "she" to "they," third person singular to third person plural, separating the shift only with a period at the end of the second sentence. When you think about it, it makes sense: in memory we sometimes become observers and in this case Farnaby is remembering Miranda ("she") but then watching himself with her ("they").

Every rule has its exceptions, and the rules of writing, the voices of the authority figures we choose, are not exceptions to that rule.

Bill Pronzini's Edgar and Hammett Award-nominated 1997 novel, *A Wasteland of Strangers*, had nineteen separate first person narrators; the only character not appearing in first person is the protagonist. It worked, sublimely.

Given the available options, and the fact that many readers seem to think that point of view shifts result from author error rather than technique or an attempt to do something different (as long as it has a point; different for the sake of different can work but it all too often gets you classified as a creative writing student, rather than a writer), let's begin our discussion with some loose definitions. They'll be very loose and they'll also be more limited than not: The topic is central to many writing classes and writing books and every teacher has another set of parameters and subtle changes. Still:

There are three basic points of view in storytelling: first and third person are the most common; second person is there for those who want to try it: Italo Calvino in *If on a winter's night a traveler . . .* and Jay McInerny in *Bright Lights, Big City* both used it, and I'm using it in *Slow Dancing to Loud Music*, as you've read.

The first person (limited) "voice" (I looked out of the window, but I didn't see any book contracts, so I went back to sleep) is one of the two most common point-of-view approaches and it's virtually a standard in certain forms: most private eye fiction, for example, serves as a perfect model. It's an ideal pov for mysteries because of the play fair tradition: since the detective cannot receive any information that isn't shared with the reader, and because the reader spends the entire novel with the narrator, the clues come to each simultaneously.

The drawback to first person stems from that same limitation: it prevents you, as the writer, from discussing what might be going on elsewhere or from "getting into the head" of other characters: everything is seen only through the eyes of "I."

There's also an assumption among non-writers that first person is somehow more "natural." (It probably arises from the fact that too many readers confuse the storyteller with the author. *We* know that the stories are entirely fabricated, right?   But readers tend to confuse us with our protagonists.)

Oh, well: where would we be without theories of writing to ponder? Probably busy writing instead of studying.

Several things occur when using first person: First, the reader tends to notice the narrator in a very specific way: The "I" is there, in front of us always, leading us, sharing with us, involving us with her actions and thoughts.

Second, there's an unstated question that sometimes crops up: Who is the narrator speaking to? Are we—the narrator and the reader—having a *tête-à-tête*? Is the story being related by one to another, leaving us as eavesdroppers? Is the storyteller talking to himself or offering a confession of sorts? Any and all variations are valid but as the author you should keep one listener in mind because it may affect how you tell your story, indicate some of the things you might have a character saying.

Third—and I find this more of a problem in the early drafts— a very strong narrator often masks inadequacies in the rest of the story: plot holes may get buried, telling rather than showing can become a bit more acceptable; whatever the faults, they become more difficult to see as you're writing. A good editor should catch and correct those errors . . . if the book is acquired.

As I said, first person is also limiting: in theory, anyway, nothing can happen that the narrator doesn't know about, which makes your job more difficult: how do you give the reader necessary background or additional information.   (We'll leave the question of whether you should have to do that for another time. Well, no, we won't: No, you shouldn't have to do that, not even for the needs of suspense. That other events have occurred will inform the actions of the other characters; your narrator either discerns them or not. You have to trust your reader to be able to do that on his own.)

One of the reasons many first person novels begin with a prologue (usually in third person, omniscient) is as the most popular contemporary solution to that difficulty. The reader receives a "backgrounder"; the narrator then picks up the tale. What I don't like about that is that I know more about the events that are taking place than the narrator does, and that doesn't strike me as fair . . . to me as the reader. (And that tells you something about my needs as a reader.)

Another approach is to break away from the storyteller, shift into third person for a short chapter, and then return. Again, I don't find that satisfying: I cannot help but think that the author could find no suitable way to relate information to me and that means, as far as I'm concerned, that the whole approach to the story was wrong from the first words put on the page.

Neither of those subjective comments means that it can't be done, though. It simply means that you have to be very careful, very much in control of your work, and that you have to have thought through what you're doing and why.

I don't think it's necessary to give examples of the standard first person approach; there is, though, a variation that I found interesting and challenging to read. Stephen Dobyns is a well-known poet and mystery writer (the "Saratoga" series). His 1997 thriller, *The Church of Dead Girls* (Metropolitan Books, Henry Holt and Company) is a first person narration about the events and effects surrounding the serial murders of three teenaged girls in a small, upstate New York town. (It bears, in that regard, more than a passing similarity to Frederick Busch's novel, *Girls*; I wouldn't doubt at all that both were inspired by a kidnaping that took place in the area in the early '90s. *Girls* was set in and around Colgate University, in Hamilton, NY, though neither was mentioned by name; the Dobyns novel does mention them, but sets the action in Aurelius. One of those little acts of synchronicity that makes reading so much fun.) Both are first person narrations; the Busch is in a traditional, limited pov, the action related to us by the protagonist, Jack, and both begin after the events that are to be related have ended.

We don't know the name of the person telling us the story of
the dead girls in the Dobyns work. But we know everything else:

> When I was in high school in the late fifties and early
> sixties, it was said that daring couples came at night to
> have sex on Hyram Peabody's slab of granite, and sever-
> al times fellow students claimed to have seen condoms
> in the grass or on the stone itself, though who knows if
> they told the truth.
>
> The granite slab was Aaron's destination. They
> would dance on it. They would drink screwdrivers, be
> obscene, and discuss Marx. As they made their way
> between the graves, Aaron teased the others by saying,
> "What's that over there?" or "Did you hear that?" Then
> they would crowd closer together.
>
> Shannon set the boom box at the base of the obelisk.
> Aaron put on the Doors. Oscar made drinks. Bob and
> Joany danced to the *Mahogonny* song about the moon
> over Alabama: "Oh, show me the way to the next
> whiskey bar." They danced jerkily, ironically. Jason
> turned his back to the others, then crossed his arms,
> putting his hands over his shoulders and undulating his
> body so that he seemed to be embracing somebody even
> thinner than he was.
>
> "Give it to her," said Shannon.

Now, there's nothing strange about that scene but for this: the narrator wasn't there! Only a few of the incidents in the story are wit-
nessed by him, and one or two, we're told, were related to him. But
. . . but, he knows all and comments on everything.

Which is a perfect transition point for us. The form used by
Dobyns might variously be called first person omniscient or authorial-omniscient. It's rarely seen and represents a certain amount of
risk: lazy readers and those simply used to "standard" storytelling

are put off by it, begin asking: "Well, if he wasn't there, how does he know?" Does it matter?

Authorial-omniscient was once the way to write; today, it appears on occasion and, most often, in a third person point of view, which is one of the things that makes Dobyns' use of it so remarkable.

If you're going to try it, you have to establish what you're doing early on. Because there are going to be lots of pov shifts in the course of the telling, you have to prepare the reader for it; after all, it's not something readers expect and if it appears suddenly in the middle of the novel, you're going to frustrate people who think they're seeing something through the eyes of a particular character, and that character alone.

The point of view also permits the author to comment and offer a gloss on what's happening: As the townspeople of Aurelius begin to panic, the narrator tells us, "Fear and ardent speculation make an unhealthy mixture." That might not be uncommon in first person; the same thing would not be part of the narrative in a third person (limited, subjective or objective) telling, however. The voice did allow Leo Tolstoy to write, "Happy families are all alike; every unhappy family is unhappy in its own way." Today, readers, reviewers and editors would consider that an intrusion, editorializing.

The omniscient viewpoint, like first person, makes the narrator visible to the reader; she plays as clear a role in the story as an "I" does. You can tell more in less time, because you don't have to establish motives and character through action and/or dialogue: You simply tell the reader what he needs to know. The price for that? Quite often you create a distance between your reader and your characters by shifting between them almost at whim. (You're not being whimsical, but it'll strike the reader that way unless he understands what you're doing.)

Here's an example from one of my favorite writers, the Booker

Award-winning Barry Unsworth, taken from the early pages of
Mooncranker's Gift (W. W. Norton & Company, Inc.; 1974):

> Mooncranker, who had not himself sat down, returned
> the smile, but with what seemed a private sense of signif-
> icance. "Umpired," he said, and then repeated the word
> with his habit of apparently ironical stress. *Umpired?* He
> placed thin hands rather gropingly on the back of a chair.
> His nausea returned as he struggled to reconcile the spent
> but optimistic feelings of convalescence with the more
> strenuous associations of umpiring. Distrust of his visitor
> came creeping back. "You say you telephoned," he said.
> "Your name is an evocative one, suggesting to my mind
> military manoeuvres and daffodils."
>
> "Oh, really?" Farnaby said, from the depths of his
> armchair. He was resolved not to betray by his manner
> any sense that the interview was going oddly. It was as
> though by entering Mooncranker's room he had stirred
> up some sort of muddy deposit or sediment in the
> other's mind. The only thing to do was wait for it to set-
> tle, affecting in the meantime to notice nothing. This
> was difficult, however, not only because of Moon-
> cranker's failure to utter any even faintly appropriate
> sentiments, but because he felt himself dislocated some-
> how by his inability to keep up a sporting tone when
> referring it. A determined jollity about the past had
> always been Uncle George's essential idiom, almost his
> distinguishing feature. And if Mooncranker had taken
> this tone, Farnaby would have adapted himself with his
> usual alacrity to it. But he did not know what was
> expected of him now.

In those two paragraphs, Unsworth has established that he's going
to shift at will, allowing us into the minds of all the characters;

knowing this from the beginning, the reader has the choice of continuing with the novel, or backing away from something out of the ordinary. And as the last three sentences show, the author has been able to give us a lot of information about young Farnaby without having to develop it . . . one of the stated advantages of the authorial-omniscient voice.

The shift in point of view is strikingly clear in that example; many contemporary popular novelists, like Arthur Hailey, do it, also: look at the opening scene of *The Moneychangers* for an example.

We'll give E. M. Forster the final word on the subject of shifting viewpoint. In *Aspects of the Novel*, he wrote:

> A novelist can shift view-point *if it comes off* . . .
> Indeed, this power to expand and contract perception
> (of which the shifting view-point is a symptom), this
> right to intermittent knowledge—I find one of the great
> advantages of the novel-form . . . this intermittence lends
> in the long run variety and colour to the experiences we
> receive. (Emphasis added)

While the majority of contemporary readers and writing teachers probably won't agree with Forster, I know that if you keep the "if it comes off" in mind, and if you have some idea in mind of why, exactly, you're doing things this way, you shouldn't have any problems with it.

And you shouldn't have any problem with the third person point of view, the most familiar approach to storytelling. It's so familiar, it's almost invisible.

As with the omniscient voice, you move over the landscape of your novel, following the various characters through their peregrinations. You are expected, at least in terms of any given scene, to remain in one character's mind, the he or she who is central to the present action, if not the entire novel. You can, from scene to scene or from chapter to chapter, switch viewpoint characters; simply by establishing the fact that we're with Jim or Betty now, you have done all you must to keep the reader centered.

There are two approaches, third person subjective and third person objective. The first is more personal: the narrator can enter the minds of the characters, telling us what they're thinking, how they're reacting internally; the thoughts and feelings of the characters are made immediate to the reader and you help the reader understand what's going on.

In the objective voice, the narrator never comments . . . there's no line ending, *she thought.* It is, for all intents and purposes, straightforward reportage: events and dialogue are presented to the reader and we are left to make our own judgments about the characters and what they're doing.

And, finally, second person. It isn't at all common and as with any technique with which the reader is unfamiliar, it calls attention to itself, creating some distance between the reader and the work, unless it's pulled off perfectly. (My daughter did her senior thesis on Calvino's *If on a winter's night* and began by discussing why the book doesn't work. The novel starts by informing the reader, "You are a man on a train . . . " As she pointed out, she was never convinced she was.)

Second person is often a disguised first person; the "you" just as easily read as "I," as you'll see in the following example, the opening of *Slow Dancing to Loud Music*:

It was cold still but finally clear, as clear as Maker's Mark can make it. You jogged across the courtyard, past concrete and glass, jogging toward the sounds, then stopped and looked at stars piercing a silk-soft sky. New constellations formed from old formations: The one over your shoulder reached down to touch you, burning. You left it nameless, imprinted with hope.

Halfway to the crowds and noise, you stopped and gasped: forty years of tar and nicotine punching from your lungs to pound your heart. You were dying. Or jealous. She was somewhere else: in a different darkness? breathing other rhythms? For a week you waltzed around her, not breathing, sticking pins in your eyes so that you wouldn't see Rachel being there, and when she isn't, as she isn't now, you knew you were right; know you are wrong.

Now you began to breathe again, began to walk infinitely more slowly because there was no place left to go; getting in touch with your feelings is like trying to tattoo a soap bubble.

One. Two. Three, four, one; two. Three, four, one . . .

Replacing "you" with "I" would make things easier; but why do it easy when you can make things more difficult for yourself? In the novella, there are two second person viewpoint characters, the one you just met, Jonathan, and a woman, Rachel. Any given section might be either one's viewpoint:

Her head is turned against your breast. What do you want, Rachel, you say, hoping she won't hear you and you hear her smile; remembering, you taste the rosemary she held.

"Surprise me." Her step is light, glides, cuts through the noise. You don't know who is leading; you know the steps, knew the steps—minimalist ballet, *plié* after *plié* after *jeté*, always on your toes, always solo—and now in the noise and heat and bourbon blanket, a new pas de deux, steps you knew, steps you know. "Surprise me," she says and you hide in the noise, pretending you don't hear anything more than one. Two. Three, four; one. . .

That's Jonathan with Rachel; he is still the "you."

The sound of the lock is the loudest noise in a night of pandemonium. You turn your back to the door, lean against it, listening. Can you hear him walk away; can you hear steps in the soft, shifting sand of your lifescape? Is he still there, waiting, hand pressed against the wood, waiting for you to open to him as all the those others must have, as there must have been all those others?

Your skin burns through the sweater where his hands touched your back, where they brushed against your face when he pushed your hair from your cheek. The memory of his face begins to melt.

You think of Walter, lying peacefully in your bed and your sons running through their innocent dreams playing with mommy who isn't there and of all the dreams you thought were of your future and smell the incense of all the Sundays of your life and the vows that echoed off cathedral walls and wonder now if they are still captured in the old stones above the altar you kneeled before and if you can pray.

You think: Ohgodwhathaveidone and you know and don't know and begin to fear the morning. You undress, thinking: Should I have let him do this? You lie on your cot naked and feel him touch you again and shake because electricity snaps between nerves sending signals you haven't felt in months or years and you listen again to all the words you said to someone you don't know and all you see in the dark are his eyes looking at you, his eyes that slid into places long untouched, that took the bands off your finger, that caressed and his smile, as if he knew your thoughts and would answer before you spoke.

A vaguely remembered trilling in your veins moves the silence of the fading night; you feel Jonathan in your room, standing over you, smiling, touching your hand.

You're too tempting, you said, and then, will I see you
again? You taste his kiss and feel fire play along your fingers, burn up your hand and you curl around your pillow
being held.

Never you. You watched him before coming into the
racket of the lounge, saw him dancing, pressing his body
against one and another, laughing and comfortable as
he'd been all week, but always somewhere else as if the
script were boring. And because you always ask questions, you asked: "Why?"

"What?"

"Why haven't you danced with me?"

"No reason. Let's dance."

And you felt him tremble against you, felt the
whiskey on his breath, felt his heart beating, one. Two.
Three, four; one. You felt everything but the cold and
then blood flowed again through arteries long blocked
and what had been numb whispered to you: *be touched*.

Talk to me, Jonathan, you think you said, leading
him into corners thick with dust and thin memories.

And that's Rachel, as "you," shortly afterward, replaying the scene in
her own mind. It might have been as easy to do the story as a multiple first person pov story, but as I was writing it, this approach seemed
to me the most effective and powerful. We'll know, certainly, when it's
finished and my agent begins to figure out what to do with it.

Having gone that far, I decided to try something else, second
person plural. Like so:

You look and wonder what your look is saying. Sleep
well? Yes, thank you. And you? Yes: and the smiles that
say I can rest later say also you're here/you're here, I
hoped . . . but the words are swallowed like honey, a
savored sweet in return for being there.

What do you say, do you speak first, what was that, excuse me: the tumble of words is awkward and you trip over them finding yourselves finally in the same place at the same time and wait together for the tests about to happen.

Can I drop you somewhere? Oh, I have a ride coming. Oh. Trip, count: one, two, one two. Smile: does mine seem pasted on? I'm glad I got to see you again. Guilt? Nervousness? Something shy, something that says was it good for you, was there anything to be good or bad and something that says yes and yes but a ride is coming and it is time to leave, leave now (don't leave).

And you leave, walk out into the cold clear morning listening to the steps echoing yours in the crunch of snowcrust. One of you will have to turn and walk away (don't let it be me) but you face each other almost but not quite touching, too close, as if all space will disappear between you, too far as your worlds say, we're here.

I'll write, I have your address here. Okay. Nods. Trip. One, two, one two. Goodbye means turning away; why don't you feel the cold you think and know; know each other, know that the dance has more steps and know that you'll try them, if these moments aren't lies, if they're not awkward looking for grace: not lies, just not truths.

I guess I should go. Uh, yeah; I wish I could ride with you, but . . . Oh, that's okay, I just thought, you know, being friends. Hmm. I had . . . I had a good time last night; it was so different from what I expected . . . and so are you, I think. What did you expect . . . no, never mind, it'll give us something to talk about, to write about.

Good bye, Rachel.

Good bye, Jonathan.

And now the growing distance, footsteps heard, then swallowed by this day. Will he write? Will she answer?

What is happening to me.

Good bye, Jonathan.

Good bye, Rachel. Soon.

But you know soon is too far away. Know that the night was desperation and bourbon; know that there was another moment born in the night.

Know that you will write.

Know that you will write.

You turn and wave, blinded by the glare of sun on ice.

I have reasons for it: Given the emotional intensity and pitch that I'm trying to create, and my sense that at moments like the one described it really doesn't matter who's talking (though for the important dialogue I think it's clear) and that what is being experienced is being experienced as much as a tumble of events as anything else, I find the approach I've taken creates exactly the effect I'm looking for. (Well, the people who've read it, and those who've heard me read from the work, tell me I've succeeded. As I said, we'll see when it's done.)

Because I also played with tenses (as well as language, syntax, and just about everything else I could play with), this might not be an inappropriate place to look at the tense you're going to use in your work.

Almost any novel you're going to pick up is written in past tense; moving from that technique immediately creates problems. Most readers are made uncomfortable and feel distanced by use of present tense, though there are more and more writers experimenting with it these days. I used to hate it; then an author named Bill Moody submitted a partial of his first novel, *Solo Hand*. It's a first person, amateur detective story, and it's told in present tense, and to make a long story short, I acquired it for my list at Walker and Company. As I expected, reviewers commented first on the fact that it was told in present tense.

I find it effective because it removes one of the walls past tense builds, especially in first person: I know the protagonist is going to come out of things okay because she's around to tell the story; present tense allows a question about the ending; in theory, "I" can die.

Another thought: I asked Reginald McKnight, author of a novel titled *I Get on the Bus*, why he chose the voice, and he said it was because as he began writing, he wasn't sure of where that bus was going to take him . . . in every sense of that phrase. For me, then, present tense adds an immediacy that many commentators don't find in it.

In a story that's burbling on my back burner right now, something that will deal equally with past and present, I found myself doing the scenes in the past in present tense and the contemporary action in the more usual past tense. I have a reason for it: the story is about the power of imagination and the cost inherent in losing it and for my character the past is more vivid and actual than the present . . . it is when the past becomes past that he's going to be in trouble.

You'll keep out of trouble if you make the decisions necessary, choosing the voice (and tense) most suitable to what you're writing, shifting points of view as necessary (but cleanly, so the reader doesn't get confused; and, yes, I do think you can have multiple points of view in a short story —"*if it comes off*"), and if you remember that you're telling the story: Dealer's choice.

Style and What
The Poet Said

"'ve written a novel in the style of . . ."

Each week brings its submissions and query letters with that phrase in it somewhere. It's almost enough to cause an immediate rejection because, along with other clues, it tells me the writer knows little about writing. So that you and I, at least, can be on the same page, let's begin with some definitions.

Discussions of what style is, exactly, take place regularly; then we complicate those talks by adding words like "voice" and "technique" to the debate. They're related but, for me, anyway, they're not the same; the difference is subtle: style has to do with writing, voice with reading. Technique is the way in which one uses style; technique can be taught, studied. Style simply *is*:

> You want to fix up your writing, parse your sentences, use the right words? Fine, pick up the little books, learn to avoid mistakes, revere taut prose and revile tautology. But do not flatter yourself that you have significantly changed your style. First, straighten out yourself so that you can then think straight and soon afterward write

straight. Your writing style is yourself in the process of thinking and the act of writing, and you cannot buy that in a bookstore or fix it up in a seminar.

— William Safire
The Language Maven Strikes Again
(Doubleday, 1990)

"Your writing style is yourself in the process of thinking and the act of writing . . . " It is something natural, something that comes very much from within, from who you are. And you cannot be someone else, especially when it comes to writing something that's going to last past the first reading.

Some years ago, Judson Jerome, who wrote the poetry column for *Writer's Digest* magazine, penned an article that echoed (and that is and always will be echoed in turn) the idea that poets pay attention to words, to their rhythm, their sound; that poets use devices like rhyme and alliteration to make what they do special and memorable. "Otherwise," he wrote, "we might as well be writing prose."

Uh-huh.

What Jerome was talking about, finally, was style and prose authors worth reading; fiction writers, essayists, all of us, have style. They don't try to develop it—it can't be done; they can improve what they have, though, and that's what we want to look at now.

Style is about language and that means it's about words, *le mot juste.*

Not too long ago I told a fresh-faced, dewy-eyed young assistant to make a manuscript go away. She wanted to know why. Fair enough.

"It doesn't work."

"   . . .   "

"It's flat."

"   . . .   "

"Okay, let's do it this way: read the first paragraph aloud to me."
And she did. It was "standard": by the guidelines, an action
scene to hook the reader; everything, in fact, that we've come to
expect from the person whose significant other and friends have
said, "Hey, why don't you write a book, you read so many of them."

There were lots of short, declarative sentences (with which, of
course, there's nothing inherently wrong; Hemingway used them to
great effect. He also knew which words to use), and the words chosen were, invariably, "common," ignoring Shakespeare's wisdom in
Hamlet: "Suit the action to the word, the word to the action." So,
instead of using a powerful, active verb, the author resorted to mod-
ifying verbs with as many as two or three adjectives or adverbs: *he
ran hard for the wall*, for instance, rather than *he raced*. (If mod-
ifiers are necessary, he might have considered *he ran* pell-mell—or
helter-skelter—*toward the wall*; they're both stronger visually.)

Okay, here's the opening paragraph of David Bradley's novel,
South Street (Grossman, 1975):

> The street lay like a snake sleeping; dull-dusty, gray-
> black in the dingy darkness. At the three-way intersec-
> tion of Twenty-second Street, Grays Ferry Avenue, and
> South Street a fountain, erected once-upon-a-year by a
> ladies' guild in fond remembrance of some dear depart-
> ed altruist, stood cracked and dry, full of dead leaves and
> cigarette butts and bent beer cans, forgotten by the city
> and the ladies' guild, functionless, except as a minor
> memorial to how They Won't Take Care Of Nice Things.
> One one side of South Street a chain food market dis-
> played neat packages of precooked food sequestered
> behind thick plate glass—a nose-thumbing temptation to
> the undernourished. On the other side of South Street
> the State Liquor Store showed back-lit bottles to tanta-
> lizing advantage and proclaimed, on a sign pasted to the

inside of the window, just behind the heavy wire screening, that the state lottery tickets were on sale, and that
you had to play to win.

What's in the paragraph? You've got your alliteration; you have
rhythm and you have word play (an "unremembered memorial").
The food is "sequestered" (a word from the Latinate, not the Anglo-
Saxon; sorry Mr. Fowler), not stored, displayed or shown.

Bradley's broken all the rules we usually hear about; the paragraph certainly isn't an action hook; it's a storytelling hook. The
language resonates, the sounds the words make by themselves and
together (the voice we hear as readers, resulting from the style in
which the author writes) echo in the mind and in the imagination.

That's what a writer does, and it doesn't matter what's being
written.

Oh, by the way: *South Street* is a first novel.

Bradley's second novel, *The Chaneysville Incident* (Harper &
Row, 1981), won the PEN-Faulkner Award. Here's how it opens:

> Sometimes you can hear the wire, hear it reaching
> out across the miles; whining with its own weight, crying
> from the cold, panting at the distance, humming with
> the phantom sounds of someone else's conversation.
> You cannot always hear it—only sometimes; when the
> night is deep and the room is dark and the sound of the
> phone's ringing has come slicing through uneasy sleep;
> when you are lying there, shivering, with the cold plas-
> tic of the receiver pressed tight against your ear. Then,
> as the rasping of your breathing fades and the hammer-
> ing of your heartbeat slows, you can hear the wire: whin-
> ing, crying, panting, humming, moaning like a live thing.

He's added here: rhythm is still there, and alliteration and certainly word choice ("whining with its own weight," "humming with the

phantom sounds . . ."); but he's added repetition: whining, hum-ming, crying—all the words used separately at the beginning are repeated at the end, yet no editor would think of striking any of them as redundant: they are emphasis, and they bring the fear of the late-night phone call with them; they foreshadow problems. Again, he's hooked us and he did it with word choices, by under-standing the weight and baggage and *meaning* of the words.

And speaking of meaning: There isn't one word in either of his paragraphs that would drive an average, adult reader to the dictio-nary. (If I'm wrong about that, everything we're trying to accom-plish here is pointless.) There's nothing pretentious about it; the alliteration isn't off-putting; there's no showing off, nothing to get in the way of the substance of what the author is trying to accomplish.

Using language with that kind of precision is not something that can be taught and I'm not even certain it can be absorbed; most writers with that kind of finesse grew up with words; you can't simply go to the thesaurus (or use the one you still haven't dumped from your word processor) because the subtlety of meaning is lost. The thesaurus doesn't allow you to arrive at this sentence from Stanley Ellin's *The Dark Fantastic:* "That was accurate enough to bruise . . ." or these from Ed Gorman's *Dark Flight*: "I went up the three broad steps to the fine red door and knocked. In the silence, the knock sounded rude."

Remarks (which is what Ellin is referring to) are usually deemed cutting or hurtful; but there should be no question in any reader's mind as to what "bruise" means. The same can be said of Gorman's "rude": The knock isn't loud or disruptive or annoying; it's rude and, again, you know exactly what the author is saying.

What we're seeing is words creating images; metaphor, simile, symbolism: tools of the poets—and of storytellers—whose work we go back to again and again.

But language alone is not enough; there has to be a story—characters and events, conflicts and resolutions (all of which will

mean something to the reader, that the reader will care about)—
and that means there has to be narrative power and sense as well:
language married to narrative. Both are gifts; both can be honed
but neither is a given.

And for all those reasons, when someone tells me they're writing in the style of an established writer, I have to look askance.

That isn't to say that we can't pick up tips and tricks,
though. If you glance back toward the beginning of this chapter,
you'll see that little dialogue I created between a reader and me;
the reader's comments (if there were any) are not indicated;
instead, I typed " . . . " It was more convenient than saying something like, "she gave me a quizzical look." The technique is something I saw in David Foster Wallace's *The Broom of the System*.
Maybe I'll use it in my future writing.

I don't think of that as style, though; instead, it's a device, a
technique, an individual quirk; it can be used or not. Cormac
McCarthy and Rick Moody, author of *The Ice Storm* and *Purple
America*, don't use quotation marks; instead dialogue is preceded
by an em-dash: —.(Lots of European writers do that too.)

In his 1998 Pushcart Prize Award-winning essay "Demonology"
and again in *Purple America*, (Little, Brown and Company, 1997)
Moody has begun using italics as emphasis in the middle of sentences
and, at casual glance, seemingly at random (though at other points
the device is used clearly to offer a quote from a conversation, separate from dialogue):

> . . . So when Hex seizes his mother's shoulders in
> the kitchen, illuminated only by the streetlamps outside
> on Flagler Drive, *Jesus, why d-d-don't we shed some
> light on the subject, huh, Mom? Now, t-t-tell me again
> what you just said, okay?*, when he switches on the
> ancient fluorescent blub over the range, he realizes
> that, in a way, he already knows, has already suspected,

was already pacing and worry, though not really gifted with insight into the chaos of domestic relations . . . Is this how he will remember the sequence later? He makes a quick survey of his mother's condition. Her chair is braked, the house is quiet, the golf cart traffic eases occasionally past their address, and there is a distant and reassuring sound of surf. His rental car, which seems to him to be *leaking fuel* in some way, is parked in the drive. And again, for a second, he gets caught upon the stupendous hurt of the crime. Think of it in sequence. His stepfather returning Wednesday night from work as usual; his stepfather dining, say, upon pork chops and applesauce and asparagus—preparing them for himself; his stepfather loading the dishwasher (overfilling the detergent cup), managing even to grind beans and to prepare the Swiss automatic coffeemaker, to set the timer so that on Thursday morning, when Aviva will arrive, Billie's *half-decaf/half-regular* will be awaiting her. Then, after lugging his large suitcase down the attic stairs to his bedroom—large suitcase as opposed to the overnight or garment bags—Sloane begins to pack. Is this how it goes? A number of such possibilities intersect—some invented, some true, some *both invented and true*—and these intersections appear and vanish in Hex as he sets out through the pantry toward the living room. Which is to say that a long story begins here . . .

A successful choice? Whether it works—for you as a writer or the public as readers—is debatable, as are most such choices. (It does work for me; that's why I quoted it.) It is something that certainly calls attention to itself, slowing the reader who will stop to think not only about the emphasized words but, for those with an interest that goes beyond "escape," to consider also why the author is doing whatever it is that's being done. So: the writing itself becomes part of the subject of the story and we approach metafiction.

Clearly, then, while what Moody has done may interest you on an intellectual level, that doesn't mean that it's something you should try to emulate, copy or use; it derives from his needs as a storyteller and, most importantly, from something more personal: from the person he is.

✍ Do our styles change? Sure: the more we learn, the more we examine ourselves and the reasons we do things. The more experience we gain, the more likely it is that that will happen. And as we grow and experiment with other forms of writing, moving from genre to genre and subject to subject, the more likely (and in commercial terms, necessary) it is that that will happen. (A hardboiled romance might be pushing the envelope a bit more than you want to try; that doesn't mean—at all—that you shouldn't do it, just that it might not be the most cost effective use of your time, personally —and do we need that word here? Of course the opinions are personal—I think what could be learned from trying it is worth the time and effort.) In fact, as an exercise, you might try writing in your favorite category in the so-called style of another writer: If nothing else, it should cure you of the habit of trying to write like someone else; when you discover that whatever makes that other writer's work sing for you doesn't seem to be part of your own voice, you will finally be free to allow your own style to evolve.

My non-fiction writing is nothing like my fiction: my use of parentheses, for instance, is not as blatant in my fiction; my use of language, however, is reasonably similar as is my use of complex and compound sentences. It is all a reflection of how I think and speak, a reflection of me. It was not developed; it did evolve, coming from a sense of security and an acknowledgement and acceptance of the fact that it is *just the way I do things*.

Don't fall into the trap, then, of worrying about *developing your style*. It will happen if you just write. If something you've read seems interesting, if the challenge of trying to do what someone else has done effectively strikes you as important, and if you understand not only why another may have done and what it may add to the work, play with it, experiment. But don't think you're writing in Moody's style, or Hemingway's, or Henry James'; whatever it is that you're about will dictate little changes and make the writing personal. (If it doesn't, there's little of you in the work; you haven't done anything creative or worthy of note.)

Saul Bellow has said that a writer's style is whatever allows her to express herself best and most easily, and that because it's natural, it frees the writer's mind for the more important aspects of the job at hand. Evelyn Waugh said, " . . . style is not a seductive decoration added to a functional structure; it is of the essence of the work of art. The necessary elements of style or lucidity, elegance and individuality."

Style can overwhelm substance and, for most of us, it is the substance of what we have to say that's important. In *The Elements of Style*, E. B. White put it this way:

> Every writer, by the way he uses language, reveals something of his spirit, his habits, his capacities, his bias. This is inevitable, as well as enjoyable. All writing is communication; creative writing is communication through revelation—it is the Self escaping into the open. No writer long remains incognito.

No writer, that is, except the one trying to be someone else.

Some Random
Thoughts
on Creativity

e arly in the manuscript of James Sallis' *Bluebottle*, the fifth
in his Lew Griffin series, the author has his protagonist—a
private eye who is also a writer, among other things—say:

> All our lives, every day, hour after hour, we're telling
> ourselves stories, threading events, collisions and recol-
> lections on a string to make sense of them, making up
> the world we live in. Writing's no different, you just do
> it from inside someone else's head.

Sure, that's all. But he's right; they're right. How do you get into
someone else's head? Everyone does it differently, I guess. What
works for me is visualization, sort of a writer's version of Method acting. It also helps with description, with finding the details that may
make the telling difference. If they don't, I can always take them out
during revision. It helps me, finally and always, to *create*.

According to the dictionary, to create is to bring into being,
to cause to exist, to produce where nothing was before, to form out

of nothing. For some of us, it's frighteningly easy; for others, depressingly difficult.

Every day of your life is filled with stimuli; some of them you're conscious of, you may even be looking for them. Others are absorbed, filed away in memory without our even being aware of them. Sometimes we make notes about them: It took me several years to "write" "The Dream that Follows Darkness": The story began one evening in synagogue, as I reread the story of David and Bathsheba; it took on a certain focus as I stood, a few years later, in a parking lot in Oklahoma City, feeling the wind scour me. There was a line that came unbidden: *And later that night, after the rain stopped, the wind began, cold and scouring the sky of clouds.* And then, one night, I sat down and began to type.

I knew the characters and their predicament, I could see the story through their eyes, how they would be experiencing events I'd never had. I saw them through their own eyes and I did what I suggested to you earlier: I turned off my computer's screen, saw the scenes play out against that otherwise accusing blackness, and translated the images into letters and words and sentences and, hours later, into a story. All the things I hadn't realized I'd been thinking about were complete and in place and the story was created.

It was relatively easy because I'd been practicing the visualization techniques for years.

For a while, back in the '70s and '80s, self-actualization programs like est, Lifespring and Silva Mind Control were all the rage; some of what they preached was nonsense, part of it, though—and probably different parts for different people—had value. Bertrand Russell, Albert Einstein, Mozart, Vincent Van Gogh and dozens of others have described the process; even though it's fallen into disfavor and even though more people swear at it than swear by it, I find it works for me.

At its simplest, visualization is simply the calling up of images; writing then becomes translating those images so that they may be shared with an audience—that's the process I described with the darkened computer screen. It also has this advantage: if you're watching the words form on the screen, you become aware of errors; instead of being completely involved in writing, part of your mind is reading what's on the screen, and most of the time you're going to stop to make corrections . . . and that means you're going backward, literally stopping midstride to fix something.

Sure, that's one of the selling points of word processing; it's also one of the drawbacks for writers: because we can correct as we go along, a lot of us feel that we've done our revisions on the fly. Once upon a time, back when we used pens or typewriters, we'd write and then actually have to rewrite, from the beginning. As we did that, we made not only the changes we'd marked, but other corrections and improvements (okay, we only hoped they were improvements). Because we no longer re-key the manuscript, we've lost a step in the revision process and, based on what I see submitted, we've also lost a measurable degree of quality. If your screen is turned off (which creates a situation akin to the way we learned how to touch type, back when we learned how to touch type: you weren't allowed to look at the page in the typewriter), all you're thinking about is the forward motion of your story. Your editor and your readers will appreciate that.

There are a number of books and audio cassettes available that teach the techniques; most of them are found in the, uh, New Age sections, though some will be available in psychology and self-help; the process is more than a shirttail relative to autohypnosis, which is being used in pain management and as a therapy technique for cancer and heart patients.

It begins with relaxation. I was asked recently, in a survey of writers seeking to learn how we prepared to work, what I might do before I begin the day's session at the keyboard. What I do is relax. My approach is to use the Lamaze procedures I first learned twenty-five years ago. What you're seeking to do is relieve muscle tension;

in fact, it doesn't hurt to do the exercises every couple of hours while you're working . . . I don't know anyone with a really good ergonomic office. So:

✍ Begin by taking a couple of deep cleansing breaths: inhale deeply through your nose and release the breath slowly through your mouth. Do that about five times then, maintaining that breathing pattern, start tensing your muscles (I start in the feet and work my way up, muscle group by muscle group), holding that tension for a count of ten, then relaxing. It takes about five minutes and not only relaxes me physically, but serves to get me focused on what I'm going to be doing.

Once you're relaxed (and each time you do the exercise, the relaxation will become deeper), look at some object: a banana, the pencil on your desk, a drawing. Study it for a few moments, then close your eyes and try to see what you've been looking at. There's no passing grade; the idea is simply to be able to see something clearly, to be able to call the image up whenever you need to.

Then, open your eyes and look at the object again: was there bruising on the banana that you missed in your image? Was the pencil point sharper than the one you saw? Close your eyes again and add the differences to your mental picture.

As you start getting more secure in your ability to see with the mind's eye, move on to more complex objects and patterns. What it will do for your recall is unbelievable; it's a lot like the game of Concentration or those puzzles in "increase your memory books"; you know the ones, we even did them as kids: you look at a picture, turn the page, and then write down everything you remember seeing.

Not only do these exercises help make you more observant, but they serve to help you recall things seen in passing, things that may have provided (or will provide) the impetus for a story.

✍ The next step is to start playing with real objects you haven't seen: take the image of a pencil and alter it in your imagination; you know what it looks like, what it should look like, and what you want it to look like: make it happen. (This isn't as silly or time wasteful as it may seem at first; one of the common flaws in manuscripts are those scenes that just can't happen the way they're described. The exercise helps to overcome that because you're seeing things fully.)

Having worked with the concrete, begin to create images of things that may never have been but that you're going to bring to life for your reader because you can see them vividly enough to share the picture with your reader.

For instance: you have a character in mind (one you're creating, not the boss you're about to kill off in your story). You know what she looks like, basically: her height and hair color, her weight, the way she dresses. Now, begin to fill in the details. What's the texture of her skin? Are there creases at the corner of her eyes? Are her nails bitten? Manicured? What shape are they, square cut or round? Is it a French manicure? Uh-oh, look at her stockings: are there any runs? Snags or catches? What kind of rings is she wearing?

Have him walk into the room. Does he walk aggressively, as if he belongs there, or is he a little more "beta" in his approach? What sort of crease do his pants hold? What are his fingernails like? Is his collar frayed? Sweat stains or yellow discolorations at the armpits?

These are all elements of description, of course, but if you can't see him, and if you can't see the details that another character might observe, how three dimensional can you make him for the reader?

✍ Now: put the characters together. You know what you want them to do in terms of the story and predicaments you're going to explore in your writing; but having seen them now, having added the final touches as it were, how do they play off each other? How do their voices sound? Let them play one of your scenes, see how it blocks. Would the character you see be able to say what you think you want him to? Would he be able to say them to her?

✍ Now you need to refine the setting. You have your notes, you know the five objects or items that you've decided to use. Do the characters fit in the room? Would that vase be better with roses in it, or wildflowers? Is the table against the wall, or was it *pushed* against the wall? The word makes an enormous amount of difference in how the reader is going to experience things. Is everything you need in the room now, or do you have to add something else, a bump in the rug or something on the floor that she'll have to bend to pick up . . . and when she does, does she do a deep-knee bend or bend from the waist? It's not a minor difference, really; if you don't believe me, picture it and see what your character sees.

As all of this is happening, sit back and be an observer: all this stuff has been crammed into your subconscious and now you have to let it come out naturally; maybe he needs a nervous habit—touching the place on his ring finger where a ring is supposed to be; maybe she needs to allow her cheek to be kissed, but never offers her lips. At this point your characters and your setting will begin to tell you the things that they need; things some part of you was already aware of, even if you haven't expressed them to yourself.

It all sounds terribly metaphysical and, I guess, maybe even nonsensical to some; after all, we're rational folks, right, sitting down to do something that's been done for years. Well, maybe. But it's been my experience (and the experience of some of the most creative minds in history) that the process of creation happens that way. Just trust yourself. After a while, you'll discover that you're doing these things automatically: standing on the elevator waiting to get to the 52nd floor, you won't be one of those people staring mindlessly at the numbers above the door; you'll be seeing the scene you're going to write tonight moving in front of you. As you sit on a plane heading somewhere you might just as soon not have to visit, you won't have to deal with that pest in the seat next to you whining about the lousy food and the fact that everything now has to be checked because you're only allowed one piece of carry-on so the check-in line is longer because everyone has to check luggage. The drone of his voice will be white noise allowing you to bring that one extra thing to your murderer's motive . . .

✍ If I have a scene that's giving me trouble, one in which the elements aren't coming together the way they should, I put up an imaginary screen, toss my characters against it, and let the thing go by itself. I usually do this when I'm going to sleep, using one of the autohypnotic techniques that I've learned. As I said, there are tapes and books available if you want to go in that direction. But you don't have to go that deeply into it. Just using the relaxation techniques we've discussed already and then going to sleep with the idea in mind that you'd really like to come up with an answer to the problem *but without concentrating on it*, you'll soon discover that when you wake up, the solution is there. (You've probably already experienced something like this, anyway.)

All of us who've decided that visualization works are pretty much agreed on one thing: the imagination works best when left on its own to do its magic. Now, that doesn't mean that when you wake up the answer will be clear and absolutely right; what you'll have are the essentials; then you revise and sharpen. It's work.

And then there are the days when we turn control over to our imaginations and what we see is, well, a little less than perfect; there are some things in the subconscious that might better be left there; they were hidden and buried, not stored. Sometimes we'll find things that we don't understand and can't (or don't want to) use. Still, no matter how frightening or threatening, they may be fascinating and worth exploring: Go ahead, do it. Maybe it'll be nothing more than a writing exercise, something that you don't think you'll be able to sell. Well, maybe you won't be able to sell it today; markets change, ideas grow. Having written down whatever it is, it's always there to be retrieved.

Nothing you create is wasted; there may not be profit in it (immediate monetary profit), but just the simple fact that you did some work on it, that you wrote it down, that you played with words long enough to record it, has value.

Bob Randisi has a powerful and frightening speech that he delivers at writer's conferences; it's called *Writing to Eat*. At some point in your career, you'll have to decide if that's what you're doing. If you are, you're going to have to follow the path of least resistance; every word you put down on paper will be there for one reason: because it is the word your market demands. You will hold your imagination in check or use it only to create proposals for new projects; if they aren't accepted, you'll pitch the next one and the next; you'll do what's expected of you.

But . . . you may choose to take the added risk of going where you want to go, to write something because it is what you want to say, and say it in the way you want to say it because, after all, that's the way you want to do it; you will have the time and energy to stretch your imagination and go with your creativity and not concern yourself with how easily it will sell or how much you'll get for it; you won't write it for the food it will bring, but for the pleasure it will bring you.

Neither approach is right or recommended (at least by me); there's just what you want to do, what you want to accomplish, and only you can make the choice. You're the only one who knows what you need, what works and whether you're right or wrong.

And you're the only one who can make the decision; never let anyone else make it for you.

 Revision

the editor who began the process of teaching me what it was I was going to do for the rest of my life is a man named Theodore Solotaroff. He's the one who pointed out that if I read every manuscript to the bitter end—and we were talking about short stories and essays!—I'd be so far behind after a month that it would take the rest of my life to catch up. That was my first editorial lesson; some time later he gave me my first writing lesson: "Writing a first draft is like groping one's way into a dark room, or overhearing a faint conversation, or telling a joke whose punchline you've forgotten. As someone said, one writes mainly to rewrite, for rewriting and revising are how one's mind comes to inhabit the material fully."

I have far too many friends and acquaintances, even in today's highly (and increasingly) competitive market, who just can't be bothered. They have contracts for too many books, deadlines crawling over each other like maggots, and a certain lack of respect for their readers and, as far as I'm concerned, too little for themselves. So, they do a sketchy outline, sit down and knock out the novel (they've written so many of them that it doesn't really take any effort), maybe run it through spell check, print, mail, and get on to the next project. They also wonder why Rodney Dangerfield gets more respect than they do.

Revision is—or should be—a fact of life for you. That doesn't mean you can allow it to become an obsession; you can revise the soul out of a piece of writing, worry every word and sentence to death. The question: how do you know when the manuscript is ready, when do you stop revising? doesn't have an answer beyond: You'll know. And later, when you see the printed piece, you'll see the other changes you could'a, should'a made; make them next time. You can't use revision as an excuse not to get that manuscript off your desk and on to mine; at the same time, you can't blithely send things out hot off the printer.

That's the first lesson here: revise on hard copy, not on the screen, even if you're young enough to have grown up doing all your writing and composition with a word processor. (And it isn't going to be long before everyone will probably be of that class.)

Sure, it may take more time, and it carries the additional expense of yet another 250 sheets of paper. (I wonder how many companies have discovered the cost to them of copy paper "liberated"—as we called it in the Army—by employees busy knocking out the great American novel at home so they can quit their jobs and spend the rest of their lives writing and touring. Some dreams die very hard.)

But, it is still the best way to do it: to have all the pages spread out in front of you, to be able to see the changes in a context of pencil on paper and paragraph next to paragraph, page next to page, looking at the lines crossed through (but still having them there, not deleted).

When you do your revision is up to you. The late Stanley Ellin, one of the best mystery short story writers the country has ever produced, wouldn't remove a page from his typewriter until it was perfect; only then did he go on to the next. Others do it chapter by chapter or, in the case of essays and short stories, wait until the first draft is done. The revisions for this book will be done when the whole book is finished. I print out each chapter as I complete it. If I stop the day's work in the middle of a chapter—something I try to avoid—I don't print out, but I do stop in the middle of a sentence; I think that was one of Hemingway's tricks to make picking up again easier. Then don't look at it again until I'm done.

It doesn't matter what method you use, as long as you have some method to your madness.

What is it that you're looking for, looking to do with your revision? Well, obviously, that's going to depend on what you see as wrong. With practice, you'll be able to start killing your darlings— those words and phrases and scenes that are there just for you— just because you like them, love them, but that you eventually come to realize don't add anything to the forward motion of the story, the scene, or the character.

You'll start seeing the misused words and the places where better words might be used and the words that don't have to be used at all. As you read your work aloud, or have it read to you which is, to my mind, much more effective, you'll find the breathless sentence that needs shortening or, at least, some punctuation. You'll find spelling errors that the spell checker I told you to dump —and you didn't—missed.

It takes time; it probably makes sense to let the material sit for at least a week or so before you go back to it, though as you gain experience you can probably work on changes in the last chapter before you begin to work on the next. But if you're doing that, don't go into the file (assuming that you are, indeed, working at a computer) and start making the changes; just note them on your hard copy and wait until everything is done before you type your final draft.

I don't imagine anyone will, these days, do things the way they had to be done when everything was being written on typewriters (and which those of us who write in longhand on pads still do): that is, retype everything. That defeats the purpose of the word processing programs, doesn't it? Yeah, but it also stops one of the essential rewriting processes: When you're retyping, you tend to make changes you hadn't thought about: new dialogue may come to you (because, remember, your subconscious has been working on the material, even if you haven't be "thinking" about it), some bit of business you hadn't considered rises to the surface and in the majority of instances, they are improvements. If you just delete a paragraph or a word and put in the new one, that isn't going to happen or, at least, not as frequently. I think work suffers because of that.

No matter: it still makes sense to wait until the work is finished before you begin revisions. What's the process like?

Just like editing.

A few lines back I talked about reading the work aloud. Here's an example of what you might find. It's taken from a published book, Healy's *Blunt Darts*, which we've looked at earlier.

> Coming out of the women's side of the locker building, Val's legs looked a little thicker than they had in the other outfits I'd seen her wear to date.

The first thing that struck me was the last two words; they aren't necessary. If I'd written the lines, or if I'd been the editor, I would have deleted them. I might even have suggested changing it to "I'd seen her in." That's a subjective call (but so is editing and writing, when you get right down to it).

More serious for me, and something that became obvious when I read the paragraph aloud, is this: Val's *legs* were coming out of the locker; what happened to the rest of her? No big deal, maybe, no reviewer jumped on it, it didn't bother Jerry's editor. But I would have recast the sentence . . . ~~unless I missed it.~~

And that strikethrough is what it's all about . . . you have to feel free to just cut (and replace, ~~if necessary~~).

Here's an example, again drawn from my editing, but something the author could have done as easily. The manuscript was

The February Trouble, by Neil Albert, the second in his Dave Garrett series.

When the manuscript first arrived, there was a problem with one scene. Garrett, a private investigator, was in the home of the man who'd hired him to investigate some threats made against his business. After breakfast, Garrett excuses himself to go to the bathroom (when I started in this business characters rarely did that; not only didn't they excuse themselves, they never seemed to have to go to the john); the scene sets up a meeting between the investigator and his client's wife.

As originally written, the scene was too long and pointless. I suggested cutting it, and that's what the author did. However, some of the things established in the original version were now gone and because Albert didn't reread the scene after printing it out, certain gaps appeared. In what follows, words struck through were deleted, words in boldface were added:

> "Hi. I'm Dave Garrett, ~~the investigator.~~"
>
> She extended her hand; the nails were perfectly groomed and painted. "Nice to meet you—can I call you Dave? ~~Call me Anne. Everyone does~~. **I'm Anne Chadwick. You're the investigator.**" **It wasn't a question.**
>
> "Pleased to meet you, Anne."
>
> She was a good deal shorter than Chadwick; and younger, too. Or perhaps she'd had a facelift; Lord knows they seemed to have the money for it. ~~"We were just running over to the restaurant," I explained. "I need to see what's been happening."~~

"The investigator" was cut because it was meaningless. He might have been with the Board of Health for all this woman knows. And since Garrett doesn't know who she is at this juncture, the introduction struck me as being just a shade too arrogant.

Anne's comment about calling him Dave serves to place her;

she's a woman in charge, something substantiated when she mentions Garrett's role: she knows he's the investigator.

Garrett's final words were deleted because they were beside the point. The trip to the restaurant is mentioned a few paragraphs later, where they belonged.

The fixes were easy; the point is that they were necessitated by the fact that the author was watching the clock and making the corrections directly on disk. If he'd printed things out and looked at them as hard copy, he would have seen the "mistakes" and fixed them before sending the pages to me. (Yes, Neil knows I'm exposing him in this way.)

Revision isn't always that easy. Here's an example from something I started as an exercise and that I may finish some day. Again, the strikethrough represents deletion; boldface indicates words that have been added:

> Kara wept. She stood looking out **over the city**, eyes blank and unfocused while ~~the city~~ **New York** sparkled below her, and wept. Without spasm or tear, she wept.
>
> She looked up, ~~now~~ violet eyes focused now on the full moon. She saw, regarded, disregarded, the halo of ice crystals and pulled the glow around herself. Her hair, **honey flowing down to** bleached silver, ~~flowing down to its natural honey,~~ turned pewter. Humming; then quietly whispering her name ~~to herself~~. She smiled, liking the small acid tingle of it. ~~Kara, with rolled French "r" or sing "cara mia."~~ **Kara mia.**
>
> Kara moved. Wrapped in white, fair skin fading back **pale** behind sultry red lips, she danced, hips circling and making love to the man who might have been her partner, to the room to the world. Caught in the lightning of exploding strobes, her eyes glowed, amethyst crackling.
>
> She danced and teased, easy laughter and showgirl

face, quick smiles and butterfly touches as she wove around her partner. The men kept coming to her, courting, smiling. ~~Lying.~~ And Kara moved through them, around them, she moved ~~and was happy.~~

Until **an athletic** ~~a slender~~ man with **grey** ~~light~~ hair moved into the circle; until she recognized that she recognized him. Then the evening began to end.

She left the **club** ~~disco~~ abruptly, running ~~along the pavement of Manhattan.~~ **through the streets.** Behind her, calling, reaching out, the ~~tall, athletic~~ man she had been dancing with tried to stop her. She turned her head, laughed. Her legs gleamed in the moonlight through hip high slits in her skirt. An ivory carving; dream flesh made quick.

~~Kara left, as she always did. It was time to leave, it is always time to leave when they close in, when the scent of rut grows heavy. The man turned away, bitter, teased, an image graven into his mind. A grail.~~

Kara's face melted, smeared, swirled down the drain. The showgirl rinsed away, leaving Joanna, translucent, looking at herself in the mirror. Green eyes studied themselves, flashed. The innocent smile, full-lipped, as her perfect body reflected in the gold and white bathroom.

She turned on the shower, set the ~~Water Pik~~ massage head on slow, the water on hot. Soaping herself, her fingers traced the pale white scar **racing from beneath her right breast to** low on her stomach: the only flaw, mark; a ~~secret~~ rosary told only by her fingers. The steaming water softened her hair, ~~drove the sticky stiffness of hair spray out~~ and the white and honey strands darkened, plastered themselves to her skull, her neck, **her** ~~and~~ back. She washed away the night, Kara, all the night-

time names the sound of prowling dancers, the smell of
drink and smoke. Joanna laughed as her fingers played
along her body, her perfect body with its secrets of night-
time names.

Then, in the steam and heat, she shivered and
hugged herself.

If I ever decide to doing anything with this piece, tentatively titled
"Virtual Reality," there'll be more changes: the story will move out
of New York, the man she runs from may be more fully described,
some word choices will be reconsidered.

Now, were any of the changes indicated here necessary? I
thought so. They improved, to my ear, the flow and sound for
which I was trying, and that was my major concern.

When I began revising those paragraphs, the first thing I did
was circle words that appeared too often. The one that stood out
was "wept." I like the sound of the word, though, and the way it
echoes "whipped," especially, and particularly in this context. Then
I have whipping meaning not only punishment, but a sense of having lost. That will be an important element of this story, ultimately.
And, finally, I was creating an emphasis on crying with no outward
manifestations; it isn't until the last sentence that Joanna reacts out-
wardly, hugging herself and shivering.

Most of the time, when it isn't being used for effect, it pays to
delete the word that appears again and again and . . . Usually, it's
some common word and it was used because it was easy not
because you were trying to create something in the reader's mind.
It happens with names, too: use pronouns when you can.

This bears repeating: If something doesn't advance the story
in some way, if it doesn't have an action that makes a difference, if
it doesn't add *substantially* and *urgently* to characterization, if you
can read the story without those words and not miss them because
nothing in them is important, cut them out. If you don't, an editor

will . . . if he isn't so put off by what he's read that he's returned the manuscript to you.

Look for non-specific words (about, almost, perhaps): if there's a reason for ambiguity, fine; otherwise, the concrete is always better.

Make certain the manuscript says what you want it to: about you, as well as about the story; that you've found the right word—the lightning and not the lightning bug.

And then mail it out.

Always Beginning

a nd now you're at the end, but also the beginning. Always, it's the beginning.

By finishing your novel, or your story (whatever it is you've written), you've done something that many—even most—dream about and talk about but never do: finish. You've written. There's a joke, a sort of bitter one, about people who want to have written, but don't want to write, to do the work or expend the effort that takes you from once upon a time to the end.

And having gotten there, your work begins: there's networking; there's getting the manuscript into the hands of those who can do something with it—something like getting it published, so that what you've written can be read: at one level or another, that's the purpose for which the piece, whatever it is, exists—unless, of course, you're writing simply for your own enjoyment and edification . . . as valid a reason to write as any other.

Still, there's this: Having written, having sent your words out to find their place in the world, you are going to write again. And this is where things change, at least for those writers who seem to make a difference in our lives.

What are you going to write next? Will it be a variation on the themes explored in the previous work? That's fine: some people spend their entire lives in search of the answer to just one question. But will the novel or story or essay be *different*, or will it, too, simply be a variation of what you did before?

If you read series fiction, the ongoing saga of a character, you'll notice that beyond the category formula the author will often create his own formula: there'll be a fight scene on page three, a damsel in distress on page five, an antagonist named at the end of the first chapter. It's easy enough to understand why that happens: a book or two has worked, found an audience: why mess with success? It makes the writer's job a bit less difficult: he knows what has to go where, and the reader knows what's going to be where, so the risk of pushing that customer out of the comfort zone is lessened: no risks, no shocks, no offense. No harm, no foul.

The risks to the author are manifold. There's a more than passing possibility that you're going to become jaded, ennui will set in, the excitement that comes with having created something new and different and special is lost—gone. (If you read series with a discerning eye, if you're looking for more than a simple escape and if you pay attention to what's happening in the world you've entered through the shaping of words on the page, you'll notice the point at which an author has tired of the character. Reviewers and discussion groups notice it. And, eventually, the editors and publishers notice it: sales fall off. Slowly perhaps, and not dramatically at first, but the loss of readers is discernable.)

A series of novels (in the sense of a serial or in the sense of a body of work) is somewhat like a river: it flows from a beginning somewhere *there* and continues to a point at which it ends, joining a larger body . . . a lake, an ocean. An author's canon. And that's why remembering something the ancient Greeks knew is important: You can't step into the same river twice.

Things change. It may be our vision of the world, it may be the world itself. Reader's tastes change; the willingness of publishers to take certain risks changes. Because we live, we change; having experienced new things, other things, our knowledge changes. (Just as we want our characters to be different at the end of a story because of the events they've "lived" through, we are affected. Even by the act of writing.)

Having changed, it's increasingly difficult to be the same writer when we begin our next works; we either tie ourselves up emotionally and intellectually, or we lie, denying what we've learned and become so as to satisfy what we were. And that is reflected in our finished stories. (For those who don't change, well, I guess it isn't a problem. Personally, I welcome the differences in myself.)

The point is this: don't get locked into anything. The beginner's mind is always filled with possibilities; in the expert's mind, though, there are few. After all, if you know everything, what's left to learn? Once you stop learning, what's left?

The lessons and exercises you've just read through to get to this page are the result of the things I've learned, through experience, in reaching this point in my life as an editor and writer. They've worked for me, and I share them at every opportunity. I know, though, that tomorrow or the next day I'll be browsing in a bookstore, or listening to someone speak at a conference, and I'll see something new—something I may never have considered or something I rejected way back when—and I'll know that it's *right*, that it's something I should at the very least try. There are dozens of writers and teachers who will, out of their own experience, argue any and all of the points I've raised. There is no right or wrong, there's only what works for you and it may only work for you right now. After all, if writing were all the same, there'd be little point in doing it and even less point to reading it.

Other things are going to begin now, too: as well prepared as you are, as experienced as you are, because things are in a constant state of flux, something that worked one day, that received glowing critiques at first and brilliant acceptance and reviews following on that, is going to fall flat; it's the nature of this beast. Even the most successful writers (and it doesn't matter how you're defining successful, it can be in terms of sales, critical acclaim, or even your own self-satisfaction with what you've wrought) awaken one morning to find that it's all gone away. For some it takes the form of "writer's block." For others, the market dries up because a form of writing has fallen into temporary disfavor. Someone else may, quite literally, discover that they have nothing more to say (which isn't a block; it's only the Self's way of telling you that this part of your life is done; there are other modes of creative expression and, truly, something else worth exploring may come to you the very next day, as you cross the street and see a cat dart under a car at the curb and you begin to wonder what it's running from).

You may also find yourself locked into something that no longer fascinates, but you're under contract and you've gotten used to the income, so you go on but the effort you expend is in direct proportion to the amount of fun you're having. If you're not having fun, as with any job, it becomes more difficult to get up each morning and face the work.

If, however, you leave yourself open to the possibilities your talent and skill and vision allow, none of these things will be a problem for more than a few hours: there's always something else you can do with the drive that brought you here. But only if you allow yourself to recognize that you're always beginning, that something else awaits when you step into that river of imagination.

The more you swim in it, the more snags you discover. None of them are insurmountable.

Reviews await you. They can be good, bad, or indifferent; there are hundreds of books that get published and receive no reviews whatsoever. There's little you can do about the last situation, and your publisher is going to be as upset as you are; for the reviews you get however, keep a certain amount of perspective.

Raves are nice, but you're not going to learn much from them, just that someone, reading your work through the veil of their own beliefs, liked what you did. You'll find comparisons made, and comments and interpretations offered, that have little or nothing to do with you and what you did . . . or thought you did. Don't think about them too much; be grateful, but don't become lazy, don't think that the applause means you can rest on your laurels. The reviewers giveth and the reviewers taketh away. A writer who believes her own press and takes it too seriously is going to find, sooner or later, that she is no longer taken seriously. (Okay, sure, there are some writers who are so brilliant, so perfect, that the acclaim never dies. It's just something you can't count on.)

Negative reviews can be devastating. Don't take them personally; they have nothing to do with you, unless you've stepped on some toes by, say, bragging too much about the good ones that came earlier. There are some petty people out there.

The bad reviews can affect sales; but think of all the extremely wealthy and popular writers scorned by reviewers time and again who laugh all the way to the bank with each and every new title. I'd suggest not making the mistake that some writers make: ignoring the bad reviews entirely. Read them, see if any of the points raised are valid, whether there is room for improvement (there almost always is). Your editor is reading the reviews, too, looking for information that may help strengthen his list or that will give him some insight into the marketplace, information that can, if absorbed, make him a better editor for the publishing house and for you.

Again, it isn't you being reviewed, it's one book and that's the only context in which you have to place it. If you are willing to accept the fact that maybe the work wasn't perfect, and if you acknowledge that the book you've started to write is something new—a new beginning—the reviews won't haunt you. They were *then*; this is *now*.

There'll be fan mail and meetings with your readers at bookstores, conventions, and conferences. They're going to be more than happy to tell you exactly what they think, the good and the bad. Readers, many of them, take it for granted that you're writing for them, to them. To a certain extent, naturally, you are; without them—in reality or as the potential that exists in an editor's mind when your work is acquired—the rewards for your efforts would be rather limited. But the ones you're convincing first are yourself and then the editor.

If the readers are happy with what you've done, and they tell you that, thank them. If they tell you what they particularly liked, remember it . . . especially if lots of them say the same thing.

If they're negative in their comments, if they tell you that a character didn't come to life, or that they liked your first book rather than your second, ask them why and remember what they say . . . especially if lots of them say the same thing.

Maintain your composure, though: it doesn't pay to argue with the reader any more than it's to your advantage to debate with a reviewer. Just remember what's said and then, later, consider the comments and whether there's anything in what was said that you can use. Some of it is going to be silly and beside the point (there are readers, as an example, who resent characters that smoke cigarettes or, more pointedly, don't like to have the fact brought up to them every time someone lights up. Are you going to change the character of your character because of that?); other points raised are going to be insightful and helpful. Only you can choose between them; it is your work, your observation and explication of the chaos around us, that is on the printed page and your value to us, as readers, lies in you, as a writer, being true to that.

If anything that's said makes you change (for whatever reason), it's another beginning.

Be prepared to receive more advice from the well-meaning than you can ever hope to use. There are those who will tell you to write something else; someone will tell you that you should get X amount more for your next book because of the reviews you received; someone else will tell you to switch categories, to go here, do that . . . everyone knows what's best for you. They may even be right. Only you know the answer; the advice is only worth the value you give it.

Publishing changes overnight. With the acquisition of companies by others and the merging of houses, markets dry up; publishers become more homogenized because there are too many of them (in a world in which there are now too few of them) and they're all competing for the same space.

Readers' tastes change.

Editorial tastes change.

Advice comes from that, from our individual observations. Each change is a chance for yet another beginning.

All those changes bring with them the possibility and reality of rejection, which isn't any more personal than anything else we've been discussing . . . except for taste and opinions: they're personal to the offerer. You may have decided to jump on a bandwagon, to listen to those who say that something is hot and by the time you've gotten it done to your satisfaction it's, well, only tepid. Which brings you to another beginning.

Don't be afraid to ask questions; it's the only way you'll get answers. Don't be afraid to ask for help; if everyone around you thinks you've got everything under control, you can drown. That's why there's a network out there (and we'll look at that network in a few moments); use it, contribute to it. Be a part of someone else's beginning.

There are thousands of people who dream of being writers, of living a life in fiction. For most, it never gets beyond being a dream. Getting that first piece done and sold is not the end of the dream; it's the beginning.

You're your own biggest roadblock. Just about everyone wants you to succeed: the agents, the editors. Everyone you deal with wants this moment to be the first, the beginning of many successful moments to follow.

We hope that you've written from your heart, with care, and done everything you can to make your manuscript as good as it can be; that you've written with integrity and understanding of the needs of fiction, of your story, of your characters.

You cannot please everybody; you are your first and most important audience.

You cannot be afraid to be wrong.

You cannot be afraid to be right.

You are a writer, know thyself.

You are a writer, to thine own self be true.

And with each word you type, you are always beginning a new adventure.

Always.

PART TWO

Networking

Networking

i went out for a walk the other day, just taking a break (there's nothing wrong with taking a break now and then, no matter how many hours you've committed to your writing), and I passed an old building with a real, old-fashioned garret apartment tucked away at the top. It was for rent; I couldn't afford it. Okay, this is New York City and the neighborhood is a good one, but what struck me as I looked at it while savoring a genuine spring day was that the artist in the garret is a wonderfully romantic image, but one that doesn't have anything to do with what we're doing these days.

Or, at least, it shouldn't.

One of the drawbacks to working alone, isolated in some little room above the city, is that without feedback, without support, without help, without a network, we're pretty much doomed to making the same mistakes again and again.

You're going to hear that there are no more Maxwell Perkinses working as editors. (If you don't know who Perkins was, there's an American Book Award-winning biography of the man who edited Hemingway, Wolfe, Fitzgerald, Lardner, Caldwell (Erskine and Taylor), James Jones, and Alan Paton among others; he remains the

Platonic ideal of the editor.   It's titled *Max Perkins: Editor of Genius*, by A. Scott Berg, published by Washington Square Press.) Given the way the industry has changed, those who say that are right to some degree, but that doesn't mean that there are no caring editors, no editors who will work with their writers to help them create the best book they're capable of at a given time.   It doesn't mean that they don't edit (a base canard popularly spoken), or that your book has to be perfect when it is submitted.   It does mean, though, that editors don't have as much time to teach individual writers their craft.   Maybe it means that you've got to be an advanced placement student.

This is a good time to bring up a touchy subject.   Because that sense of the necessity of the perfect manuscript is so much a part of what young writers are hearing now, the topic of the book doctor has to be discussed.

Book doctors are freelance editors, many of whom have had long and reputable publishing careers and who, having been downsized or retired by choice, offer their services to writers worried about the condition of their manuscripts.   For fees as low as five dollars a page and rising to whatever the market will bear, they advertise that they will help get your manuscript into publishable shape.

Can they do it?   Yes, many of them can or, at worst, can direct you in your work so that some of the more egregious errors disappear.   Some of the better ones work with you almost as teachers, offering suggestions, reading and rereading, shaping the work as best they—and you—can.   (And they won't take you on if they don't feel they can do anything for you.)   That doesn't mean a publisher will acquire the manuscript when the work is done or that an agent will represent you.   No one can guarantee that; anyone who does should probably be avoided.

There are agents who will respond to a submission by telling you to send your work to a book doctor and, possibly, recommend one. They should be avoided; there are too many scams out there, too many people willing to take advantage of your desire.

There are book doctors who, for whatever the fee, really don't do very much more than copyedit (and in this case it doesn't mean any more than correct your spelling and grammar) and give you cryptic notes: "Show, don't tell," without giving you any indication of how to go about that task.

They should be avoided, too, but how are you going to know before you become involved? Do the same thing that's suggested when you're searching for an agent: ask for recommendations, ask the book doctor about former (or present) clients, then ask them what was done and what the results were.

There are some excellent people working on a freelance basis with writers. I haven't seen any of them advertise in the writing magazines; they get clients through recommendations from other clients. Unfortunately, a few bad apples have ruined the reputations of some very honorable men and women, so you have to approach the consideration to hire one carefully, slowly and thoughtfully.

There's only one thing assured when you're dealing with book doctors and other freelance editors: your bank account will be lighter when the process is done. If you're working with someone good, you will also have learned something about writing. If you're working with someone who can't really do the job, you'll have learned another kind of lesson.

Back in the good old days (when were they for you?), writers had an opportunity to learn and hone their craft in the magazines— all those pulps that so many decried, but that offered income, editorial guidance and a place to publish and be seen.

Short stories are much more difficult to write than novels; you have much less room to accomplish the same task. Today's short story market is infinitely smaller and offers less recompense: many of them pay in copies and in the rush to get the check, lots of writers just don't want to be bothered doing the get kind of work necessary to create a good short story for that kind of payment. Even within the categories, where there are paying markets, the numbers are down and competition for space is fierce.

Space in the "little" magazines, the literary quarterlies—some of which pay handsomely—is also at a premium and the editorial guidelines are such that for most writers, people interested in genre and popular fiction, they aren't a career option. (They're a wonderful writing option, though.)

What it all means is that the reactions we need in order to learn where we may be making mistakes have to come from somewhere else. (I'm not going to discuss the various electronic and cyber-magazines because, at this point, I'm not convinced of their value. Some writers I've spoken to like the license and anarchy many of those "publications" represent; I don't because at most of the sites I've visited I don't sense any editorial judgment or control at all. That might be fine there, but it isn't fine in my corner of the publishing world and I have serious questions about the quality and value of the feedback writers receive. I know there are some excellent e-mags—though I haven't seen much fiction in the ones I've been to; there's just so much time and I don't spend mine surfing, much as I might enjoy it—but it's my bias based on what I've seen so far.) Fortunately, that network for support does exist and can be entered easily.

Workshops, writers groups and critique groups can be found in every part of the country, and major conferences and workshops are held year round. There are also classes and courses at schools; some are part of a curriculum, others are conducted on the campuses and with the support of the institutions involved. That's where you can begin.

Writing and critique groups are started by people interested either in a form of writing or the field generally. They can be as small as four or five people (even two writing "partners," people who sit down together once a week to look over each other's work and comment on it, qualifies). A local library or bookstore can probably give you leads to groups in your area, and certainly to classes. In fact, the June 1998 edition of *Writer's Digest* has a list of bookstores around the country that are involved with groups; the magazine also offers a starter kit for Writers' Groups; you can e-mail them at wdwg@fwpubs.com or call 1.800.289.0963, ext. 424.

I don't know what they're offering in the way of information, but based on my experience with groups, I'll tell you what I look for and what seems important to me.

First, you have to know what you're looking for in the group. Feedback and commentary are important, but what kind of information are you looking for? Many groups have published writers as members; the tendency, as I've experienced it, is for those members to tell you what's worked for them and, unfortunately, to think that because it worked for them, it's right. But that isn't necessarily so, especially if you're writing a different kind of book.

Are you looking for ways to make your book more commercial to become a better writer? Sadly, the two don't always go hand-in-hand; witness the ongoing debates between those who say that literary/mainstream fiction is too downbeat or not fully enough "plotted."

So, again: know what you want and expect; it may be that you're better off taking some classes in creative writing than joining a critique group. (The slam against them is that you may only learn what you need to know in order to teach the class yourself.)

Second, there's trust between the members. The critique group setting places a writer in a vulnerable position: you are reading your work, or having it read, and receiving feedback and commentary from the other members. Is what you're hearing correct? Useful? Is the group dominated by a couple of know-it-alls, people who refuse to discuss their comments but insist that they're right because . . . well, because they've been published, or because they heard an editor say something once, or just because they have an attitude?

When scouting a group, sit in on a couple of sessions, listen to the byplay between members, listen to the advice: does what you're hearing people say jibe with your own feelings about the work being critiqued? Does it make sense to you, as a writer and in terms of your own work? Remember: just because someone is saying something, it doesn't mean that it's right for you.

Third, how does the group work? Most seem to follow one of two approaches: members take work home with them, read, make notes, and then everyone joins at the next meeting to discuss what's been read. At others, copies are distributed but the author reads aloud for a fixed amount of time. When the time is up, the critique begins. (I prefer a variation on that: I'd rather have someone else read the work because the author is going to read what she wants you to hear, dramatizing, acting, enhancing the words on the page. The experience of reading, however, is different: we have to add those enhancements, cued by what's written. If I read your work aloud—and I do in the critique sessions I run—I'm reciting cold and you, as the author, hear the places where I trip over an unfelicitous phrase; it makes an enormous difference in the perception of the work.)

As a rule, once the critique begins, the author remains silent, making note of whatever has been said. You can respond only when asked a direct question. If someone says your character isn't coming alive and doesn't go any further than that, that particular critique is valueless. You should, at the very least, be allowed to ask why. What you can't do is defend the work against the comments, at least during the meeting. (I've got mixed feelings about that; I enjoy debate. On the other hand, everyone wants a turn and arguing takes time away from other people.) After the meeting, however, there should be time to discuss things, and that time should be taken.

What you have to learn to do is sift the information you receive, saving what makes sense and ignoring the rest. I once received a manuscript I'd requested after hearing a portion of it read at a critique group I was visiting. It took several months to arrive; once it did, I understood why. The author kept reading at meetings, trying to make the manuscript suit everyone's taste, fulfill everyone's directions. The resulting mess was unpublishable.

Again, trusting the people to know what they're talking about and making certain that they recognize what you're trying to accomplish, is of paramount importance. If you're writing in a category, but trying to stretch the envelope, being told that that you can't do that in a mystery doesn't help you at all. (That's an example of what happens in a strictly commercially oriented group; what you're trying may make your job harder, but if you succeed, you become the bandwagon, rather than the person jumping aboard.)

Listen carefully to the praise being doled out, as well. (Critique does not mean negative; it implies a consideration of the work in a particular context.) Some groups lavish accolades; I cringe when I hear it. That isn't to say that strokes aren't nice, we all like to be appreciated. For me, honesty is best; nice turns of phrase should be applauded, but if they aren't there, I'd rather keep silent. You're not doing a writer a service by encouraging them to submit something (and that's what the praise leads to, unless carefully couched) if they're not ready.

Another thing I've learned: you often get more from listening to or reading another person's work and discovering the things you don't want to do than you do from the comments made about your own work. So, pay attention to everything.

Like any group, a writer's group has a dynamic, and its success depends on the members and leadership. Schisms are regular happenings; so is backbiting and all other forms of social nastiness. If you're in with some people and see this happening, you've got two choices: cut your losses and run or try to mediate and bring things back into focus, restating the goals of being together.

But as long as you have confidence in what you're getting as feedback and feel that your writing is improving because of it, you've taken a first step on the road to publication.

☞   ✎   ☞

While your network has begun, you still have some building to do, however. If you have published writers in your group, you may be able to get an introduction to their editors or agents; there've been times when one of my writers has asked me to fly out and address her group and I'm always happy to do it as long as it is understood that I'm not taking manuscripts home with me. Things don't always work that way, though, so your next step is to start attending conferences and/or workshops . . . there's one almost every weekend somewhere in the country and both *Writer's Digest* and *The Writer* publish lists of them every spring; and lots of writer's group newsletters include that information; larger groups often sponsor conferences as well.

Conferences (as opposed to workshops) are panel and/or lecture oriented, with as many as eight tracks going on at once. (Fortunately, tapes are usually made so that you can still hear what's being said at the panels you can't attend.)

In addition to writers speaking to you from the perspective of their experience and careers, there will be editors and agents attending. The publishing pros not only speak about what they're looking for (no matter what they say, the answer is something they can sell), but will offer talks on their specialties and areas of expertise. If your writing interest is in whatever a particular pro is talking about, it pays to put their panel down on your list of must-do items for the conference. It's not only for the insight you'll gain, but because most con organizers also arrange for the editors and agents to be available for one-on-one meetings.

These are arranged before the conference begins; with your

application you're given the opportunity to request a meeting with the people of your choice. (Early registration becomes important; the slots are filled quickly.) We'll talk about how to handle these meetings in a bit; for now, you just want to know they're available.

Additionally, at some of the conferences I've spoken at in the last few years, critique opportunities are being offered: your work is read by or to one of the guest speakers and comments offered. This feedback has a special value because a person who may be considering your work at some future point is telling you, right now and to your face, exactly what they think and why. It can be grueling and disheartening; it can open doors. Remember: what you hear is still only one person's reaction; just because I don't like something doesn't mean that another editor won't—just a look at the different lists published each season is proof of that. And if arguing is forbidden in the critique group setting, it's twice the sin here. Just swallow your pride and get on with your work.

Another popular offering: for a small entry fee, most conferences now sponsor contests: you submit an outline and the first chapter of your work in progress, it's read by a screening committee, and those that get the nod are passed up to the next level and, finally, to the guest editors and agents who pick winners. There are cash prizes and scrolls awarded at a dinner and the knowledge that your work was deemed best of breed or best in show.

The best contests give the judges the chance to comment on the work; those that make it to the final round get the insights (for whatever they're worth) of the publishing professionals. So, in addition to the prize you may or may not win, you will learn what others think of what you've done, and they're not people you know (your name isn't on the work you submit), so the judgments are unbiased (beyond the biases we all bring to our reading).

The value of the contest is not really in the winning; we've all judged too many to think that a prize-winner is necessarily publishable (thus, my admonition not to make winning a conference prize an issue in your submission letter); it is in the analyses you receive. Before submitting, you might want to check with the organizers to make certain that they are part of the package you'll receive once the contest is over.

I realize I've just painted a pretty bleak picture of how the professionals may react. Unfortunately, most of what we see and hear isn't ready (and that has nothing to do with the conference system; most of what we receive as submissions isn't ready, either) but every conference has its success stories: requests for manuscripts and contracts offered. Think of it as part of the network you're building and keep your expectations in check.

The conferences I enjoy most are the ones held at hotels or conference centers over a period of two or three days. In the evenings, many of the editors and agents hang out in the lounge (or in a hospitality suite if the conference is wise enough to provide one), and they are approachable and more than happy to speak to you. (In April, 1998, I sat in a bar at the Pike's Peak Writers Conference at midnight, working with a writer on a manuscript. That's me; we're not all that commitable. But the others were there, sitting in small groups, talking.) It's been my experience that you can learn as much, if not more, during these late night bull sessions than you can in a panel. And you learn a very important lesson: the editors and agents are as human as you are.

If the conference you're going to attend doesn't provide that kind of opportunity, take a chance during the day and ask an editor to lunch or dinner (they're often part of the program; at some conferences the speakers are assigned tables for meals and you can seek out the table of interest), or offer to buy her a drink. Unless something's been planned, they're usually happy to say yes. At the very worst, if none of these options are open to you, don't be afraid to go up to a speaker who may be sitting doing nothing and opening a conversation; as long as they're not involved in something, they'll welcome the attention and courtesy.

How do you pick a conference? Well, time and finances play a role; using one of the lists, you can find those that fall within all your budgetary needs. Call the organizers and find out who the guests will be, whether there's a contest or one-on-one, whatever is of concern to you. (If you're writing horror and nothing on the program deals with that area, it may not be the right conference for you.)

Having chosen, registered, and arrived on site, go to the registration desk and get your membership packet. It will have the schedule of all the panels and other events, and you'll get the other information you need (when your one-on-one is, for instance, or where to sign up for them). Choose the panels you have to see and, if you're traveling with a friend, perhaps arrange to have one of you go to one panel, the other to another, and you can swap notes if the cost of all the tapes is going to be too high.

I'd also suggest something radical, especially to people who attend conferences regularly: don't go to the "how to create suspense" panel for the third time, even if you're writing mysteries. You've been there and heard most of it. Instead, go to a panel on creating a sensuous scene or a panel on dialogue . . . as a writer, you have to know how to do it all and, don't forget, each opportunity presents a new beginning, a new chance. I wound up writing "The Dream that Follows Darkness" because I went to a horror panel, something I had no previous interest in. Okay, it didn't end up as a horror story, but that's because I don't write horror; what I learned in that panel, though, created an opportunity and channel to try something new, something that in this case worked out. If I'd gone to the plotting discussion, it wouldn't have happened.

Once you've got your schedule worked out, start meeting people. Everyone milling around in that registration area shares a basic interest with you and almost all of them will be happy to meet someone new, to talk about what they're doing and what you're doing. They may have attended the conference previously (there are lots of repeat offenders at these gatherings) and they might very well be able to steer you toward something that'll be of interest, maybe recommend a particular speaker . . . or know where the men's room is. It all counts.

What you should bring: comfortable clothes, first of all and, just in case, a sweater; some of those meeting rooms can get awfully cold, especially in states where they keep the air conditioning on Arctic.

Pads, pencils, and business cards are always in order. Some speakers have no objection to you taping them, others do. (After all, those speeches are a form of writing and we have no control over what you may do with the tape once you leave. At least the organization's tapes carry a copyright notice. And, of course, the organization may not want you to tape panels because they're doing it themselves. So, check with the registrars and the speakers before you turn on the tape recorder.)

Bring two or three copies of your synopsis and the first chapter or two of your work. You'll need them for the critique session, if there is one, and you'll need them just in case someone asks to see your work. Don't offer to show it; let us ask. As a rule, the editors and agents don't want to carry material back with them and they don't have the time, at the conference, to do a thorough reading. During a one-on-one, however, you may be asked if you have anything with you; at that time, whip it out. (It's in your bag, not in your room.) After that, it's in the hands of the Muse.

I like taking my laptop with me (and before the laptop, a portable typewriter, and before that a pad and pencil) because conferences can be wondrously energizing; you might very well find yourself up half the night, writing away either on the material you brought or something new.

For all the camaraderie and laughter that goes on (and there's lots of it) this is a professional event; carry yourself appropriately. If you have an appointment with an agent and for some reason you can't make it, make sure you cancel. (The editors and agents talk to each other and to the organizers. There's only so much time available and everyone resents it if you're a no show. So we talk about our resentments. There's nothing wrong in deciding that a particular person can't help you; just let others know so that someone else can have your time.)

At the appointment, be prepared. Know what you want to pitch, what you want to say . . . and don't worry. Believe me, we know how scared you are and what this represents to you. As I said, we're human and forgiving (under the right circumstances). We know how hard it is to prepare a good synopsis, we know how hard it is to talk about your work not only to a stranger, but to one you're hoping will take you and your dreams as seriously as you do. (We do.)

One of the reasons I suggested listening to a speaker you're going to meet with is this: if you know what I'm looking for (or claim to be looking for) and your work doesn't meet that "guideline," you'll have an opportunity to change your pitch, to find another angle. Or, you may simply say that you realize your work doesn't suit my needs, but you hope I wouldn't mind discussing this or some other aspect of your work or the field in general. We won't mind and you'll get five or ten uninterrupted minutes in which to talk about your concerns with no one listening in. (We also recognize that people are often too shy to speak up in a panel situation; that's another reason to hang around and catch us alone, when we're all rather more relaxed. Editors and agents suffer stage fright, too.)

Ask questions; the only stupid question is the one you don't get answered. We've heard them all, answered them time and again, and will continue answering them. That's why the speakers are there; we're taking time from work (and the manuscripts keep rolling in and we know this appearance will bring a fresh onslaught) because some quirk in our personalities makes us want to help. (Trust me, it's not for the money.)

And even though I said don't argue, that doesn't mean you can't discuss or even debate an issue. If you disagree with a speaker, don't hesitate to voice your opinion, though it may be better to wait until the panel is over, just so that you don't take time away from someone who needs an answer. If an editor or agent says no to a project, you're not going to change his mind; he knows his needs. But if you believe in some aspect of writing that the speaker has dismissed, I see nothing wrong with talking about it. You'll both learn, even if neither is convinced, and as long as your arguments are cogent, you may even make a favorable impression. If you couch things in terms of an attitude, however, he's going to turn away from you.

Attend as many sessions as you can, participate as much as you can, meet people, and learn. If someone has been particularly helpful, drop them a note after the conference, thanking them. (It doesn't hurt to write to everyone you've met with, thanking them for their time. That way, if you have something for them someday, they'll remember you with a smile, rather than dismiss you. It's only human.)

A last note: every conference has an evaluation sheet that they ask you to fill out before you leave. Do it. Let them know what you liked and didn't like, let them know who you found effective and helpful and who you found rude, uninterested or otherwise a waste of your time. The conference chairs look at all that material and take it very seriously; your comments may serve to make the next conference a better one for you.

Workshops, real workshops as opposed to conferences that use that word in their title, differ in several important aspects.

They're much more hands on and for me, that's the most critical difference. You meet with a teacher for several days running (most workshops are at least a week long), do writing exercises, do rewriting based on critique, have longer one-on-one sessions with your instructors and, in the evenings, participate in readings and other activities designed to improve your writing skills. While you are going to panels and listening to lectures at most conferences, you're really working at a workshop.

You also have much more time to talk to writers, to discuss what you're doing, and to pick up insights and information that will help you.   The intensity of what happens during that week is exhausting, but the rewards are worth it. In addition to your writing, you're going to have to read, carefully, the work of the others in your class and be ready to comment on it.

Having a computer or typewriter at a workshop is really necessary, because of the amount of writing you're going to do—and the amount of material you may have to submit during the course of the week. Doing it longhand is a possibility, but not the best of all possible worlds. At those workshops conducted under the auspices of a university, it's often possible to use the school's computer lab, but there's no guarantee of that, so you're better off prepared. Information about the availability of computers can be obtained before you register.

Again, check the faculty: most workshops are more mainstream in orientation, if not literary. Make sure the program offers you what you think you need; then consider whether there's anything to be learned by attending anyway. (Most of the time, there is.) Many workshops require the submission of material before acceptance; they want to be certain that you'll be able to contribute to discussions and the learning process of the other students. So, if you're not working on anything, if you're just starting out, the workshop approach may not be for you.

My two favorites among the workshops, the Green River Writers Novels-in-Progress Workshop in Louisville, Kentucky and the Stonecoast Writers Workshop run by the University of Southern Maine, both bring in editors and agents for brief appearances, so the marketing aspects of the business are considered as well.

An excellent resource for information about the various options available to you is Eileen Malone's *The Complete Guide to Writers Groups, Conferences and Workshops*, published by John Wiley & Sons; the Appendix to this volume lists the programs I know best and have enjoyed most; they worked for me.

If you can't get to a conference or workshop, you're still not cut off from the information you need: Every genre has an organization representing the people writing in the category. Malone's book offers an extensive listing of these, and they can also be found in *Literary Market Place*. Not all of these organizations accept unpublished writers, but they'll all respond to your request for information.

Keeping up with what's happening isn't difficult, either. Magazines such as *Writer's Digest*, *The Writer* and *Byline*, as well as others, are available everywhere, as is *Pubishers Weekly*, the bible of the book trade. *PW* offers reviews, bookselling and publishing information, interviews, and market surveys—it's really indispensable, and while everyone can't afford a personal subscription, a group could subscribe. As always, there's the public library. (*PW* is also available, in part, on-line.)

The reference shelves are loaded with guides to the markets and the needs of the various publishers; there are also publications like the *Gila Queen's Guide to the Markets* that keep you up to date.

And don't forget the online services available: lists of agents and publishers, discussion groups, newslists: it's all out there, choosing what's right for you is up to you. A decent place to begin is www.writersclub.com; AOL has a writers area . . . or did when I typed these words. The point: It's volatile, so check it out.

What it takes from you is getting out there, out of the garret and into the streets, paying attention to everything, winnowing what you need, and becoming part of the community. You're not going to do it on your own.

And now, having written and networked, it's time to get down to business.

PART THREE

The Business of Publishing

An Introduction
to Publishing

he writing's done, or as done as you're going to get it. You've written and rewritten, studied the markets, met the people who can help and who will help. Now it's time to get down to business.

And publishing is a business: bottom line, profit driven, run by people who spend a large part of their days looking at numbers. (I fought when they said that my tests and profiles showed that I should be an accountant. Today, I spend as much time with a calculator as I do with words. Okay, almost as much. Fine, a lot.)

The industry has changed dramatically since I took my first seat behind an editor's desk in 1968. There were more houses: I worked for Signet, a part of New American Library, owned by the Times Mirror Corporation of Los Angeles. Today, Signet is part of a conglomerate that includes what used to be E. P. Dutton, Penguin, and the entire Putnam group—including Ace, Berkley and Grossett & Dunlap (another company I worked for, which included . . . oh, never mind).

I went to work for Fawcett (then part of a magazine empire). It combined with Ballantine (another paperback house), became part of the group that includes Random House, Knopf, Pantheon, and other imprints. Random House has just been acquired by the Bertlesmann people, which already own Bantam, Doubleday and Dell.

The Mysterious Press was bought by Warner Books, owned by Time-Warner, which also owns Little, Brown.

You can't tell the publishers without a scorecard. Or, sometimes, with one.

Methods of getting books to the reader have changed, too. Many of the paperback wholesalers have either gone out of business or been absorbed by larger companies. Distributors like Ingram and Baker and Taylor have become the leading suppliers of books to the trade. The independent booksellers have found it difficult—often impossible—to compete with the chains: Barnes and Noble, Border's, Walden, and Dalton; and 1997 saw the rise of on-line booksellers, led by amazon.com. (And as we go to press, Ingram has been bought by the on-line arm of Barnes and Noble, creating a furor in the industry, and not only because Bertlesmann owns a large part of barnesandnoble.com.)

Word processing has given rise to growing numbers of people trying to write for publication . . . or it may just appear that way because the ease of the process (rewrites, when they occur, being more a matter of making corrections on screen rather than retyping manuscripts, which are then printed out at a rate of three or more pages a minute) has simplified things.

Agents are more powerful than ever: with editorial workloads increasing because of layoffs and downsizing—coupled with corporate demands for books that perform "better"—very few of the major publishing houses will accept unsolicited manuscripts and, at many houses, the agents are virtual first readers, choosing what gets to an editor's desk for consideration.

No qualitative judgments here, they're beside the point: this is the situation as it exists today and we have to make the necessary accommodations. Complaints—yours and mine—fall on deaf ears.

There's been an increase in small and regional presses, specializing in a category or a type of book. They're not trying to compete head to head with the bigger houses; they represent niche publishing, fulfilling the needs of certain writers and markets.

Many writers have turned to self-publishing (as opposed to vanity press publishing which we're not going to talk about beyond saying, don't do it); it gives the author total control . . . and total responsibility. All the risks, from beginning to end, are the writer's. And so are the profits.

Both small press and self-published books have had successes; some, like *The Celestine Prophesy*, have gone on to mainstream renown.

Still, and logically, the dream shared by most writers is to be accepted for publication by one of the "New York houses." It comes true every day.

In the pages that follow, then, we're going to look at what happens from the day a manuscript arrives at a publishing house (with a little backstory, where necessary) to that moment—about a year after publication—when we all gather in the publisher's office to look at the previous year's list and hold a post-mortem meeting, looking at our successes and failures, and trying to figure out why.

At this point, you've become the supplier of a raw material to an industry that turns it into a particular product: a book. Knowing how the business works helps you become a better supplier.

And that's to everyone's advantage.

The Gentle
Art of
Submission

nothing is going to happen until you get your manuscript—in the proper form and shape—into the hands of the right editor.

There are several routes, not all of them guaranteeing success, but all of them workable. They all begin with research.

Unless you've managed to meet an editor somewhere and interest her in your book, your best bet is to find an agent and get him on your side. Of course, these days, finding an agent is almost as difficult as finding an editor. (If it were easy, everyone would be doing it . . .)

As already mentioned, meeting agents through conferences is one of the best approaches: it gives you an opportunity to see each other, to talk, to get a feel of the person and to gauge levels of interest. The relationship between agent and author, just like the one between you and your editor, should be a close one built on trust and mutual interest in your success. An agent's income depends on his ability to sell your work: it's the commissions that keep an agency going. That said, it's time to say this: An agent should not charge any upfront fees whatsoever. Period. No exceptions. There are agents out there these days who have told writers directly that current practice accepts the charging of reading fees, editing fees, and other expenses before they're incurred . . . No. If any agent with whom you're in touch even broaches the subject, run, don't walk. I can't make it any clearer nor emphasize it any more than that.

What's happened is this: Because agents have become so important to the process, lots of people with nothing more than a post office box and a letterhead have set themselves up as agents. They don't have any more access to editors than you do; the editors know who they are and when manuscripts arrive from them, they go to the bottom of the pile.

Ideally, you want an agent who is a member of the Association of Author's Representatives; it's no guarantee of happiness, but membership does mean that the agency subscribes to the AAR's Code of Ethics (a copy of which is available from the organization: 10 Astor Place, New York, NY 10003; 212.353.3709. Include a business size SASE). This doesn't mean that non-member agencies are bad or should be avoided; many good agents have chosen not to join. You're just going to have to use your common sense.

Agency fees are generally 15% of all earnings from the sale of a project: that includes advances, royalties, subsidiary rights sales—any and all income. Many, if not most, agencies also pay a commission of their own to their representatives in foreign climes—if your agent has retained all translation and British Commonwealth rights, for instance, her agents in the various countries charge a commission for sale and you'll be charged for a portion of that; it's perfectly legitimate.

Your agent will also discuss expenses with you before you have your final handshake on the deal. Long distance phone calls, photocopying and special mailing costs are expenses you often share with the agent. Those monies are repaid from the advance; they are not paid beforehand. No exceptions. If someone asks for three hundred dollars to help defray those expenses, say thanks and goodbye. (One agent asked an author for several hundred dollars so that she could fly to New York to present the author's work. Fortunately, the writer spoke to some of us at the conference and we were able to dissuade her from signing.)

Does your agent *have* to be in New York? No more than your publisher has to be. My agent, Kimberley Cameron, lives in California. Through the miracles of the telephone and e-mail (and frequent flyer miles), she's in touch with her contacts in New York on a regular basis. Like others who know what they're about, she talks to the editors here and comes into New York twice a year, spending a very intense week meeting with the people she already knows and making appointments to see the people she wants to know. I have no complaints and have sent several of my unagented writers to her. She takes some and rejects others—even knowing that they have an editor's interest—because she only represents work that "speaks" to her.

That means that when she sends me something I can be confident that she believes in the work, cares about it, and that she has every reason to believe that I'm going to be interested in the manuscript or writer. That doesn't mean that I'm going to acquire the project (there are so many variables in that, as you'll soon see); it does mean that it's worth my time looking.

And I speak with her far more often than I speak with many of the agents in New York, just as I'm in more frequent touch with many of the out-of-towners.

Agents also meet with editors at the conferences; we often joke about the fact that even though our offices are just across town from each other, we only meet on the road. Additionally, I'll meet with agents specializing in mystery fiction at various conventions: Bouchercon, Left Coast Crime, Magna cum Murder: all grand celebrations of the genre. The advantage is that the agent and the writer are both there and a meeting between the three of us allows for lots of the discussion that might otherwise require calls back and forth. (Every genre has its conventions; there aren't quite as many face-to-face opportunities for mainstream writers, sadly.)

Your agent can be anywhere in the country (or even in the world); what's urgent is the confidence you have in her and her faith in your work.

If you've met at a conference and the proper expressions of interest have been made—and you're certain there's no scam involved—there are some questions you'll want answered. They're the same answers you'll look for no matter how the contact is made.

You want to know how many clients the agent represents: if it is a one person agency and there are hundreds of writers on the list, you have a legitimate concern: how much time will be spent on your work?

Listen to the agent at the conference, and to the gossip: is he asking everyone he meets to submit material? That may (and it is conjecture) mean that he's just trying to be Mr. Nice Guy, hoping to find something, anything, in the submissions that will arrive over the next few weeks. It strikes me as a rather scatter-gun approach and I'd be wary. I'd also wonder how long it's going to take to get a response.

Ask the agent about her other clients. Have you heard of any of them? Is the agency making sales? To which publishers? Which editors are at the top of that agent's submission list: are the editors people you may have heard of (through your network and familiarity with your genre)? Does the agent specialize in your category and will you take a back seat to some other client. (Of course you are, to some degree; what you don't want to do is find yourself ghettoized, held back because of someone else on the list.)

Try to find out whether the agent uses multiple submissions, trying to create a buzz and auction for your work, or does he pick and choose the editor, based on knowledge of the editor's interests and the quality of the work the editor does.

Does the agent insist on a contract or a handshake? No value judgment here, just a question and an answer that has to make you comfortable.

And see if you can get a feel of the agent's involvement in your career, generally. Is she going to keep you locked into your genre, insisting that you write to market (which may be your desire) or is she someone who is going to look beyond the moment and allow you to grow and change? What does the agent expect from you in terms of sale and growth and development? Does it jibe with your desires?

Your relationship with your agent should be a partnership: you both want the best for you. At the same time, your agent works for you, you are employing him, paying him for a service rendered and if that service isn't there, you can't hesitate to leave. A bad agent is worse than no agent at all. Be sure that you'll be kept apprised on a regular basis of what's going on with your work: where it is, what the reactions have been, who's seen your manuscript and what they've said. You want that information so that you can keep track of where you are in the scheme of things and, too, so that if you have to leave the agency, you'll be able to tell the next agent you hire who has seen your work; that'll help the new agent prepare a game plan. (And keep this in mind: an editor might not consider a submission from one agent as seriously as she does from another. There is a hierarchy there, based on the editor's knowledge of the agent. I can't guarantee that an editor will tell you exactly what they think of a particular agent; when asked—and I am—if I don't care for an agent, I'll hem and haw and say something like, "Yeah, I know him. Haven't done any business with him that I can remember." You can take that to mean whatever you want it to mean; there are lots of agents I haven't done business with. Generally, we'll speak highly of the ones we like and remain relatively silent about the others.)

After talking to the agent, talk to your friends. Does anyone know her, does anyone have an opinion, an experience to share. A lot of what you'll hear is gossip and rumor; some of it will be fact. You'll have to use your common sense, your knowledge of people, and measure your needs and then make a decision.

After signing on with someone, the agent will direct you and tell you what he needs from you. The partnership has begun. From now on, all you should have to think about is your writing. But, at any point in the process, don't hesitate to ask questions *of the agent.* I worry about writers who sign and then start second guessing, running helter-skelter, asking everyone if this, that, or the other thing is right or the way it should be. The people you're asking don't necessarily know any more than you do. So, if something strikes you as amiss, if, after five months, you haven't heard anything, if you're uncomfortable, talk to the agent first and if you're not satisfied with the answers, take the steps to cancel the agreement. This is your career, not mine or your best friend's or anyone else's. A little common sense will go a long way toward keeping you happy and your writing on track.

If you haven't had the opportunity to meet an agent, you're still in the game. Just as writers have forever submitted directly to publishers, you can go directly to an agent, with many of the same steps and traditions.

What you'd want to do first is see if somewhere among your friends you have someone who will either introduce you to his agent or who might suggest agents, based on some information they've picked up at a conference. If you're all alone, there are guidebooks available and listings in the writer's magazines, as well as the addresses listed in *Literary Market Place.* I'd hesitate to get in touch with an agency that runs a classified ad; it's been my experience that someone soliciting manuscripts (an agent or a publisher) is going to take more than they're going to give. Your experience may be different, but in a marketplace so crowded with potential clients, it strikes me that an agency that has to advertise—and that couples the solicitation with promises of "advances between $5,000 and $100,000"—just isn't doing things right: if they're getting clients with those six figure advances, they don't need more clients . . . they already have more than enough to do.

Many writers suggest looking at the acknowledgments and dedication pages of published books because authors often thank their agents (and editors). If the book is something you might have written, the agent is a possibility. You can also find agents named in the pages of *PW*, usually after some big deal has gone down and become newsworthy. The downside there is that just about everyone else in the search is going to be writing to that agency. After all, if they could get one writer a deal like that, imagine what they could get for you. Then get realistic; confidence is good, it's even important. But don't let it turn to cockiness.

The various guide books will not only give you the names and addresses of agents, they'll also offer profiles of the agency, perhaps tell you how many clients are signed, and will present the most important information you need: the submission guidelines and what the agent may or definitely isn't looking for. Pay attention to that data; you don't want to waste your time or the agent's (or an editor's) with submissions that are so far off the mark that they're returned unread.

Having chosen the agents you want to go to first, prepare your submission package based on what the agency lists as its requirements. Begin with a query letter.

There are dozens of books about submitting material, and an article on the subject appears with boring regularity in every writing magazine; it's also a standard panel or lecture at conferences. Having read lots of them and having listened to even more presentations about the subject, the most important advice I can give you is this: Present yourself with calm professionalism.

Don't hype yourself or the work you want represented; the only thing that sells your manuscript is the manuscript itself. Describe the manuscript (a cozy mystery with an amateur sleuth, set in Dubuque; a second in the series is under way), offer any pertinent credentials (three short stories, one featuring the same character, in one of the mystery magazines), the word count, and a thanks in advance for considering this request to send the material along. Include an SASE and/or an e-mail address, sign the letter and send it on its way.

There's no reason to include a photograph, no reason to talk about your age, sex, education . . . the only thing that counts right now is the manuscript.

You can, if it's not specifically forbidden, try to call the agent for submission information and interest, or e-mail them; many of us find a certain ease in just clicking on "Reply" and dealing with our correspondence that way. Don't, however, fax or e-mail more than a one page letter, unless requested to do so.

The question of humor in query letters crops up like dandelions on an unkempt lawn. I don't like it and think the risks far outweigh any possibility of standing out from the crowd. Cute's for when you're alone with your friends . . . this is business. Take a cue from advertising, where they've discovered that those funny, wonderful commercials and ads may get attention, but they don't succeed in increasing sales. Can you imagine some oil company sending a funny letter to you, asking you to switch to their product? They'll tell you, instead, about their prices, about their quality, about their service. That is, in essence, what you want to accomplish when you get in touch with an agent or an editor.

Another mistake I see too often: Don't tell us that your next book is something dramatically different from the one you're pitching now. We are all looking for writers we can build and continue with; if you're submitting a horror novel now, but your next is a romantic suspense, we're not going to sense continuity. You're better off saying nothing about future work (unless it evolves directly from the present one) and discussing what comes next once contact is made and a relationship established.

Some agencies and publishers ask for a synopsis and one to three chapters as the submission package. The synopsis, usually, is best kept short and simple; no more than two or three pages; the romance publishers ask for more, so check the guidelines. And those chapters: they're the first three, not three assorted. I'll never forget the time a writer sent me chapters seven, eight, and nine, because they showed his writing to the best advantage. Unfortunately, if we don't like the first three, no one will get to those later in the book . . . and since we'll see the first three eventually if your plans come together . . .

There's as much said about synopses and manuscript format as about the problems with health care. I don't know any editor who cares whether your name is on the upper left or upper right, if your social security number appears on the first page, if there's a copyright notice (we all know that you own the copyright), or how many spaces you leave from the top of the page before you type "chapter one."

We do care that the manuscript's in a readable typeface (which means that it's not sans serif) and large enough to read comfortably, that it's double-spaced, that paragraphs are indented, and that the margins are decent—I use an inch left and right; an inch and a quarter top and bottom. No one's ever complained. I generally use either Times or Bookman Old Style, with a font size of 12. There are still, I'm told, some editors who insist that you use Courier (a monospaced face, the "l" and the "m", for instance, taking up the same amount of space on the page; the faces I use are proportional. I don't mind reading manuscripts presented that way as long as everything else is clean); if it's mentioned in a guideline, follow directions, otherwise, use common sense. And don't use fancy fonts or bother with things like running the first sentence of a chapter in small caps. You've got lots of bells and whistles at your command thanks to word processing; unless you're doing desktop publishing, however, you don't need them in preparing manuscripts and they only serve to clutter the page and tell us that you're not professional. Every publishing house has designers on staff to make the interior of the book look as they want it to. As with copyediting, there's a house style that takes precedence unless formatting is somehow integral to your text.

And speaking of publishers, let's look at what you should and shouldn't do in approaching a publisher directly and unsolicited.

You've heard, time and again, that you should study a publication before you submit to them: it only makes sense; after all, if your material isn't right, you're wasting your money and time, and the editor's. The same holds true when you're submitting to a book publishing house. I'll use Walker and Company—and my desk—as an example; you can and should project from there.

I edit mystery fiction, but what does that mean? As we define our program, mysteries are series-oriented, 70,000 words in length, and play fair: clues presented, red herrings strewn, and the resulting game between author and reader is the point. It's clear, and any mystery writer who reads crime fiction (and they all should, obviously) will be able to see exactly what it is we do by reading the books (at best) or, at the very least, skimming them in a bookstore.

However, I receive 100,000-word romantic suspense novels, 90,000-word adventures and thrillers, 50,000-word horror tales, and every other conceivable variation on the theme. What do you think happens? In short, the manuscript or proposal isn't even read; it's put right into the SASE, along with a form letter, and returned.

"Oh," you say, "well, if you had a guideline sheet . . ." We did. It was detailed, explained fully what it is we looked for and what we didn't want, and those rules of the game appear regularly in every marketing guide book out there. And the manuscripts arrive with notes saying that the manuscript fulfills our listed needs. Writers have to read, it's that simple. I've even had writers tell me that after careful examination of my current catalogue, the submission is just what we're looking for. And it isn't.

So, pay careful attention to the lists, to the books that are being released; you may still be wrong, because lists change with the phases of the moon, but we can tell if you've done your research and make allowances for that; your rejection letter may include a handwritten postscript explaining the situation, or encouraging you to submit something else.

Reading the books serves another purpose: you begin to discern an editor's style, the things an editor likes or doesn't like, allows, accepts or doesn't want. If the books are all cozy mysteries, don't submit a gritty police procedural; if the language is rated "G" you wouldn't want to send something filled with hyper-realistic street talk.

Knowing the lists that you want to join involves other decisions. Do you want to go to a big house, where your book is one of dozens, or a small house, where you stand a chance of being noticed? The advances offered are likely to be close enough, that that kind of positioning can make a difference, and the possibility of $1,500 more may not be worth the loss of identity.

Do you know of a particular editor's work and reputation? Do you think that working with a particular editor can be good for your writing and your career?

Consider the physical package. Does one house seem to offer better covers? Better flap copy? These aren't minor factors: the cover is the first thing the buyer sees in the stores and if there's a likelihood of getting a better jacket, which can mean better sales (other things being equal), you might weigh that into your decision. It's not just a matter, then, of picking a house that publishes, generally, what you write, you have to find the house to which your work is best suited. That's one of the things a good agent can do for you, but it's not impossible to do it on your own, if you're smart enough to take the time necessary to do the job . . . and given the amount of time it's taken you to produce the manuscript, there's no reason not to take more and finish the job properly.

THE AUTHOR
ANYPLACE, U.S.A.

Dear *The Editors:*

Thank you for taking the time to remove my query from the envelope in which I mailed it, stick it into my SASE, and put it in the mailbox (you didn't strain yourself, did you?)

Your letter said that my manuscript does not sound right for your list "at this time". At what time *will* it be right for your list?

Furthermore, you forwarded your "best wishes" for my success elsewhere. I somehow doubt the sincerity of your statement, for if you really wished me to succeed, you would have published my work.

Finally, I would like to mention that editors, agents, other writers, and writing instructors are constantly harping on how we would-be authors should always be "professional" in our work, our queries, our submissions, and all dealings with publishers. I am still waiting for some indication of professionalism on the part of the publishers and their editors, though. How professional does an unaddressed, unsigned form letter look to you. How professional is it to respond in this manner to someone who has put months of his life and his best effort into a manuscript, even if the end result isn't worth publication? If you have the time it takes to read the query letter, the outline, and/or the sample chapters, how much more of your valuable time would it take to add just a note to your form letter to let the author know *why* you rejected his work, and to sign your name so he'll know he's dealing with an actual human being?

Remember, authors who really want to write could write and publish their own work if all publishers and editors vanished from the face of the earth tomorrow, but if all the authors vanished, you'd be out of a job! Try to keep things in prespective. [sic]

> Sincerely,
> The Author

Being rejected (and it's your manuscript that's being rejected, not you, unless you've managed to offend someone) is going to happen but it doesn't mean that you can't go back to that house or that editor at some other time. I received the letter reproduced above from an obviously frustrated writer, one who considers form letters unprofessional (though being a professional writer means knowing that the form letter is traditional because it does take a lot of time to respond to each writer you're rejecting, offering the reasons why; read down a bit and you'll see what happens when an editor does go that extra step).

Now, this guy was being cute, I guess, sending me a form letter; if he'd been as clever in writing his novel, maybe something else would have happened.

But why didn't he send it to the editor to whom he'd submitted his work? Is it possible, do you think, that he just sent the work originally to "Submissions Editor," rather than finding out who might be interested in seeing the work?

When will the manuscript be right for my list? I don't know: maybe tomorrow, maybe never, but given my inventory, marketing direction, publisher's dictates, it *isn't* right for my list today.

The writer questions my best wishes for his success; if I'd meant them, I'd have done the book. Wrong: it could be in a category we don't publish, or we might be over-inventoried; the editor might not have felt qualified to edit the work properly (depends on what work was necessary). Success is finding the right editor for your work; we really aren't interchangeable.

Do you really want me to tell you why the book was rejected, what I really think of your work? Think about it; if I do tell you I'm not going to pull any punches or soften the blow—there's no time for that.

I'd guess that this author has been rejected more than once, and that he's been receiving form rejection letters, even though his spouse and critique group (and everyone else who's seen the work) has been encouraging him and he just can't understand what's wrong. Believe me, if I tell him he won't believe me.

Agent Donald Maass has estimated that agents take on about two percent of the material they receive and that the publishers take two percent of that. As much as publishers need good manuscripts to stay in business, there are far more writers producing material than the industry can absorb. That means you don't want to do anything to increase the odds against you.

And that means you want to remain polite and businesslike, recognizing that when an editor says no, it means just that.

It means that you don't want to argue the finer points of your writing in an attempt to prove that the editor is wrong.

And it means that you don't want to insult the editor.

I rejected a manuscript during my early days at Walker and Company, and did it not with a form letter, but with a letter suggesting some improvements. In response, I got a letter saying that improving the work was my job as the editor. The writer's name is on my bulletin board.

I received a single-spaced manuscript (well, a partial) of about 100 pages; that represented a tenth of the total pages . . . The margins were about a quarter of an inch all around, there was no spacing between paragraphs (though there were indents) . . . Instead of a form letter, I wrote offering some basic information about the gentle art of submission. I heard back: someone at St. Martin's Press had read it all, offered an in-depth analysis and requested the balance of the manuscript. (So why, I wondered, was I seeing it, too?) And, I was told, the reason it was single-spaced was because the author didn't want an editor to be intimidated by the size of the manuscript! I was also informed that I was callous and uncaring and not doing my job properly. The author's name is on my bulletin board.

A submission arrived, offering a novel about a drug dealer (the Cali cartel, just in case you were wondering); instead of a form letter, I wrote, explaining that I had too many p.i. manuscripts in inventory and that as an editor I'd grown really tired of drug trade adventures; there were just too many of them. The writer wrote back, saying that I'd clearly not read the material and was obviously not interested in doing my job correctly, because my comments were entirely inappropriate. The writer's name is on my bulletin board.

Finally, there's this letter; it speaks for itself, and appears exactly as I received it:

> I have your kind letter outline the requirments Walker makes for the submission of a novel.
>
> I thank you but I must decline the offer. I have not time to do an outline, or futz around with your internal guidelines. I'm fully aware that you do not need me. You have an abundance of masochistic writers to swallow up. But the great truth is that as much as you don't need me—I sure don't need you, or any other publisher or editor and especailly any agent.
>
> To ask that of me, a published writer of long standing, to do the requirements you put forth, is insulting.

But this feels good, an expression of independence, no longer waiting breathlessly (with pounding heart) for some son of a bitch publisher to decide my fate.

I don't cry anymore, Mike. Isn't that wonderful? The field of writing, which once made suffer and never provide a living wage is paying me back for all my tears and suffering. I operate a very lucrative ghostwriting business that removes me (and my Ego) from parasitic agents, ten percenters who don't know their asses from a hole in the ground. If they knew, they wouldn't be agents. They'd be living in penthouses. Do I hate agents? No. They do what they have to do, however clumsy, in an aggressive way with limited ability.

I am a veteran of the writing wars. I've been through it all and I know the score. I can tell you a good book from a bad book just by reading the first few pages. Because my judgment is based on long experience and extensive success. Between my editor and me, we turn out over 20 books a year, with very high percentage of success for my clients.

If you want to see the *full script*, I'll be pleased to send it to you. I know you're loaded with reading material, but I don't aim to let my work sit in Walker's office for eight months gathering dust.

So my question to you is: what do you want to see from me? An outline is out. A brief resume is in. Do you want the full script, half a script, one third of a script? You got it. Say what and when.

I'm afraid I responded childishly. I returned his letter to him copy-edited, even though I knew I should have ignored it. And I sent my own letter, suggesting that he first consider the edits and telling him that even his letter didn't meet my basic needs.

I pointed out that if he weren't so down on agents, he could have saved himself bunches of woe, because the agent wouldn't have let him insult me by calling me Mike . . . or a sonofabitch. (I did tell him that while I denied that title, I was one mean mother.) I mentioned that I'd checked his listing in *Books in Print*, and that I wasn't exactly overawed by his accomplishments.

And I said, "So, my answer to your question is this: I don't want to see anything from you, not now, not ever. I'm certain there are hundreds of wiser editors waiting for you to grace them with your presence. I'd suggest you write to them. Perhaps they'll be more understanding of your needs and requirements for submission."

His name is on my bulletin board. And every editor and agent has one . . . and every now and then, we share the names posted on them.

Unless you are one of the blessed ones upon whom the heavens smile, you are beginning to take steps that can lead to frustration, anger, misunderstanding, success, fame, glory, satisfaction . . . Keep the idea of calm professionalism in mind, ask questions, listen to the answers, follow the dictates of common sense, keep writing and improving, keep beginning.

And now, if you'll follow me, we'll step into my office and you'll spend a day in an editor's life, a day like all days, a day that represents about a year in the life of your manuscript as it goes from the mailroom to publication.

Beginning
the Process

everything that follows happens pretty much every day; submissions arrive, books go into production, others are contracted for, some are rejected; copy is being written, profit and loss statements produced, covers designed. Somewhere in the course of that day, your material is being read, and while the agented submissions are looked at first, there is, as I mentioned, a hierarchy there and some may be looked at after the day's slush.

There's a strong feeling in the writing community that authors want their work read by the editor, not an assistant or a reader or whoever else might be tapped for the job. I'll tell you why that's wrong:

The assistants are looking to make their mark, to discover the next big book. And that means they may read more carefully, or more thoroughly. Experienced editors make decisions quickly: they may read a couple of pages or a chapter, and move on to the next envelope. Younger staffers are not as confident (or cocky); still unsure of themselves and of what works, afraid of making mistakes, they take longer, read more. Now, before you get cranky, think about yourself as a reader. You pick up a book in the bookstore, leaf through it, make a decision as to whether to buy and move down the shelves. (If you don't believe me, spend an afternoon at a bookstore, watching others.) How many times have you picked up a book at the library, or from a friend's bookshelf, read ten pages or fifty, and then decided not to continue?

The editor stands in for the reader. She knows what "works" for her, the kind of writing she likes, feels hooked or not. We don't have to read the whole book, any more than you do as a purchaser . . . and as a purchaser, don't forget: You're looking at something that's gone through a long process to reach the shelves.

So, even if you don't consider it fair or right, it's a fact of life, proven over the years.

Sure, we make mistakes. The history of publishing is filled with stories about manuscripts that have been rejected time and again, only to become bestsellers. There are also stories about books for which too much money was advanced that have disappeared without a trace, forgotten by everyone except the author and the editorial staff that's looking at the figures a year after publication date. The idea is to make fewer mistakes, especially the kind that cost money. There's a belief that, if asked, an attorney will always advise against doing something; if you don't do it, you can't be "wrong." There are times when editors may be doing the same thing. Not a pretty picture, and not one seen frequently, but as the bean counters take more control, and jobs become scarce due to all the mergers, making the wrong decision takes on some frightening prospects.

(Now, if the government cared enough about the written word, and could be trusted to subsidize while maintaining a hands-off stance . . . But that's all better left to a fantasy writer.)

The reading process changes from house to house, of course, but my daily routine is pretty much set by now. The full manuscripts (sent by agents or unsolicited) are put in one pile and the query letters, partials, and proposals in another. Those are looked at first: I usually do it at about four in the afternoon. If an idea strikes me, I'll knock out a quick note to the author, requesting the balance of the material or, in the case of queries, requesting a partial or, on rare occasions, the entire manuscript. (If the author has supplied an e-mail address, all the better.)

The full manuscripts are then sorted: Requested manuscripts, agented manuscripts, option books, are put to the top of the pile; the unsolicited manuscripts are, these days, opened, a prepared letter informing the writer that we no longer accept unsolicited manuscripts placed on top of the material, and the package moved out. Sadly, I've had to join with other publishers in doing that, and the reason is simple: I receive close to a hundred submissions a week; there's just no time to read everything, even if we're only considering those manuscripts that have been requested or arriving from agents.

If there's a reader or editorial assistant available, some of the material is placed on his desk to be read; I'll read the works that I'm particularly interested in: established writers I've been romancing, the work I've requested at a conference and agented material from people I've come to respect over years of working with them. (If there's no reader, I deal with it all, when and as I can.)

When the pile of submissions gets out of hand (all too often for anyone's peace of mind), we may hold a slush party: a group of editors sit around a table—all the submissions in tumbled stacks in front of them—and start reading. The rejected material gets a form letter.

There simply isn't time to write a letter to everyone who sends a manuscript, and, as I said, when we send an in-depth letter it often leads to more correspondence, arguments, and problems. Sure, the phrase "not right for our list at the present time," may not tell you very much but there often isn't anything more that we're comfortable saying.

If we're interested in your work or if we see a potential that strikes a responsive chord, you will get a personal letter, one either suggesting changes that might make the book acceptable or asking to see something else because we can't, for whatever reason, use what you submitted. Those reasons could be inventory problems (too many novels about time-traveling cats under contract), a desire not to compete in a certain market (trial novels a la John Grisham) or a realization that a particular market has dried up or that the house doesn't have the right foundation to sell the book successfully—or because you've sent a particular type of story but said that your next book is something different (your letter might say that if you have another book like the first sketched out, we might be interested). But because the editor thinks you write well enough and have stories to tell, you'll be encouraged to send more or send different, but definitely to send.

Agents get what is, in essence, a form letter, too; it's just rather more personalized.

While it may seem interminable to you, waiting for word, and while editors really do want to get those manuscripts off their floors and shelves to make room for the next day's influx, it is almost impossible for an editor to keep up with the mail, even with form letters, readers, and three page decisions. Calling the editor may not work (he just won't take the call), but sending a letter asking for an update is an accepted approach. (Sometimes you'll get an answer, sometimes you won't, but guilt is a marvelous tool.)

Lots of writers are enclosing postcards with their submissions, asking that we let them know that the material has arrived. There's a problem with that: If the package isn't opened immediately (and in all likelihood it won't be) you're not going to hear anything.

Oh, and while I'm grousing: sending unsolicited material via Express Mail, Priority Mail, FedEx or any other special service doesn't make any difference, because, well, that doesn't mean it's going to be opened any sooner.

And another personal quirk: if I have to spend five minutes trying to open the package, duct-taped to a fare-thee-well, how happy do you think I'm going to be?

Finally, we're left with your manuscript—the one that we're interested in—that we might want to acquire. That one is read and the considerations begin. It may have been read by the editor first, or passed along to her by a subordinate with a report and recommendation; the route doesn't matter, what counts is that your writing has the editor's attention.

By this point, you should have a pretty good idea of what makes a manuscript appealing, that combination of writing, story, marketability and editorial taste that provides the match between your work and the editor's needs. You've done it and I'm reading it . . . the publication process has begun.

Several things occur simultaneously as an editor reads and becomes involved in your story. We're considering the editing needs and time that will go into getting the book to market. How will I market this, where does it fit in the house's game plan? How will I package it, what kind of cover treatment can we come up with? What's the competition? Can we break new ground? Will the author continue with a series or other books of this kind? How long is the book likely to be and can it be cut or expanded if necessary, cut or expanded without ruining the structure? What will it cost?

All the questions have to be answered before anything else can happen; with the answers in hand, the editor moves on to the next step; getting permission to acquire the book.

In most of the big houses, that calls for an appearance in front of an editorial board or committee. The manuscript may have to be read by others on the staff or by the publisher; there may have to be a discussion—especially in hardcover houses—with the subsidiary rights director or the marketing department. There may be a request for research: what else is out there like this, what's the competition, do you see the author growing, can we get quotes and blurbs? Eventually, the decision to go ahead is made.

Smaller, non-corporate houses, often bypass all of that or, at least (thankfully for me) reduce the discussion to a meeting between the editor and the publisher. The same information may be exchanged, the publisher may want to read the book, but a process that can take a couple of weeks in a larger house takes a few days in a smaller one. (If everything is going right; sometimes mere mortals are toyed with and the best laid plans of mice, men, and editors . . . .)

Before I make an offer, I have some other bureaucratic needs to fulfill: getting a cast-off, the term for the figures—length, prices, manufacturing information—that have to be known before a profit and loss statement can be produced and then doing the P&L (even in small houses). Before I do that, however, I'm probably going to call you; it's time for you to meet your editor.

What is it, exactly, that an editor *does*? Let's define the job (as editor, rather than acquirer of manuscripts) this way: We help the writer produce the best book she is capable of at the moment. We are not there to teach the basics of writing, to rewrite or ghostwrite; my job is to see to it that when your book is published it is as good as we can, between us, make it. That may involve some of the things we're not there to do—we've all done some rewriting, for instance, and we do "teach," at least in the sense that we share our ideas of what makes writing good and hope that the author, while working on the next manuscript, will take those "lessons" to heart.

The process is different for each editor and for each editor it may change from writer to writer and also change based on the point at which the work is beginning: if I'm recommending changes on a manuscript that I haven't acquired (with an eye toward accepting it if the alterations can be made successfully), my approach is much broader and, in a way, simpler. Working with a delivered manuscript, however, involves, for me, much more detail.

With the novel you want me to buy, I might say that it should be a little longer or shorter; I won't necessarily tell you how to do that, though; instead, I may be suggesting that a subplot can be gotten rid of, or that a character needs to be developed more fully. Or I might simply say, you're fifteen thousand words over my limit; cut it back and we'll see what happens. We could discuss the fact that, in a mystery, certain clues are too obvious (I never worry about them being too obscure); that the police procedure is wrong or that the sleuth's activities are too unrealistic.

If there are too many problems of that nature, difficulties with the concept(s) of the novel, I won't be talking to you, though, unless the writing itself, the storytelling, the use of language, and the theme are so far superior to everything else that I'm seeing, that I can't risk letting you get away. So, as you've heard time and again, especially over the last few years, you have to have the manuscript in near perfect condition. The competition is stiff and with the number of manuscripts editors are seeing—even with the "agented submissions only" guidelines—you have to be close to perfect. That doesn't mean, by any stretch of the imagination, that you won't be edited, or that editors aren't doing their jobs; that we only acquire books but don't work on them. (Yes, there are some editors who do only that; but they're working at an entirely different level, going after Oprah for the diary of her beef trial or some such other really important work of literature.) What it does mean is that the process begins at a later stage: when an acquired manuscript arrives on the desk.

The terms we use change frequently and haphazardly: I've seen what I call line-editing now being called copyediting; concept editing called editing . . . so, here are my definitions:

The first editing I described, that broad overview of changes is concept editing: it deals with plot, with structure, with storyline, and with character development in their totality but not on a word-by-word basis.

Line editing is, as the name implies, a process during which the manuscript is gone over word-by-word, line-by-line. Concept editing considerations may come into play (though we'd hope not; it depends on how much work was done before the contract was signed. If the manuscript is the third in a three book contract, there may have been no discussion whatsoever, beyond the general idea that it will be an historical romance, a novel of the frontier, the third in a series about a character), but the bulk of the work now involves tweaking and fine-tuning.

Copyediting is a separate process: the copyeditors read the manuscript for continuity (did eye color change, are the dates correct in terms of ages given, can you get there from here in that amount of time). Yes, they'll also think about word usage, grammar, house style (is the preferred usage "toward" or "towards") and design elements (how should an extract from a letter or newspaper story be presented). They do a form of proofreading. And they see to it that neither you, the editor, or the publishing house are embarrassed by the kinds of silly, stupid errors that always creep into a work, and to which heavily rewritten and edited works are particularly prone. So many changes may have been made that not everything is caught by the editor and author.

Let's look at the line-editing process. We have a delivered manuscript, already owned, but with no prior editorial discussion between the writer and the editor. There'll be some minor differences in what happens, based on whether I've worked with the author before: trust has developed—he knows I'm not going to make gratuitous changes, just for the sake of making a change. I know that he has certain habits, things I may not like: "Said Bookisms" are high on that list for me. But it could be too many "he said"/"she said" constructions; it could even be a very simple typo that appears again and again . . . some people just spell weird, weirdly. Knowing about that beforehand, and knowing that those kinds of changes are not going to affect the structure of the novel, I'm comfortable reading with a pencil in hand, making the corrections ('cause that's how I see'em, as corrections) as I go along. But I have a stack of Post-it Notes at my side, just in case.

In case of what? Well, let's say (because it just did) that as I'm reading, I realize that the author has an opportunity to do something a little different in this book. Because there are two central characters, both revealed through third person, it's conceivable that the author could use two completely different styles: Bill is driven, on a quest, racing time, an almost noir creation. Tom, the target, doesn't know he's being stalked; his life is, right now, relatively simple. (Well, there is "the other woman," but that isn't a problem. Yet. But even seventy-five pages into the manuscript, I'm developing a strong dislike for her; that's the author's intent.) Bill's story, then, might be told with short, punchy sentences, something that speeds up the reading, while Tom's story is more leisurely—longer sentences, maybe even more observation: it's a relaxed storytelling, just as the character is, for now, relaxed. The reader may not be aware of how she's being manipulated (most won't be), but we'll create a wave-like story, at least in the beginning. I make a note and stick it on the first page, something to discuss, later.

Hmm . . . what's this? As we drive along one night with Bill, the forward action is slowed, no, stopped! as we get some background. Can't have that, can't be slowed that way at this point. A note gets put on the page. But, a-ha, Bill, later that night, writes a letter. Okay, back story can be revealed, slowly, piece by piece, through these letters—they occur frequently enough. And by revealing it in increments, starting with trivialities and moving up through the crisis to the confrontation, we keep the reader in suspense. Back to the previous note, note the suggestion. Keep reading.

Question for author: you say that Bill finds . . . (well, I'm not going to tell you, here, what it is, but he finds something). Can it be located that easily, in a town such as you're describing, by someone blowing through? (This could be a copyediting question, but having found it early, we may be able to take care of it without causing massive rewrites later.)

Some of what I've described is concept editing, some is line editing: as I continue through the manuscript, I may change words, strike sentences (or add them; I've worked with the writer long enough to know his cadences, his language). If a character isn't strong enough for his role, or too strong for hers, I'll ask the author to look at making the needed change; I'm not going to do that immediately. I could be wrong and won't know until I reach the end of the manuscript and can see how the role played out.

Obviously, if we've discussed these conceptual concerns before acquisition, as I read now I'll be looking for other things, taking it for granted that if the author couldn't or wouldn't make the changes that I thought stood in the way of acquisition, I wouldn't be seeing the manuscript now.

The editorial process at that point, then, is a matter of looking for everything that trips me, that brings me out of the story and, at the same time, considering everything I think will make the book stronger, better.

Once all my notes are in place and, given that I'm looking for some structural changes, a virtual rewrite of certain sections, I'll either write to the author or call him to discuss my suggestions. (They are, for the most part, just that: suggestions. I may be adamant about some, less so about others.) I prefer making a call because it allows for an immediate back and forth; as the ideas are talked about, other ideas flow: "Yeah, I can change the pacing, but how about if we only see so-and-so at night, emphasizing the fact that he's hiding . . . without saying it in so many words?"

"Okay, but that means, doesn't it . . .?" And so it goes. The author agrees to some, disagrees with others, and comes up with his own variations. At some point, we're in agreement about what we think has to be done, decide on a delivery date, and go on with our lives.

That kind of editing not only goes on with a finished manuscript but can come into play (quite happily) when delivery is being made in increments: if I'm seeing fifty pages at a time (because some writers like to work that way and the editor should adapt his approach to the author's needs); catching a character gone awry early, for instance, makes the rest of the writing easier. It's like preventive medicine: fix it now and you don't have to do major surgery later.

Some writers like to send their first drafts to the editor so that they can get feedback before they begin their own rewrites and fixes. Again, whatever works for the writer becomes the editor's job description for that project. Or it should be that way: part of your job, when an offer is made to you, is to discuss the editor's m.o. with her and make sure you're comfortable with what you hear because, while some things are supposed to be a certain way, they're often something else.

If you're agented, discuss what you need as a writer before the manuscript starts making the rounds: the good agents—the ones you will want to have representing you—know the editors and the way they work and will use those considerations when deciding who should see your project.

The next manuscript on my stack is not so complex and presents no real problems: it's part of a series, the essential characters are well-established and the others will be playing out their assigned parts. I saw an outline before the author began to work— she sends them in, three at a time, and we buy the three books— and she's a polished professional.

I read that manuscript, making those changes in text, sentence structure—whatever—without even thinking about it.   I know what the readers of this series expect and what they won't stand for. My job, as much as anything else, is to see to it that they

get what they want: that's what the writer wants, what the bookseller wants, so it's what I want (whether I want it or not; if I want
the author to go in some other direction, to try something new, we
talk about it and then decide on how we'll proceed; if necessary,
that's also discussed with the agent. The three players are all committed to one thing: the writer's future and career and how they tie
into the business needs of the publishing house).

In the meantime, the first author, the one with the heavy
rewrites, has finished his work and sent it on to me. I now read it
again, in much the same way I've just worked on the series book: a
quick read through for language or any glaring errors, making corrections as necessary.

Both manuscripts are transmitted to the production department, and the copyediting and other processes that guarantee a
finished book we're all happy with, begins. Both authors will have
the opportunity to see the manuscript, to see what I've done (my
marks are in black pencil; the copyeditors, these days, use the
infamous blue—or green or red. The writers respond to the questions the copyeditor may ask, to the changes any of us may have
made to the text, and are free to question any of those decisions.
If everything is in order, the manuscript is sent back, and the
printing process begins.

Also beginning, the editor's work on whatever is next on her
plate and your work on whatever's next on yours. It just keeps on
keepin' on . . . we hope.

Though not part of the editorial process, I want to remind you
that your contract should not only offer you the chance to see both
the copyedited manuscript and the page proofs, it should require it
of you. If it doesn't, you have lost control of your work, changes
may be made with which you disagree for any number of valid (or
invalid) reasons, but you're not going to know about it until the
book is published. And there's nothing you'll be able to do about
it but complain.

There are some houses that refuse (or have refused in the past) to give the author this opportunity, usually pleading the schedule as the reason for it. That may be, but it's still something you should think about very seriously.

And consider this: there are editors who think you should be writing the book they envision, rather than the one you want to do, and they will either make or suggest changes that dramatically change what you've done. (A friend of mine, a romance writer, discovered that her reincarnation romance had become an angelic romance, because on the day the manuscript arrived, that's what was hot. She didn't care. You may.) If your contract is for a particular kind of book, or if your style and approach were known to the editor before delivery, and you are faced with making those kinds of drastic changes, you're again faced with a choice. And you'll have to make it pretty much on the spur of the moment. So, be certain before you do the deal that you and the editor are looking for the same finished product.

And that's what an editor does, when she's functioning as an editor. But as you've probably decided by now, we have lots of other functions.

I've mentioned word count and manuscript length a few times. Since they become part of that P&L that I'm going to have to do, let's examine some figures. Remember this: these numbers are not only just examples (and drawn from hardcover estimates; they'll be different for paperback, but the principle remains the same), but they're only valid in terms of the day they were typed. Prices change so radically and so quickly that I feel almost guilty offering any as examples.

We'll consider two novels. The cast-off, the production department's estimate of the length of the finished novel, in type, with all the front matter (title and half title pages, dedications, acknowledgments, copyright page and whatever else is going to precede the beginning of the text), are for books of 204 and 276 pages. Being clever, we'll title the first one *Short* and the second *Long*.

The plant costs (composition, copyediting, proofreading, design revisions—setting the copyright page and other front matter—cover art and design and press preparation) will come to, for our purposes, $4,300. It breaks down this way:

Composition of Text:	$1,620.00
Copyedit and Proofing	600.00
Front Matter	260.00
Cover Design & Type (this figure is provided by the Art Director.)	500.00
Cover Preparation	1,270.00
Dies	50.00

Now we look at the manufacturing costs: paper and printing the cover, based on projected print orders for the book. That figure is guess work, an estimate arrived at through a number of considerations: a house's track record with a particular kind of title, author's past performance, and whatever other information can be gathered.

These are the figures I'll use for *Short*, based on three print estimates:

Quantity	3,000	4,000	5,000
Paper & Print	$5,190.00	$6,230.00	$7,270.00
Jacket	$1,150.00	$1,380.00	$1,580.00
Manufacturing Total:	**$6,340.00**	**$7,610.00**	**$8,850.00**

Total Costs:

Plant per copy	$1.433	$ 1.075	$0.86
Manufacturing per copy	$2.113	$1.903	$1.77
Freight	$ .10	$ .10	$ .10
Total Cost Per Copy:	**$ 3.65**	**$3.08**	**$ 2.73**

It doesn't take a particularly keen-eyed observer to see the drop in total cost as the print order goes up. One would think, then, that we'd just order more copies, but it isn't that simple; we'll see why in a while.

Here's the same kind of breakdown for *Long*:

Composition of Text:	$2,200.00
Copyedit and Proofing:	830.00
Front Matter:	320.00
Cover Design & Type:	1,000.00
Cover Preparation:	1,300.00
Dies:	50.00

Quantity	3,000	4,000
Paper & Print	$6,080.00	$7,270.00
Jacket	$1,100.00	$1,300.00
Manufacturing Total:	**$7,180.00**	**$8,570.00**

Total Costs:

Plant per copy	$1.90	$1.425
Manufacturing per copy	$2.39	$2.143
Freight	$ .10	$ .10
Total Cost Per Copy:	$4.39	$3.67

Again, the prices go down as print quantity goes up, but the cost per copy for the 276 page *Long* is almost a dollar more. (There's no 5,000 copy figure given here, because I've chosen for the example to make it a book later in an established series and we know the sales figures well enough to be certain that we won't print that many copies.)

If you look carefully, you'll notice that the cost for printing the cover of the second book is a bit less than for the first; that's because we've decided that there'll be a metallic ink used for *Short*, although the art itself will cost less; we're going with a piece of "found" art: an old photograph for which the rights are available at a decent price.

Remember, these figures are all estimates, prepared before the book is acquired or anything is done; most houses, just before going to press, run them again. Some costs may have gone up (you can be pretty certain that none of them will have gone down), something may have happened that will require a change in print order (the author won the Pulitzer Prize for his previous novel); whatever the variable, we make every effort to take it into account before the printing process begins.

With the numbers in front of me, I set to work next on the P&L, and attempt to determine the profitability of this project based on known costs and estimated sales, list prices, discounts, and business expenses.

The factors here are:

Estimated list price: varies according to length, market, etc.

Average discount: most hardcover houses figure 50%

Net price: the list price less the discount. We're assuming, then, that we'll be getting $11.00 on a $22.00 book.

Net units sold: Return rates vary; some houses use a figure as high as 33 1/3%; others as low as 20%. Paperback return numbers can be as high as 50%. Those figures remain constant; it doesn't matter if you're printing 2,000 copies or 7,500 copies or, in mass market, 15,000 copies or 100,000.

Using those numbers, we come up with an estimated net regular (i.e., book) sales in dollars (simple multiplication; or, thanks to software applications like Excel, a matter of pressing a key.)

Added to that is an estimate of what the subsidiary rights sales might come to: a sale to paperback, a book club, or a foreign publisher, and you arrive at your total net sales in dollars. Here's an example of what the P&L for *Long* might look like:

Sales

List price	$22.95	
Average discount		50%
Net price	$11.48	
Net units sold		3,100
Free copies (reviews, etc.)		100
Return units (@ 20%)		800
Net sales ($)	$35,588.00	
Sub rights monies	$4,000.00	
Total Net Sales	$39,588.00	

Production

Unit cost	$3.67	
Print (quantity)		4,000
Total	$14,680.00	
Royalty @ 10%	$ 7,115.00	
Sub rights monies	$2,000.00	
Advance	$5,000.00	
Total royalty payment	$ 9,115.00	
Total Cost of Sale	$23,795.00	
Gross Margin	$15,793.00	
Gross margin percentage		0.398

Almost a forty percent profit, right? And the author is earning $7,100 in royalties and I'm only offering a $5,000 advance.
Time to tar and feather the publishers, I guess.

Except . . . Traditional publishing procedure has been the allo-
cation of the first fifty percent of profit (not fifty percent of the profits) to certain fixed expenses: The sales manager gets a salary; the
sales reps get salaries and/or commissions; your editor has to eat (so
that she has the strength to keep entering all those figures); the people in the production department; the guy in the mail room who sees
to it that your manuscript gets to the editor's desk in the first place;
all the other general and administrative personnel: everyone wants
to get paid and each book has to contribute to that.

And then there are other things that go on: you'll want galleys
of your book to get to reviewers and bookstores; maybe they'll be
sent out for pre-publication blurbs, maybe the publisher will just
send copies of the manuscript, but those copies have to come from
someplace, and that someplace is going to cost money. Not to mention postage.

How long did you spend on the phone with your editor, the
last time he called to discuss some changes?

Want copies of your reviews mailed to you?

Want to do signings at a couple of bookstores . . . and have the
publisher pay for the trip?

The money necessary to keep the company running so that
your book can be put in the hands of the readers has to come from
somewhere, and each book has to contribute to those expenses.

And, finally, consider this: the total cost of sale was $23,795,
and 3,100 copies of the book were sold; that makes the cost of sale
for each copy $7.675; and the publisher is only receiving $11.48 (on
average) per copy: that's about $3.80 "profit" on the $22.95 book.

Royalties, the money you're making on each copy sold, are a
business expense for the publisher, part of the cost of publishing the
book. In the hardcover business, the royalties are pretty much

standard: you get 10% of the list price on the first 5,000 copies sold; 12 1/2 on the next 5,000 copies, and 15% thereafter. I've gotta repeat this here: we're selling the book at an average 50% discount, so we're getting $11.00 on a $22.00 book; you're getting your royalty, however, based on the full list price: $2.20 per book on the first 5,000 copies and if everything goes according to our fantasy, more on the next 5,000 and if we get up to fifteen thousand copies, your getting $3.30 on each copy . . . and the publisher is still getting $11.00. I'm not suggesting you cry for us, but you have to know that in order to understand some of the other things that happen, like a "net royalty" offer or lowered royalties on certain higher discount sales . . . all of which we'll cover when we get to the contract negotiation discussion.

The figures done, all responsible parties having signed off on them, and having received the go ahead from the powers-that-be, it's time for me to call you and start the negotiation.

Oh, you have an agent. Well, then, I'll call her. The negotiation is pretty much the same; it's been easier with agents because they've always known the information I just shared with you. Now you know it, too. And you may not have an agent. Because we want you ready for anything and everything, in the next section we'll look at a contract and walk through a negotiation, just in case you need the information.

Negotiating
a Contract

Getting, Giving
Whys and Wherefores

f inally, the call comes: we want to acquire the rights to publish your manuscript.

Sticklers, please note: I want to *acquire* the rights to publish your *Work*. I am not buying the rights to publish your book. It's a subtle difference and it doesn't mean all that much, at least not to you, but it leads me neatly into an important segue, and that is one of the reasons so many publishers prefer to deal with agents. We speak the same language, which makes negotiation a lot easier and more pleasant. It also makes it quicker, as you'll see in a moment.

Once upon a time, when I was with Tor Books, we had a deal pending with an unagented author. Nothing new or special there. But the author, having agreed to the terms as offered over the phone then put everything on hold as he went off to consult with an attorney—an attorney with no knowledge of publishing whatsoever. The contract came back to us with lots of changes (none of which had been discussed; i.e., none had been negotiated, and that's what this is about). Among the changes, the lawyer changed the word

"Work," (publishing contracts refer to the Work) to Book. But a manuscript isn't a book, a book is what the publisher produces. It took several weeks to get everything straightened out, to point out the differences between "buy" and "acquire"; in reality, a publisher is leasing the right to publish your Work as a book, for a certain amount of time; contracts should have clauses allowing you to revert the rights under certain conditions.

If an agent had been involved from the beginning, the deal would have been completed immediately. If the author had taken the time to research a little before submitting the manuscript, he'd have known what questions to ask when the editor called him with the offer. You will be prepared.

There's a downside to negotiation, and you should be aware of it before you do anything else: the publisher has almost all of the power when it comes to dealing with a first time author, and has a lot of it still even with an author who is three or five or ten books into a career. And it doesn't matter if we're dealing with you directly or through an agent; there's only so far you can push, and you have to know which items make enough of a difference to you that you're willing to risk having the deal fall through.

I've been acquiring publication rights since January, 1968. I've had deals fall apart; I've never regretted those occasions: *there's always another manuscript waiting in the wings*, always another writer ready to fill the slot.

During my tenure as Editorial Director of Zebra Books, the Horror Writers of America let it be known that books published by Zebra would not be considered for awards because HWA didn't like our business practices. A mass market house, Zebra's publishing schedule was slot-driven: we had to have so many romances, so many horror titles, so many westerns, so many this or that, each month: it's how the annual budget was established. We knew that horror fiction accounted for a fixed percentage of sales each month and we had to have the titles to generate those sales.

The HWA threat may have kept some writers from submitting (though as the horror market began to fold, some of them began to reconsider their moral stand) but there was never a slot unfilled and the sales were not affected at all.

Editors are regularly confronted by similar situations: an author feels she can get a better deal elsewhere, or her editor isn't holding her hand enough, or someone else on the list is getting special treatment (that this other writer may be selling better is a consideration that is discounted by: "Well, if they treated me that way, I'd do better, too"), and decides to go elsewhere. At first it's just a threat to leave but, when it doesn't bring the desired results, pride demands motion. Some find new houses, some don't; the editor's list, however, goes on. There may be a dip in the sales line on that chart up in the accountants' offices, but almost always we can say this: No writer is the franchise; Stephen King has left several of his previous publishers, so has Dean Koontz and James Ellroy—writers move these days almost as if publishing had a free agency clause—but the publishers they've left stay in business. A hole is nothing more than something to be filled.

The moral is this: if the negotiation is more trouble than it's worth, it's not worth the trouble. Yes, we want to go ahead, but we're not going to give up anything we need in order to keep you. Agents understand that and if you're unagented, you have to know it, as well; you also have to remember this: an agent may promise certain things, but if the editor doesn't want to give them, whatever they are, the promise is just words.

This isn't said to pour cold water on your dreams; it's just that when we get down to business, dreams have to be put on hold.

✏︎   ✎   ✏︎

Every negotiation begins with the boilerplate, the basic contract devised by the publisher's attorneys. (Some organizations—The Author's Guild and Science Fiction Writers of America are better known examples—have developed suggested contracts; I don't know how many publishers pay serious attention to them.) As we deal with agents, a new standard contract emerges: I know that one agent insists on certain wording for a particular clause; another agent refuses to accept one demand or another; when I deal with those agents, the only thing left to be negotiated is the advance. Two minutes later, the contract is being formatted.

If you've become a member of a critique group that has published members, they may be willing to discuss their contracts with the membership; don't be offended if they delete things like the advance. Seeing those contracts will give you some idea of how one publisher sees the business. If you have access to two or three contracts, you'll also become aware of another fact of life: almost all the contracts are the same. They can run six pages or fourteen, but once you get past the verbiage, they're saying the same thing.

Generally, they begin by delineating the grant of rights: what it is that is being acquired. That's followed by the warranty and liability clauses: you are guaranteeing that you own the Work and have the right to dispose of rights, also that there is nothing obscene, injurious, libelous or otherwise prone to get the publisher and bookseller sued.

Then we get to money: the advance, the way it will be paid out, the royalties and various royalty schedule alterations, as well as subsidiary rights payments.

Your requirements: delivery dates, what it is you will deliver and the form in which it will be (including things like permissions, map, and indices); delivery of requested changes and things that will happen if you miss those dates or don't make the changes; checking of copyedit and proofs, charges for changes in proofs, and options.

The publisher's obligations: how the book will be published, copies to author and/or agent, things that might prevent publication and what can be done about them. The option clause may appear here, too.

There may be an Agency Clause: this states who the agent is and the agency's rights in terms of the Work.

And that's about it; clean, simple, and to the point.

More or less detail, more or fewer words, but every contract contains all of these items.

When you get the call, though, you'll be told the advance, the *basic* royalty schedule and the option details. As a rule, an editor won't discuss the various subsidiary rights with you; we'll take it for granted that if you aren't agented you won't want to hold on to the rights because, well, what are you going to do with them?

As we go through the contract, I'll be pointing out where an agent can make a difference and where they can't. Having studied what follows, you'll know the questions to ask and with a little common sense and good will on both sides, be able to negotiate the changes that make you happy and keep the editor on your side.

The Grant of Rights

After some introductory comments (contract between, dates), THE PARTIES AGREE AS FOLLOWS:

The Author hereby grants and assigns exclusively to the Publisher and its successors, representatives and assigns the rights in and to an unpublished work of fiction (or nonfiction) tentatively titled . . .

I know you've spent hours coming up with just the right title for your manuscript. It's tentative nonetheless. There may be another book with the same title being released about the same time, certain words may no longer be working or may carry baggage that the Publisher thinks will hurt sales; whatever the reason, the title is something that will be decided by the Publisher. Most of the time, your editor will work with you to arrive at something that's mutually acceptable, but the final decision is the publisher's: they're the ones who have to sell the book.

The title having been typed, it's the last time it will appear in the contract; from now in, we refer only to the Work.

The Publisher acquires the Work for the full term of copyright and all renewals and extensions thereof *in all languages throughout the World, the right to print, publish and/or license and sell the Work, in a hardcover and/or paperback edition or any part or abridgment thereof. And the rights of digest, condensation, anthology, quotation, book club, serialization before or after publication, TV and performance rights, with exclusive authority to dispose of such rights.*

There may also be wording about electronic rights, large print and Braille editions for the visually impaired, and just about anything else that can be thought of. In fact, some contracts also include a clause that reads: *All rights not specifically reserved by the Author, whether now in existence or hereafter coming into existence, are granted to the Publisher.*

Now the fun begins. An agent is not going to grant "all languages throughout the world." Translation rights can be lucrative— if they can be sold, and that's a mighty big *if*. Some companies, and certain genres, are sold successfully; others are mere possibilities, fruition fondly to be desired. Most agents will grant English language rights throughout the World, excluding the British Commonwealth of Nations.

If you don't have an agent, though, what are you going to do with those rights? You don't have the contacts to make the sales, to get the book into the hands of a Japanese publisher, say, and negotiate a contract.

If the agent makes a foreign deal, you get whatever that advance is, less your agent's commission and less the commission the agent pays to his foreign agent. If we make a deal for you, you get only 50% of the advance, and there may be an agent's commission involved there, too.

What I suggest is this: grant the rights, but have a clause added to the effect that if those rights haven't been sold within eighteen to twenty-four months after publication, they will revert to you. If anything happens, you've got the money (plus earned royalties from those publications, still split with the publisher); by the time you have your second book in the pipeline, you'll probably have an agent, and the rights on the second book will rest with him.

If nothing happens, you'll probably still have an agent for the subsequent books, the rights will revert to you and your agent will be able to try to sell them in conjunction with the rights to the second book.

It's win/win and most editors will go along with that. There are some houses, though, generally mass market publishers and especially certain genre specialists, who will not give an inch (on anything). That's where your common sense has to come into play: Your manuscript, your career, your call.

The assortment of other rights (other than performance, for the moment) are minor items, really. Most agents will reserve first serial rights (publication of a chapter or portion in a magazine before publication) for themselves, and let the other things go. Because of the timing involved in much of publishing these days (the book appearing within a year or eighteen months of delivery), there isn't all that much time to place serial rights, and it seems that while a chapter of a new Rabbit book by John Updike might appear in a magazine, how many other excerpts do you see? I think most editors will give up first serial; you can try if it makes a difference or, as happens, if you've already placed an excerpt, making the clause moot.

Performance rights are tricky. An editor is going to feel that you have no chance of placing them at all if a book isn't published. I've negotiated contracts with agents that give the publisher a small percentage of the performance rights (whatever they may be); others retain all rights. My advice again: ask that the rights revert to you after a certain amount of time, just as you did with translation rights—unless you've established early on that you have contacts in the industry.

Publishers want to sell these rights: we cannot really make enough money just on the sale of a book. So, the subsidiary rights department is going to do everything it can to place them. If it works, everyone makes money. If it doesn't, you get them back and can try on your own.

I do recommend one change: Remember that clause I mentioned: *All rights not specifically reserved by the Author, whether now in existence or hereafter coming into existence, are granted to the Publisher.* Suggest that it read: *The Author reserves all rights not specifically granted to the Publisher.*

None of us knows what tomorrow's technology is going to bring (most of us, really, don't know what the potential of electronic rights is as things stand now); before audio books hit their stride, the rights were routinely granted to the publisher, specifically or not. Now, agents will retain them, just as routinely. The change in the clause keeps you safe.

A reminder: read the grant of rights carefully, or ask about it in detail early in your talks. Ask questions, and then make an informed decision. And if the editor doesn't answer, waffles, says don't worry about it, or otherwise seems not to be playing straight, consider seriously whether you want to hitch your wagon to her star.

The next major clause is the warranty and liability guarantees. The wording varies to some degree, but they generally follow along these lines:

The Author warrants that the Author is the sole author and proprietor of the Work, that the Author is the sole owner of all the rights granted herein and has full power to enter into this Agreement; that the Work is original and is not in the public domain; that the Work does not violate the right of privacy or publicity of any person; that the Work is not libelous or obscene and that the Work does not infringe upon, invade, or violate the statutory or common-law copyright, trademark, or patent of anyone.

These representations and warranties are in effect as of the date of this Agreement and shall remain in effect on the date of the Work's first publication and on the dates of any subsequent editions of the Work. The Publisher may rely absolutely on the accuracy of these presentations and warranties when negotiating with any third party for the disposition of any rights in the Work held by the Publisher.

The Author shall indemnify and hold the Publisher and any assignees or licensees of the Work harmless against any loss, damage, liability or expense arising out of, or for the purpose of, resolving or avoiding any claim, suit, proceeding, or demand made or brought against the Publisher by reason of the publication, sale, distribution, or disposition of rights in respect to the Work, which, if sustained, would constitute a breach of any of the Author's representations and warranties.

The Publisher and Author shall give each other prompt written notice of any claim about which either of them obtains knowledge.

If any such claim, suit, proceeding, or demand is brought or made based upon a violation finally sustained of any of the foregoing warranties, the Publisher may elect (1) to undertake the defense thereof, or (2) to notify the Author to undertake the defense. If the Publisher does so notify the Author, the Author shall undertake such defense; the Publisher may, at its option, join in the defense. In any event, the cost and expense of any defense shall be borne by the Author, unless (a) such claim, suit, proceeding, or demand arises solely out of an act or omission of the Publisher, in which case the cost and expense shall be borne by the Publisher, or (b) the Author has, pursuant to notification from the Publisher, undertaken the defense and the Publisher at its option elects to join with the Author in the defense, in which case the total cost and expense (including reasonable attorney's fees) shall be shared equally by the Publisher and the Author.

Whenever any such claim, suit, proceeding, or demand is instituted, the Publisher may withhold payments due the Author under this or any other agreement between the Author and the Publisher, subject, however, to the Author's right to draw on such sums to defray the Author's expenses in connection with such claim, suit, proceeding, or demand. The amount withheld shall be in amounts necessary in the reasonable opinion of Publisher's counsel to defray the likely expense of litigation and either settlement or adverse judgment. If a final adverse judgment is rendered and is not discharged by the Author, the Publisher may apply the payments so withheld to the satisfaction and discharge of such judgment. If no action is commenced within two years of receipt of a claim, amounts so withheld shall be released at the end of such two years.

These representations and warranties shall survive the termination of this Agreement.

No editor has the authority to change this clause; even discussing changes can make life unpleasant. It's necessary, especially these days, when people sue for no more valid reason than because their bunions hurt that morning.

You might want to have the word "obscene" stricken; that's a minor issue. This version of the clause doesn't say that nothing injurious is in the Work. That one gets tricky, especially if you write mysteries and have someone poisoned; its primary purpose is to protect cookbook publishers. Authors of some action books and certain self-protection manuals might want to pay attention to words of that nature as well.

Larger publishers often have insurance to protect against these kinds of suits; for most of the smaller houses, the cost is prohibitive. And while there's no protection against nuisance suits, there's nothing wrong with this clause if you're not doing anything illegal.

Although the editor's call was to offer you a certain amount of money, that information doesn't appear in the contract until now. (Unless it appears sooner or later; there's no industry template.)

The clause begins simply: *The Publisher agrees to pay the*

Author as an advance against all earnings hereunder the sum of
_____ *payable as follows:*

The usual formula is that the author will receive half of the advance on signing of the contract and the balance upon delivery and acceptance of the finished manuscript. As advances get higher, or in multibook deals, other formulas will be used: part on signing, part on acceptance, part on publication. In multibook deals, payments may be keyed to delivery of outlines; for one author, on a series contract, payment may be made on the basis of a certain amount every month (the author is, obviously, important to the house, successful; accommodations are made as necessary).

Editors may have a certain amount of room to play, but as you've seen, the advances are arrived at through the P&L statement and while we'll try to pay less, you can ask for more if you want to, or try to get a different payout. What you should never do is use someone else's advance as a guideline; there are too many factors involved in arriving at an offer and the editor isn't buying that other writer; it is your work and your position in the particular publisher's universe.

Don't forget, either, that the advance is really a loan against future earnings: the royalties you earn go first toward paying that advance back. If you're insisting on a very high advance (with nothing in the way of history to back you up), you're not going to reach an earn-out position, that point at which the royalties start going into your pocket. That leaves a bad taste in the publisher's mouth and you don't want the boss to cringe when your editor walks in with your next project.

There's a feeling that if the publisher pays more, you'll get more, better and stronger support. That's true at certain levels: more goes into a book that we've paid $75,000 for than one we've paid $7,500 for; but the difference between five grand and seventy-five hundred isn't going to mean anything. While your manuscript may be worth whatever figure you care to put on it for you, it's only worth what we think it's worth, based on projected sales and our experience selling books of that kind . . . whatever that kind is.

The results that other houses have with a particular type fiction don't mean anything to your editor, unless he's had the same results.

That brings us to a discussion of placement on the list. I'm sure you've been hearing about the death of the midlist author, the one who isn't a celebrity, who isn't receiving the high five and six figure advances. Category writers are generally not midlist; that's much more a mainstream consideration; midlist authors are the ones most publishing houses think are going to breakout, transcend genre. Category fiction is just that: it sells within certain ranges that are understood by all the players, into a pretty fixed market.

Yes, you can go beyond that if, for reasons no one can really pinpoint, for all the "how to write a bestseller" books available to you (if it were that easy, wouldn't there be a lot more bestsellers? Think about it before you invest); if you're lucky and something about your book appeals to a greater readership, those people who don't read "that stuff," you'll move up. (Again, pick any category you'd care to investigate and try to find some definable parallel between the breakout books in that genre. What's the similarity between Mary Higgins Clark and Sue Grafton and Robert B. Parker? Why do they make it but Donald E. Westlake doesn't? Why does Larry Block but not Don? Then stop worrying about it and go back to your own writing, trying always to make it better.)

I can guarantee that if you try to get a bigger advance based on the fact that some other writer is getting more, you'll get one of two responses: a polite discussion of all those who are making what you were offered . . . or less, or a rather curt: "Well, when you sell like she does, you'll make it also. Now, are you going to accept this offer or not?"

An agent may be able to get you a slightly better deal, but I wouldn't spend that extra money just yet; it may be the difference between $4,000 and $5,000 but it isn't going to be anything that will take you to a new income bracket, at least not when you're starting your career.

Oh, all those writers who get onto the talk shows because they're getting huge advances? They get on because they're news. They're news because they've beaten the odds and gotten the deal; there are 50,000 new books published every year; how many writers get on the shows? (If you've followed my advice and started reading *PW*, you are also familiar with their annual survey of the big money books that flopped.)

Back to business: the advance is against all earnings; that includes royalties and subsidiary rights income. Let's say that you've accepted a deal for $5,000; that's the amount that has to be earned back before you begin to see a royalty check.

Things are going nicely: the hardcover house has been able to sell mass market rights for $2,500. The split is 50/50, so you've earned back $1,250. You still have to earn $3,750 in book sales (or other subsidiary rights monies). If your book is selling for $20.00, you're getting two dollars a book in royalties (on the first five thousand copies sold, less a reserve for returns . . . another twist we'll get to). That means we have to have net sales of at least 1,875 copies before you see any further income. (We're counting on selling more than that, but these are figures for explanation. Unfortunately, there are books that don't sell that many copies. Just so you know.) With copy 1,876, however, you start earning money above your advance.

Paperback royalties are all over the board: Six percent, eight, ten (sometimes, but rarely, higher) and there are houses that will offer less. While there's nothing you can effectively do in terms of your hardcover rates, there is room to negotiate with most mass market houses; try to get at least six percent, with one or two splits, kicking up to eight at 75,000 or 100,000 copies, and maybe ten at 250,000. There's lots of room to maneuver here, at least with reputable houses. How far and hard to push is, again, your call. Don't settle for anything less than six percent, however.

Why the big difference in the numbers? First, we're dealing with lower cover prices, and then because mass market is a game of big numbers. A hardcover house can effectively print 5,000 copies of a book and start your career rolling; the generally accepted minimum print in paperback is 15,000; they want to begin at 25,000 copies. Most paperback books (we're not talking about the bestsellers here, just most of the books you see on the racks) sell less than 50,000 copies (with returns, don't forget, approaching the fifty percent mark).

As publishing houses have become part of conglomerates, more and more of them are making hard/soft deals. They're acquiring rights to do the book in various formats and their contract offers will reflect that: in addition to the hardcover royalty, paperback royalties will be mentioned. Again, you want to try to get at least six percent as your royalty.

Other considerations: If a paperback reprinter buys the rights to your book from a hardcover house, the advance can range from $2,000 (as an example only) up to, well up to just about anything, depending on what happens. When you get a hard/soft offer, however, you're not going to get an advance that represents those kinds of combined numbers; the extra two grand won't necessarily be added to the advance, though it might be a little higher.

Because you're earning back one advance with the two editions, your royalties are "pooled"; if the hardcover doesn't do well, the paperback earnings will be applied against the total monies paid up front. Pooling sometimes comes into play when you make a multiple book deal, as well. It works like this: I offer you fifteen thousand dollars for two books, at a standard hardcover royalty. However, you have to earn the entire advance back before you see a royalty check. If the first book doesn't work as well as we'd all like, the publisher sees the second book as protection on the investment. If it works better than expected, it'll be a nice Christmas for everyone involved.

I prefer, as a writer and as an editor, to separate the books, assign a specific amount as an advance on each manuscript and let each stand alone. (This isn't going to be an issue for most people, but since we're trying to cover as much as possible, I'm throwing it in for your consideration.) Agents tend to dislike pooled royalties as well, so editors are used to deleting it from contracts.

Finally, a trade paperback royalty may be mentioned in the contract. Most houses have been offering seven-and-a-half percent on the first 10,000 copies and ten percent thereafter; I think you can settle for as little as six percent without feeling cheated.

That isn't all there is to those earnings hereunder, however. In addition to the sub rights, there may be a premium sale to a company that wants to use your book for promotion; there are school and library sales; and there are high discount sales, all of which carry reduced royalty payments.

You'll remember the discounts publishers are forced to give; they can run over fifty percent or be as low as forty percent. New writers, especially, are haunted by that problem: in order to get an untried author onto the shelves, we have to offer higher discounts. (Booksellers want to use their display space for the things they already know will sell; if we want them to take a chance on you, we have to give them an incentive; the high discount is an incentive.) On a first contract, or even a second unless you've become a best-selling author overnight, there's little you can do about that clause. Later, when you have some clout, you might try to get the reduced royalty to kick in when the discount is above fifty percent.

That high discount situation has given rise to another twist on the royalty scheme. By contemporary standards, royalties are based on the list price of the book. Many publishers are suggesting what are called "net contracts": the author receives a given percentage of the net income derived from the sale of the book. If the publisher is getting ten dollars per copy (a $20.00 book), and sells five hundred copies, the net receipts are $5,000. You would receive anywhere from six to ten percent of that figure—at best $500. On a list contract, you'd receive ten percent of the list price ($2.00) multiplied by copies sold, or $1,000.

The net royalty approach helps the publisher and is found in the contracts of lots of smaller houses, where cash flow is a problem; while some larger houses have tried to establish it over the last few years, they haven't met with much success.

Depending on the project, I'm willing to consider net revenue contracts, and have written for publishers under those terms. I do insist, though, that it be for ten percent of receipts.

It'll be difficult to ask questions about all of those clauses when the offer is first tendered; once you get the contract, though, you should be able to call your editor to discuss anything that bothers you, and to receive whatever clarifications you need or want.

Money out of the way, we get to the obligations of both parties. The publisher will guarantee to publish the book within a specified period of time, barring acts of war, strikes, and other events outside of its control. They also have the right to publish the book in the manner and format of their choice. That means your editor will edit the work until it is satisfactory according to his definitions. The publisher will also make the final decision about the cover, art, copy—everything that defines the finished product as they produce it.

You commit to a specific delivery date (of a full manuscript, or a rewritten one, based on your conversations with the editor. There is invariably wording here stating that if the revisions are unacceptable, *in the sole judgment of the Publisher*, the contract can be terminated and all monies advanced must be repaid. You will, eventually, be able to get that changed to what's known as a "first proceeds" clause: the contract is cancelled, but you can repay from the advance you receive from another publisher for the same Work. Unless there's a reasonable amount of confidence on the Publisher's part that you will be able to sell the Work elsewhere, they're not going to agree to a first proceeds amendment); supply the manuscript, sometimes a computer disk, any necessary permissions, *and to read and approve the copyedited manuscript and page proofs.* No hemming or hawing, here: if that clause is not in your contract, demand it. If you don't, or if the editor refuses, you've lost any control you might have over the finished text. If the editor refuses, find out why and if you're not satisfied with the explanation, consider making it a deal breaker. (That's how strongly I feel about the issue, anyway. I'm more than comfortable suggesting caution about every other point, but on this one, I throw caution to the wind. And my contract out the window.)

The option clause is another pet peeve. There are writers who feel that an option clause makes them indentured servants of the publishing house. The publishers feel that they are making an investment in an author, that the acquisition of the manuscript is just a beginning. Profits, for both the writer and the publisher, come over a period of time: the idea is to build a following. That can't be done if there's no guarantee that the publisher has at least a fair shot at acquiring the next work. (It isn't unheard of, either, for a publishing house to be less enthusiastic about a soon-to-be-released work if it's known that the author is leaving for other pastures.)

There are countless variations on the wording in this clause; as a writer, I prefer one that reads: *The Author agrees to submit to the Publisher the Author's next book-length work or proposal before submitting the same to any other publisher. For a period of thirty days after the submission of the completed manuscript or proposal, the Publisher shall have an exclusive opportunity to acquire the said work on mutually agreeable terms.* All this commits you to is showing the next work and negotiating in good faith.

A common alteration reads . . . *next book-length work or proposal in this series* or *of the same category.* That frees you up: if you've written a romance and your next book is a western, you're free to show it elsewhere. Most editors will readily agree to this change, because our interest, as I said, is in developing a following for you, and a book in a different genre doesn't do that effectively. It also means that if you're doing one series, and want to create a second one, you don't have to show it to your editor, even if it's in the same category. My suggestion: do the moral thing and let your publisher see the new series first; there's a certain crankiness that develops when we discover that you've gone into competition with yourself; indeed, some contracts prohibit the publication of competing works. (If you show it to your editor, however, and it's turned down, you're free to shop it elsewhere. This is another instance in which having a agent is helpful, if for no other reason than having a publishing savvy individual advising you. There's a pitfall in having too many series out there: readers begin to wonder just how much time and effort is going into the work and have been known to shy away. This doesn't mean it can't work, just that you have to think about it very seriously.)

From the publisher's point of view, a better option clause ends with the words . . . *at terms no less favorable than those offered by another publisher*. The intent here is to allow you to show the work around if you can't make a deal, but allows the publisher to come back and acquire the work without it costing you anything. That's called a "matching" option; there's also a "topping" clause; it stipulates that the publisher can acquire the manuscript for an amount equal to (usually) ten percent more than your highest offer.

Each editor has his own way of dealing with the clause; what you don't want is something that forces you to sell the new work to the same publisher for the same amount as the original sale.

Occasionally an option clause will specify that you can't submit the new work until thirty days (or some other arbitrary figure) after publication of "the Work hereunder." If the first book's going to be published soon after the deal is made, there isn't too much to worry about; if, though, the book's two years down the road, that phrase pretty much shuts you down. The publisher is hedging bets:

how will book one sell, what're the reviews going to be like, the pre-pub buzz? By waiting, we have some idea of what's happening, and that means we can, possibly, raise the advance.

If the new proposal arrives a week after delivery of the first manuscript, we're shooting in the dark; how can we logically offer more if we don't know what's going to happen? From your point of view, the wait may mean a substantially better advance on the second contract.

What to do? Compromise. If there is an attempt to control when a new proposal can be delivered, try to get a time period you're comfortable with, based on conversations you've had with your editor. Keep in mind that we don't want too long a wait between books; certainly in the early stages of a publishing relationship, anything more than eighteen months is too long and ideally we'd want book two on sale a year after the first one ships.

Discuss the details with your editor, explain your writing patterns and how long it might take you to finish a new manuscript, and come up with a date that works for both of you.

Another thing you don't want (and I haven't seen it in a while, but that doesn't mean it isn't going to happen again) is a clause that allows the publisher to name another author to take over a series if you can't come to terms. That wording will be clear (though it may not be in the option clause itself), and that's another one you should consider a dealbreaker.

Most publishers offer the writer ten free copies of the book; you can get that bumped up (as long as the number remains reasonable) and most editors will send you a few extra as you may need them. (Those are part of that hundred free copies mentioned in the P&L; you don't get royalties on free copies and the publisher doesn't make anything on them, either.)

Back at the top of the contract, we looked at a clause that gave the publisher rights to your Work for at least the term of copyright. Here's where your protection comes in: the reversion clause.

Again, with variations from house to house, this clause states that if the book goes out of print (*not* out of stock), you can write and demand a reprint and the Publisher has sixty days to respond. If they decide not to go along with your request, the rights revert. They then have a year in which to get the book back into print; if they fail to do so, the rights revert.

A paperback edition, published by another house, is a form of in print, so licenses become important considerations here; the Publisher may revert the rights but will still participate in any income from such subsidiary sales.

Sometimes, no matter how careful we are, publishers over-print; those extra copies are what eventually go onto the street as "remainders." You want a clause that gives you the right of first refusal; usually those books will be offered to you at about a seventy-five percent discount.

You want a clause that gives you permission to examine the Publisher's books of account as they pertain to your Work. This is at your expense, unless there's an error of at least five percent. Most publishers already have wording for this, and I've been seeing it pretty regularly in boilerplate.

A last sticking point: the reserve against returns. During the first year of a book's life, copies are shipped out, but because booksellers can return their overstock (at least within certain timeframes), the publisher can't be sure the books are actually "sold." You're royalty statement will, therefore, indicate that a certain percentage of the shipped books are being held as a reserve against returns. The reasoning is simple: if we pay you as if these books were in the hands of readers, and they come back, you would owe us money. And we both know you won't have it. Rather than overpay, then, we reserve. See if you can get a clause in your contract guaranteeing that all reserves will be released by the third royalty period. (By that time, most of the books that are coming back will have arrived; the rule of thumb is that ninety percent of the returns will have been made at the end of the first year on sale.)

There are going to be lots of other clauses, of course; read them and ask the editor about anything you don't understand. I'd guess that just about any change you request is one that's been requested by others. If you've come up with something completely new, you'll hear the phone dropping from your editor's hands.

With the contract out of the way, I can get on with the rest of my work.

Marketing Art

With the contract done and signed, the editor begins the process of taking you from printout to published. The editing may be complete or you may be making suggested changes, keeping your delivery date in mind. Once the manuscript arrives, the final line edits will be done and the manuscript will begin to move through the production department, being copyedited, and having the interior designed (will there be running heads . . . the title of the book and the author's name appearing at the top of respective pages? What typeface will be used, how much leading—space—will there be between lines? Will chapters begin "new right"—each starting on a right hand page—or will they begin wherever they begin, even in the middle of a page?)

While the decision to publish as a mass market or trade paperback or as a hardcover will probably have been made at the time of acquisition (and it is subject to change; once the manuscript is in it might be decided that it's so good, so special, that it makes sense to get the extra attention a hardcover will bring in terms of reviews and the increased sales potential of doing the book in two formats), the publisher, today, has other options.

The standard hardcover, for instance, has dimensions of about 5 1/4 and 8 1/2 inches. Certain titles, though, are done in a slightly larger format, measuring 6 1/2 x 9 1/2 inches. Usually, these are books with bestseller or breakout potential. While the reason may not make sense, it does seem to have been proven in the marketplace: the larger book is taken more seriously because it looks more important and seems more substantial. A quick look through the shelves at your favorite bookstore will prove the point. (New to my bookshelf today: John Irving's *A Widow for One Year* and Brian Morton's *Starting Out in the Evening*. Irving's well established, a bestselling author; Morton is a newcomer with excellent pre-pub quotes and reviews; one of them is in the larger format. Want to venture a guess?)

As you're browsing, however, you'll notice that there are an increasing number of hardcover books in a much smaller format; Dava Sobel's *Longitude* is approximately 5 x 7 1/2 inches. Good things come in small packages, too; that book was an international bestseller. These smaller sizes, rarely used for general fiction, are popular for certain non-fiction, novellas, and other titles to which a publisher wants to call special attention; again, through marketing, the consumer's perception of these books is that they're different, not like the other titles on the shelves. (They're also a pleasure to hold and read; they have the convenience of a paperback and the substantiality of a hardcover . . . and I don't doubt at all that that is a factor in their popularity.)

Having a bound book means nothing, though, if the book can't get to the bookseller and, ultimately, into the hands of the readers. All of the elements that go into that part of the process are functions of marketing. One of the primary concerns is the cover of the book—the jacket or wrapper.

Once the editor has enough material in hand, and that could be a substantial enough outline or an entire manuscript, depending on the complexity of the book, those pages are passed along to the art director, often with a memo outlining the editor's ideas for the art. Since there seem to be regular and loud complaints about cover art, it seems logical to take a few minutes now to discuss the process.

The cover of your book is considered a billboard, calling for attention while surrounded by 50,000 others. While budget considerations can play an enormous role in the decisions being made, no publisher goes out of its way to release a bad package. Striking art can sway a bookseller so that he will display the book cover out, or to put a stack of copies toward the front of the store so that the consumer will see it immediately and, if you remember how books are bought (with the art being what attracts the browser's eye), the importance of the cover becomes a paramount consideration. In fact, in certain paperback romance operations it's not unheard of for the cover artist to receive more than the author did as an advance; the artist doesn't get royalties, of course. If the cover attracts enough readers the author is on her way to success—and in the case of certain artists, the authors know they've "made it" if a particular artist is tapped for their covers. (They've been known to get jealous and/or to try to make the artist part of a negotiation.)

The art director usually has not only fine art training, but a commercial background as well: this is advertising, this is selling, this is marketing a product. Additionally, both the director and the sales manager know, through experience, what is working, what's hot, at a particular time, from such urban myths as green covers don't sell, to necessities: don't give away clues in the cover art of a mystery. They know that a rearing stallion helps sell a romance, that certain hardware is an effective tool in selling science fiction. Just as the advance you were offered isn't arbitrary, neither is the art.

That's one of the reasons you're advised not to bother submitting your cover concept with your manuscript. The art may be pretty, it may have been done by your significant other, your child, by you, yourself; if it doesn't suit the marketing needs and niche of your publisher it's beside the point. There are times when a good editor will consult with you. If your book is set in an historical period or focuses on certain technical matters (a submarine or a specific jet; a particular computer or part of the world), you may be asked to supply sample art of those factors so that they may be accurately portrayed. In those instances, you may also be given an opportunity to see sketches or the final rendering, to "vet" it so that experts (real or self-proclaimed) won't look at it and decide that none of us (especially you) don't know what we're talking about.

We also have to take into account whether the book is part of a series and changes in the readership. Even if you didn't read Gothics, you recognized the books immediately: the tower on the cliff, one light in a window, the dark and stormy night, the woman in a cape running downhill (usually toward the sea), looking over her shoulder. If an art director had a Gothic to work on, the job was three quarters done before the manuscript was taken out of the envelope.

The lurid paperback original covers of the 1950s and '60s worked well in their time; the kind of book was immediately identifiable. When I was growing up, we knew immediately which were the j.d. (juvenile delinquent) novels, the *Amboy Dukes* and *Blackboard Jungle* type novels that we had to sneak into the house. Today, those covers are parts of exhibitions and the history of publishing, but they're not used.

Something like that has happened in the romance genre: As the category was beginning to dominate the market, the so-called "nursing mother" cover art was so much a part of the genre that I could go into a bookstore (as editorial director of Zebra, one of the leading houses in the field and one known particularly for the quality of its cover art) and not tell my covers from Avon's or Silhouette's or anyone else's. That treatment also contributed to the jokes, insults, and disdain that met the field in almost every venue.

On the one hand, the covers worked (that rearing white horse, a pirate or cowboy—bare, or nearly so, to the waist—the woman whose bosom was just contained by the bodice of her torn dress); at the same time the writers were becoming disenchanted (this wasn't the way to be taken seriously as writers) and the readers were beginning to complain that some of the covers were going too far. That brought a new approach; some of us called it "wallpaper"; nice colors, pretty patterns, nothing to offend any sensibility. But appealing. Today you can find both—and other variations on the theme.

That's series as category; within categories, though, there are also series, the continuing adventures of a particular character. One of the jobs the publisher has is establishing the series. That not only means having new books on a regular basis, but making them immediately identifiable to the reader. A logo may be created, some object that becomes a symbol for the series: books about the Lone Ranger might use his mask; a series about Merlin could use his staff.

One publisher recently faced what has become known as the "bloody balls" fiasco. A mystery series by Harlan Coben, featuring a sports agent (Myron Bolitar) as sleuth revolved, not so amazingly, around events in the world of professional athletics. The covers (these were paperback originals) all had the ball particular to the story covered with blood toward the center of the jacket. They looked a little silly and while there was violence in the novels, these books looked like those that had contributed to the demise of the horror market.

When the series moved into hardcover, the wrappers went upmarket: *One False Move* was not only in the larger format, it featured a type solution (no illustration) and a simple graphic: the x and o of a chalkboard a coach might use to diagram a play. The paperbacks were reissued with new covers, too.

The connecting element might also be a portrait of the character, a form of art, anything we think—based on past experience and current events—will let the reader know that this is the same author they've enjoyed before.

There's also the question of whether we want to have art at all, whether it should be an illustration, a graphic element, whether the art should "bleed"—go from edge to edge—or be "spot"—a small illustration placed on some part of the cover, or if it should be a type solution: The title and the author's name and perhaps some copy and nothing else. Painting, computer generated art, photograph, collage? Should the art wrap around and continue on the back of the volume? Each kind of book and each marketing approach will call for something else, and the art director will be told if something special is to be done.

As if those choices aren't enough, there are ways of tarting up the cover, most of which were created by art directors in mass market houses for rack-sized paperbacks where the competition for the eye is stronger. You've seen them all: embossing or debossing the type or art elements, metallic inks or foil lettering, die-cuts (cutting holes in the cover, with a second piece of art as the first "page" of the book or trimming the edges (again using a second piece of art), and playing with textures (combining a matte finish on the cover with the art glossy), are now standards seen regularly on hardcover books as well.

Each bit adds expense (with die-cuts you pay the expense of a second piece of cover art), represents another step in production (and may not be accounted for in the P&L or initial production breakdown; they're added at the suggestion of the sales department or at the encouragement of the editor who has been campaigning for more attention for the book); their purpose is simple: catch the eye of the browser, make the book look more important.

Of course, anything that's overused loses its value, and there are other problems: Certain black covers pick up fingerprints; by the time the third or fourth person has handled the volume. It begins to look tacky, and that defeats the purpose. The die-cut covers tend to tear and be left behind. Very light covers may look dirty or aged. (One of the reasons paperbacks used to have the upper edges of the pages dyed yellow or red was so that they wouldn't show aging.)

Eventually, a decision is made and the cover is commissioned; all we're hoping for at this point is that the idea can be executed successfully; every art director has tales of terror about the artist who didn't deliver, or of the elements not coming together (not to mention something happening during the printing process and the colors shifting to a prism never before seen). Whatever is going on, though, everyone is going to be paying attention to the progress of the cover: it's one of the most important tools we give the sales reps, as you'll see soon.

Speaking of elements not coming together, though this isn't part of the art, it is a crucial part of the cover, so we'll talk about copy here, too.

Many of the bigger houses have departments to deal with copywriting: whether for the cover, the catalogue or sales materials, there's a staffer that reads the manuscript and creates the words that we hope will entrance you enough after you've picked up the book because of the art, that you'll start reading the author's words and buy whatever it is you're holding. Smaller houses leave the task to the editor. I've been writing my own copy since 1977 and I think my authors benefit from that.

After all, I've been involved with the book from the beginning. I know it better than anyone but the author does, I have a greater interest in it (even if it's one of many, there are fewer on my plate and my involvement with each is more intimate than is the case for a copywriter), so my approach to the job is different. That isn't to say that the copy departments can't or don't do the job right, just that the editor brings something else to the formula.

The copy has to hold the readers' attention, convince them that they want to read this book rather than any of the others that are calling out for attention. As with art, in general the copy has to give enough information without giving away too much and has to synopsize the important elements of the novel in two or three paragraphs.

In a series, there may be a cover line, just in case the reader missed the connection between covers or never saw a previous book in the series. So, we say: A So-and-So Mystery; it reminds previous readers and lets the new reader know that there are others in the series available now or soon to be released.

And there are the blurbs: quotes from other writers or taken from reviews of earlier books by the author.

Pick and choose, put it together, keep it succinct.

We write the copy, using the buzzwords we've come to know will sell in a particular market, and the art director tells us to cut it because there's no room. (There have been times when I've been asked if a title can be changed because it is too long and interferes with the painting.)

Whatever it takes, no book goes out naked . . .and most of the time, anyway, we're all pleased with the way they're dressed.

Marketing

Publicity, Promotion and Advertising

We want people to know about your book; we do not want to waste money in the effort, and it's very easy to throw money away. But if you don't spend any, you won't get any attention. So, how much should you spend, and how?

One of the thoughts you've had pounded into you again and again is that the more you receive as an advance, the more that will be spent in support of the book. That's true, at least to a degree: the difference between $7,500 and $10,000 is not enough to make any kind of dent in the marketing budget and a book that's worth only a few thousand dollars is not going to get a six figure offer. (That some which get the big advance should have received less is subjective; you'll disagree with the premise, of course. Unless you're a reader or an editor and not the writer or the agent. That's what makes this all so much fun.)

In addition to the figures we worked on earlier, one of the determining factors in arriving at an advance is the positioning of the title on the publisher's list. Is it a lead title (that will be defined differently by every publisher in terms of numbers; they'll all agree that the lead is the book from which they're expecting the best performance), a midlist title, a category or below-the-line entry? Those are decisions made by the editor, publisher and marketing people, based on lots of different factors: past performance of the writer, performance of the category, special interest or timeliness, competition and what's probably thought of as gut instinct, but which is really years of experience and sense.

Midlist is a word that gets used a lot these days and I'm not certain that the people using it really know what it means, at least in terms of figures. Let's try this: In larger (hardcover) houses, a midlist title is one that's expected to net a minimum of 15,000 copies; smaller houses probably cut that figure in half. The hope with which we begin is that a writer will start there; for genre writers, the hope is that they move up to that level; then we want everyone to keep moving up the ladder. Because we hear so much these days about the death of the midlist, and because a lot of the writers who are finding themselves cut are category writers, they seem to have decided they're midlist authors. They're not, and it doesn't matter what size house we're talking about, or whether we're discussing hardcover or paperback publication.

What has happened is that publishers have been betting on writers they think will graduate, and that bet means a higher advance. But if the books aren't selling at the right level (and most midlist writers receive some kind of marketing support—at least small ads, for instance, in carefully chosen journals), the publisher has no choice but to stop throwing good money after bad. The writer gets cut, not because he's midlist—but because he actually isn't. And it doesn't have anything to do, really, with the amount of support, though we (as writers) would like to think so. It has much more to do with how many people are interested in reading the kind of book you've written.

There may be 50,000 mystery readers in the country or 150,000 romance readers; it doesn't matter because they do not read everything within a genre, whether we are talking about the classic categories or about kinds of books, generally. The market has a mind and it picks and chooses, according to it's taste.

It doesn't take much to realize that if you're having your debut novel released and one of the household names is on the same list at the same time, you're not the one who's going to get the marketing budget. (Does King really need it? That's arguable; but most viewers of the talk shows, for instance, are going to prefer seeing him being interviewed than you.)

At the same time, your manuscript wasn't acquired so that it could sink without a trace; the idea is to make money and that means selling a sufficient number of copies; everything that's done is done to assure that result.

We know—because we do it every month—what a new novel, of any kind, is likely to sell. We know what can be done to promote it, because we've done it before. We know that ads don't really sell the books of unknowns, because we've tried and because in this country, today, books are not a necessity for most people . . . they cannot be made to buy something they don't think they need. What does sell books is word-of-mouth: when Oprah picks a book, people rush out to buy it, but she picks the books she'll get behind based on, well, whatever it is that drives her. Most of the books she's made bestsellers were books that had been published, some advertised, and none of which had gone anywhere. There's no way a publisher can make that happen for you.

Yes, every now and then a publisher spends an obscene amount of money on a book because of things that are happening outside of the industry. Maybe the manuscript began as a screenplay for which a producer has paid too much and made a lot of promises. The publisher has decided to bet with the producer; because a couple of million has been advanced, the acquisition becomes newsworthy and the author gets on the shows and the public hears about the book again and again. When publication date hits, enough of them rush out to buy the book ("Hey, that's the book we've been hearing about, it must be good";) and it hits the lists for a few weeks, but then everyone who bought it begins talking about it and what they're saying is, "Why?"

We see the syndrome all the time: the hype for a movie that closes the next week, the "big" book that sinks quickly after the loud splash, the Hollywood star or singer or tv series favorite who gets a movie (or writes a book) that no one cares about, even with the noise surrounding the release. Yes, it sells and money is made (though usually not enough), but what happens next? Generally, a step back.

The point of this rant, the thing I want you to take away with you, is that for all you hear and will hear about the power of promotion, the truth is that it does very little. What counts is sales; if your book has "legs" and begins to run, if your sales go up markedly on your next book because people want to read it because they've enjoyed the last one, then all that marketing money begins to come your way, it begins to support everyone's effort to move you to the next level.

Until then, you're not being ignored. That attention comes from the promotion, publicity and advertising department(s). You and your editor are not the only ones watching what's being done: so is the subsidiary rights director.

You remember those subsidiary rights, don't you? All that stuff I tried to get you to let me acquire when we were negotiating, those rights we're going to try to sell for you (and us); everything that's done for your book becomes a tool in the sub rights director's arsenal. If she can tell a paperback house or a book club that you're going to be signing somewhere or that you've been on a local tv show, she's a step closer to making a deal. One of the first things she's going to want (after your sales figures, if they exist) are reviews. They're generated by the people dealing with your publicity. And this might be a good point at which to discuss the differences between the three marketing aspects we're discussing now.

Publicity is "free": it's reviews and interviews and signings (as opposed to a tour, which is promotion), anything that calls attention to your work without any expense. Well, there's some expense: the reviews, particularly the pre-publication reviews in *Publishers Weekly*, *Library Journal*, *Booklist*, and *Kirkus Reviews*, are generated by galleys, bound proofs of the uncorrected text. Galleys are expensive (relatively) but they're an indispensable part of the publication process.

After the manuscript has been set in type (about the same time you're receiving your page proofs for checking), a set of pages are given to someone in the publicity department who sends them out to have a chosen number bound in cheap cardboard or colored paper. The number varies, of course, but there'll be copies made to send to major review sources, key bookseller accounts, maybe for the sales reps, to writers from whom we want to solicit quotes, and a few for your agent. (Remember those rights the agent didn't let us have? Well, now we're supplying galleys to her, so that she can sell the rights for you. Hey, no problem, glad to do you the favor.)

The covers have the title, proposed pub date, maybe some of the catalogue or cover copy: whatever information we think the recipients need.

A trend seen over the last few years is the production of advanced reading copies, called ARCs. They're galleys, but bound in higher quality stock, usually with the proposed cover art; in effect, they look like trade paperback editions, although the back covers carry advertising and promotional promises, rather than selling copy. It's an additional investment, makes the book look more important and, obviously, they're done for those books that seem to have a better shot in the marketplace.

Another wait begins: what will *PW* say? Are there going to be calls from booksellers, trying to order early or letting us know we made a mistake. Are the sales reps excited? We wait, you wait . . . but the process of starting word of mouth has begun. Don't forget, *Bridges of Madison County* became a bestseller because the booksellers loved it, promoted it, on their own, to their customers. That buzz began when they received the galleys of a book that wasn't getting any special attention from the publisher until the buzz started.

The publicist also sends finished books out for review; the galleys were to prime the pump, the book itself should get things flowing. There is very little a publisher can do to guarantee a review, in any media. Book review editors choose books according to the profile they have of their readers; sometimes there's an agenda involved, sometimes a reviewer just doesn't like someone and won't bother with their books . . . there are no controls; we're all at the whim of someone else.

But I can tell you this, having spent time on the staff of a major book review: paperbacks have a hard time getting reviewed because advertising departments don't think their advertisers appeal to mass market readers. It does not have anything to do with the amount of advertising a publisher takes in the review section; it has everything to do with the paper's perception of itself. Couple that with the attitude you might expect to find in someone editing an "arts" section, and with the notion that paperbacks are somehow less than books, and you'll understand the situation. There's nothing to approve of; it's tacky and nasty and pretty awful. But it's out there and, at the very least, if we know the enemy, it can't sneak up behind us as easily.

It's not only mass market books that suffer: genre reviews are not usually a regular part of a review section. Most major papers will do mystery reviews a couple of times a month, science-fiction once a month, children's books now and then, but that's it. (The category writer who has transcended genre is reviewed as fiction.) There's nothing we can do about that, either.

Promotion costs, and it's point of sale: Is there a special display box or carton near the cash register at your bookstore, maybe holding five or six copies of a book? The box is a promotional item; and the space on which it's displayed is paid for: no retailer displays something unless there's a profit to be made and if you want some extra real estate in his store, you're going to pay for it. The payment is in the form of incentives: put up the display, and we'll send you two extra copies of the book, free. Take something else, we'll raise your discount another point. Whatever the formula (and sales managers spend a lot of time coming up with new, ever more attractive ones), there's a *quid pro quo* involved.

One of the most obvious and common of the promotional tools is a dump, one of those large display stands, often with the publisher's name on it, sometimes with a riser, a piece of cardboard with art or other sales hype. Publishers also have generic dumps: the box without the riser, just its own name; they're a little less expensive and, if it's decided to do a riser, the boxes are already in stock.

As with the counter pack, the publisher pays for the space on which the dump stands, through discounts and incentives. They give the publisher that many more copies in the store, allow for backlist titles to be displayed along with a new one (most often in paperback), and give the publisher and the title a presence in the store.

Publishers can offer as many displays as they can create; they can't do anything to force someone to take one: the bookseller knows what's going to work for him and two free copies of a book that won't be sold may not be incentive enough; if another publisher is offering a display of a potentially more popular title, well . . . (That's why scheduling is so important. You don't ever want to compete with yourself; if you can avoid going one-on-one with John Grisham, you'll do that. It's just like tv programming: if there's a big football game scheduled, you slot something to appeal to women. And don't give me a hard time about women liking football, too.)

Bookmarks, bags imprinted with the title of your book, book-
lets with a chapter from an upcoming book, those are all examples
of promotional items, some of which may work (if nothing else,
they let people know about your book); what no one can do is guarantee that the bookseller will use these items, or for how long.

Advertising is, well, advertising. We see book ads all the time:
some are for books we never hear of again; others are for books that
don't seem to need it (Stephen King, again). Ads do let casual readers know that an old favorite is back, and they may inform a reader that something of interest has been released; that usually works
best for non-fiction titles. Most of the people I know and have spoken to at conferences are more likely to buy a book because of a
review or a favorable comment than because of an advertisement.

If there is an advertising budget, the money has to be spent
wisely. Would you rather have your novel advertised in the *Times
Book Review* (where the budget may allow for one small, very
small, ad), or get a series of ads in journals where your name or
what you've written may make a difference? That's where local
newspapers play a role and, especially in category fiction, where the
fanzines are important. Some well-placed ads will, at least, guarantee that readers interested in you will have the opportunity to know
you and your work exist. That doesn't mean they'll buy it, but at
least they were targeted.

The rule of thumb used to be that advertising dollars equaled
copies printed; if you're getting a 5,000 copy first printing, an ad
budget in the same amount is virtually worthless. And, no, we
won't add 20,000 copies to the print order because the ad isn't
going to sell those copies.

One of the things you might be asked to do at the time that
you sign your contract is to fill out a biographical notes form. There
are lots of boring questions on it, but there are a few important
ones: do you have any contacts with local media (which is where
we have the best chance of getting attention for you), former

schools, favorite bookstores—each of them offers an opportunity for us to exploit you, to get you publicity. Using the information you supply, the publicist will get in touch with the people who might be interested in you or your book; if you live in a small town, one in which the newspaper might not be on our galley list, we'll be sure someone there gets a copy of the book. (You've seen the cost of books, now, so you can understand why we might not normally send them to places that don't usually review; but you're a potential feature story: LOCAL BOY MAKES GOOD.)

The publicity people also see to it that catalogues get into the hands of people who make decisions: bookstore owners, book reviewers, fan magazines, whoever we think may be interested in our product.   If we know that there's someone in your town who might be interested, we'll send one to him, too.

The catalogue is prepared in time for sales conference, so that the reps have it; again, the copy is either generated by copywriters or by the editors, then everything is laid out by the publicity department, often leading to the same complications we saw with the cover: too much copy, too little copy, do it over. Most catalogue copy is very light on plot; you'll learn why when we go to a sales conference and out on the road with a rep.

The decision as to whether a book gets a full page in the catalogue is another one of those that comes from your placement on the list: leads get more attention, they generally have more past reviews and may require more hype to sell because more is expected of them. None of those positioning decisions are made lightly and first novels can get the attention if there's a sense (because of the writing, because of in-house enthusiasm) that something can happen. The bookseller and reviewer see the attention being paid, they (we hope) pay more attention.

And so it goes. Does that mean that if you don't get a full page you're being discounted, ignored, written off? Not at all. Again, we know what a new mystery is going to do and what a regency romance will do. It all goes back to the question I asked you to answer earlier: why your book rather than another one? The books that get the attention are the ones that stand out somehow, that show a special promise beyond usual expectation, either because of what they are or because of what you've done.

This isn't a bad time to remind you of something, and I'll use the mystery genre for my examples because it's the one I watch most closely: Robert B. Parker, Tony Hillerman, Sara Paretsky, Sue Grafton, Julie Smith, James Lee Burke and Elmore Leonard are all well-known bestselling authors . . . today. None of them received any special attention when they began. Leonard had been writing since 1951 before *Glitz* became his first novel to hit the lists in the '80s.

The Alienist, Bridges of Madison County, Snow Falling on Cedars, Smilla's Sense of Snow and *Midnight in the Garden of Good and Evil* are only some of the recent titles of books that were published with no special expectations or support.

Today, the authors are established, have earned a special position in contemporary popular literature by virtue of having produced work that exceeded all hopes (except, perhaps, the writers'). It wasn't publicity that made them who and what they are: it was the writing. It was the writing that got them the first attention of an agent and/or an editor, that got them a place on the list (and a half page in the catalogue). The rest happened because they wrote books that spoke to the readers. And that, without exception, is the best and most valuable publicity, promotion and advertising you can get . . . especially if you want to last, rather than just be a shooting star.

Marketing
Sales

everything we've done to this point has had one purpose: to get a product ready for the sales department to run with. The editing and copyediting were done to prepare a product that a market would want and enjoy. The art was designed, and copy written, to attract, engage, and compel both the buyer for a bookstore and the ultimate consumer to buy the product. The efforts thus far of the people in marketing, the folks doing the publicity, promotion and advertising (and those efforts will continue until and after the book is on the shelves) had and will have as their goal focusing the attention of those buyers. With all of that done, it's time for the sales director and reps to do their jobs: selling the book to the bookstores.

And to some places that aren't bookstores. Let's take a look:

There are two people an editor (at a hardcover house) may turn to for support when considering an acquisition: the sub rights director, who'll offer an opinion as to the odds on selling the book to book clubs and a reprint house, and the sales manager, who will have a good sense of how particular books are selling, what the current figures are (and the return and reorder rates), and other intelligence about the marketplace. He may tell the editor that something's a difficult sell right now because the market is glutted, or that he's being told that certain settings or kinds of book are doing well or poorly, he may even have some insight into reactions to particular cover art, and will share that information so that the art director's job isn't made more difficult. (Good editors—those who are paying attention beyond the world of their own desks—usually know most of this; still, by involving the sales director from the beginning, his enthusiasm may be heightened. And it's just plain good office politics: it's not that he'll let a book fall between the cracks—the sales department has a budget to meet, just as all the others do—but having him on your side never hurts.)

The sales effort begins at the sales conference, a meeting with all of the company's sales representatives. Many companies, especially the larger ones, have their own force to go out on the road; if it publishes both hardcover and mass market titles it could have several: one to deal with rack jobbers and wholesalers for paperback, another to deal with direct hardcover accounts and distributors. Some companies also become distributors or representatives for other, smaller houses.

Houses that don't have their own sales force either sign agreements with the larger firms or use commission reps: groups of sales people that represent several publishers in their territories. (Each group works a part of the country; the publishers hire four or five of them to make sure that no part of the nation is left uncovered. There are also national rep groups, like Publishers Group West; its staff works everywhere for its client publishers.)

Back in the '70s and '80s, sales conferences were great parties. Held at resort hotels, the sales force, editors, marketing people and whoever else the publisher invited would spend a week presenting the titles to the reps, showing slides of covers, and giving the editors an opportunity to meet the salespeople, answer their questions and build relationships that were useful to both.

Today, most of the conferences are held in places like New York and New Jersey, are much shorter (which means more intense) and don't allow for as much personal interaction. Sometimes, particularly if presentations are being made to several rep groups, the editors (or publisher's representative) present the same books two or three times. They make certain they don't get bored because the reps are being bombarded with information, being told of possibly hundreds of books, and toward the end of a conference, no matter how good the intentions, everyone is tired and the reps close to being overwhelmed.

The job still gets done.

The sales force isn't interested in what the books (well, the novels) are about, they're not interested in plots or storylines. They want to know if it is part of a series, they want to know where it's set and where the author lives (ideally, the same place), the author's past performance and they want a one line keynote, something they can use when they're presenting the book to their account.

The material they receive includes catalogues, tip sheets (a listing of the important information, a capsule synopsis of the book, reviews and sales figures of previous titles, and sales handles: single line entries that can be used to pitch a book. These may include awards won, the fact that you have your own tv show, whatever helps show that your book stands a competitive chance), covers, galleys of key titles and—for picture books—samples of the artwork included.

The temptation faced by most editors the first time they present is to wax eloquent and rhapsodize about a favorite book or, even more harmful, all the books they're discussing. We learn quickly that that's a good way to lose the audience. While everyone is fresh when the conference begins, if the reps are hearing about several hundred titles in only a day or two, it's impossible for them to absorb everything.

Talking about each book as if it were the best thing ever written is also an act of futility: they're not going to believe the editors and while they may pick up on someone's excitement about one title, if the book doesn't live up to expectations (or the editor's hype), they're going to be wary the next time.

If you're invited to speak at a sales conference (and writers sometimes are, though not as frequently as they once were), be sparkling, talk about how excited you are, thank them in advance for their support, tell them a little about the book, smile, sit down, and drink some of that coffee cooling in the cup in front of you.

It's a bit different for non-fiction writers: talking about how you deciphered the Dead Sea Scrolls, about the threats you received after turning state's evidence, or how you uncovered a major scandal. It's interesting and may provide sales handles.

The reps ask questions about sales or special interests, looking for the details they think will help and that we didn't think of providing. They may also tell us that in their territory a particular kind of book isn't selling and ask if we know any way around the problem; it could be a packaging solution or taking a different tack on the cover copy.

They'll be told how many copies we want them to sell in their area, and we'll warn them if we think certain accounts should or most definitely shouldn't be skipped on a given title. (Again, that's usually in terms of non-fiction.)

The reps will also be provided with the various incentive plans and discounts and other financial bonuses like co-op advertising (if the bookstore has a signing and advertises it, the publisher may kick some money in to defray some of the expense) being offered to booksellers, based on size of order or amount of returns—anything we've been able to think of to get books out there and keep them out: I've worked for companies that have offered prizes for the best window display of a specific title.

Then the reps either go home (or to another meeting) and begin the drive through their territories, calling on accounts. The editors and others at the meeting return to the office to get ready to start the process again for the next season. They also correct problems that have been pointed out. For example, at one sales meeting I attended, we were told that swastikas and the hammer and sickle emblems on books (these were paperbacks) were no longer working, as evidenced by high returns even on otherwise good selling authors. Flags were also being returned. And we had dozens of covers like that because that was what had been working. It meant going back and doing new covers, at least for those books far enough down the schedule that there was still time.

We might also have to reschedule a title because we learn that a particularly strong novel is being released in the same month by another house and because the two books are similar, ours is going to suffer. Do we go out earlier? Later? Let's have a meeting . . .

And before the reps make their first call, let's talk about print orders. I know you've seen ads that talk about 100,000 copy first printings, or have talked to writers who were disappointed because they were told that there was going to be a 15,000 copy printing and only 7,500 were done. Except in the case of a brand-name author, those print figures are targets. When the reps are told we want them to sell a certain number of copies, the plan is to get sufficient orders that we can print as many as we promised. If those figures don't come in, though, the printing is reduced. (We'll talk about the impact of jobbers and distributors in a bit.) Publishers cannot afford to overprint; inventory warehousing is very expensive and because of the Thor Machine Tool ruling, after which inventory couldn't be amortized, overstock became a huge drain on a publisher's resources. Selling those remainders also costs money; it's wiser to print conservatively and go back to press as necessary, and that's the way it's being done today.

Each publisher uses its own formula, based on sales history, but in addition to looking at what the independent bookstores are ordering, we also look at the figures from chains like Barnes & Noble and distributors like Ingram and use their figures to estimate what we might need. Ingram, for one house, might represent ten percent of what they usually sell, so if the Ingram order is for 1,000 copies, the publisher is confident that 10,000 copies might be enough for the first print. (If they'd taken 10,000, that 100,000 copy first printing would have been viable.)

What are you doing while all of this is going on? You've checked your page proofs and sent them back, you've discussed your next book with your editor and begun to work on it, and you've been talking your book up wherever possible. If you're on-line and have a web page, you may have posted a chapter of the book and mentioned the release date. If you go to chat rooms or post to a newslist or bulletin board, you've directed people to your web site and added publication information to you signature.

You have been in touch with the managers of local bookstores, telling them about the book, looking into the possibility of a party once the book arrives or, at least, arranged to go in and sign stock. And you've coordinated these activities with the publicist, letting her know what you've done and, if necessary, asking for help: could you send three copies of the cover to this store for a display, could you send me one so that I can use it to make a postcard that I'm going to mail to all my friends (and those who refused to be; revenge is a dish best served cold).

Publicity budgets aren't what they used to be; I doubt that they were ever what we think they used to be. The gala publication party thrown by publishers are pretty much a thing of the past; they happen for the stars and newsworthy, not for the rest of us. (And they don't sell books.) Tours usually aren't cost effective; rarely are enough copies of the book sold to meet the expense of the tour. (There's nothing sadder than a signing to which only three or four people come; the value of those events is in meeting the bookstore owners and, if you impress them sufficiently, having them pay closer attention to your book, perhaps hand selling it, recommending it to their customers.)

Most publishers will, however, help you if you're doing these things on your own (and most of us will be doing them on our own): we'll see to it that a bookstore knows you're coming and make sure they have copies, we might pick up some part of the expense. But that's about all, so keep the fantasy on a short leash; don't give it up, just don't let it run away with you.

And keep working on that next book.

⇒　✎　⇒

When I was in mass market publishing, I used to go out on a sell trip at least once a year. Of course, I was also at a house that had its own sales force, so it was easy. The reps who are selling a publisher's list on commission aren't quite as happy about squiring an editor around. Actually, I don't think the reps I went out with were particularly thrilled, either: no one likes to have someone looking over their shoulder as they go about their job.

I could never be a sales rep.

What's a rep's life on the road like? It starts early, ends late, and is filled with . . .

Okay, let's begin here: The rep, Lee, is calling on a general, independent account, PageBoy, a bookstore that tries to sell "everything"; well, everything that the manager/buyer/owner thinks her customers want to read; we have to trust the merchant to know.

An appointment has been made; whether it will be kept as scheduled is anyone's guess: a salesperson from another house may be there and take a bit more time than expected (or maybe started late because of the rep before him).

Over breakfast, or lunch, or at a roadside stop, Lee's looked at PageBoy's figures for the last season: what they bought, what they reordered, what they returned, what incentives they participated in: Lee's looking for clues as to what to pitch harder, what to soft-pedal. No book is going to be ignored: Lee's income depends on commissions and commissions result from selling books. Returns from an account, however, are deducted from Lee's check, just as they are from the author's. So, if Lee knows that PageBoy cannot sell New Age self-help effectively, she's not going to insist the store take ten copies. Because those figures show that the store sells cookbooks particularly well, the cookbook on the list will get a bit more attention during the presentation.

What follows now is much the same, no matter what type of account (and there are many) is being called upon. There are variations, sure, but one thing remains paramount: the buyer cannot be sold; offers can be made, some cajoling take place, but in almost every case, the person buying the books already knows what he wants (he may have seen galleys, he's certainly received the catalogue; we can only hope he's read it).

Our visit is to an independent bookstore—a place like Denver's Tattered Cover or New York's Coliseum or a specialty store: The Mysterious Bookshop in Manhattan or Once Upon a Crime in Minneapolis. (There's a specialty store for just about any interest.)

The call could be made, however, to the home office of one of the chains: Borders (about 220, nationwide, as of this writing), Barnes & Noble (500), Waldenbooks (900, mostly in malls), Dalton (700, also in malls) and Hastings (150) are among the leaders. You've heard a lot about the chains, about how they're driving independents out of business, about how the staff doesn't know anything (or care anything about books) and about how they're (especially the bigger ones) beginning to dictate what publisher's publish.

There's a certain amount of truth to the horror stories. It's hard for a small, independent bookstore, one that catered to a carriage trade up until now to compete: they can't order in sufficient quantity to get the higher discount, which means they can't sell at a discount; on the other hand, they offer a personal service the chains can't begin to compete with; they know their customers, know Susan's tastes and can recommend a book to her the minute she walks through the door, and they do seem to be much more amenable to special ordering—getting the book you want if they don't have it in stock.

Specialty stores have it a bit easier; the chains can't carry an extensive backlist (no one can; as I mentioned earlier, there are only so many feet of shelf space and a store will only carry what sells) in say, mystery. Poisoned Pen can because they don't have to carry everything else. So, the mystery reader, looking for earlier works by someone they've just discovered, will go to the specialty shop rather than the Waldenbooks at the mall.

What the chains have done, and what is often ignored when talking about them, is bring books to areas that haven't had many (or any) bookstores. Sure, they may choose a location near an established retailer; they know there are customers there and they're going to make it difficult to compete. But that's business and as nice as it is to think that there's something special and holy about books, they're a product and if someone wants to make money selling a product they're going where the customers are.

Although the chains do hold signings and readings, the independent store is more likely to—it's a way of bringing readers in. At the same time, if a chain is supporting a title, for whatever reason, they're going to order more copies and that means the display will be larger and the larger display attracts the consumer's eye, increasing the chances of selling copies.

Do the chains dictate what we're going to publish? Perhaps. It is not unheard of for a sales director (the chains are usually serviced by in-house personnel, regardless of how the rest of the industry is sold) to call and ask the B&N buyer how much support will be received for a certain book. But that isn't the case with general fiction or category entries (we already know—been there, done that—

what they're going to take of a first novel or the latest entry in a series); it applies usually to big budget items or books that may not have a long shelf life, something tied into today's news, for instance. (I'd give an example, but by the time you read this, it probably won't be news and we'll have forgotten all about it.) The influence of the chains in those cases really doesn't have any impact on what's happening to the rest of us, and the money spent on those big books won't destroy your chances of getting acquired: we need the big seller to support the rest of the list and blockbusters are important because they bring people into the bookstore. Some of them may only buy the hot ticket, but enough will continue to browse, even if the book they want is displayed right up front.

How important is that display space in terms of business? Consider this: how many bookstores (of any kind) have you been in that have had book bags or CDs or Beanie Babies or magnets or greeting cards or other non-book (though book related) items on display? The money they generate more than makes up for the lost book display, in the store manager's mind.

Remember, too: bookseller feedback has always been a part of the business; I'll call certain independent booksellers to ask them about the sales of an author I may be romancing, or about a particular subgenre or "new" idea. (They're a much more important source of information for genre titles than the chains will be because they don't only look at sales figures, but have talked to the customers and have good feel for the pulse of the targeted readers.)

And for both the chains and the independent, display space costs money; if they're devoting a table to a book, it's because they think they can sell it. They're not going to devote that real estate to something they don't believe in.

There's something about our psyche that makes us to want to gang up on the big guy, the one perceived as a bully, and that's what's happened with the chains. Like them or not, they're important and they're not going away and they do carry a lot of books.

Distributors (also serviced by the home office) have as much influence as the chains; if Baker & Taylor or Ingram gets behind a book, it's going to help a lot. They don't really "sell" books, but they can and will, when one of their accounts calls to reorder, ask if they have enough of copies of whatever they're behind and suggest reordering *now* because copies are moving out of the warehouse very quickly.

They're also among the major suppliers for almost all bookstores and libraries in the country. Discounts are dictated by quantity; if a bookstore needs only one or two copies of a title (or books from a specific publisher), they're not going to get a discount. But they can order those two books, and five of something else, and gang it with three of another, and get the quantity discount from the distributor. They'll also get the books much more quickly, because the national distributors have warehouses all over the country, and there are regional distributors as well; where it may take a week or two to get books from the publisher, it might take only two days from the distributor.

(There's also the unfortunate instance of a bookstore being "on hold," not being shipped because they've not paid their bills for a while; publishers won't sell to them—no surprise—but they do keep their accounts current with the distributors, so they can keep up with customer demand.)

Baker & Taylor and Brodart specialize in library sales; again, for the libraries it is a far more cost effective way of ordering. And they offer another service, called "Brodarting" because that company led the way. The library distributors will put the Mylar protectors on the books before shipping, as well as taking care of the card pockets, Dewey Decimal tags, and stamps. When the books arrive, they're library ready. Even with the additional charge for the service, in these days of library budget cutbacks, it's an important and cost effective service and something the publisher could not do.

Brodart offers something called the McNaughton Plan, and if a book gets taken for it, it's usually an indication that the title has nice potential. The plan is, ultimately, a lend-lease operation for libraries. Brodart takes six or seven hundred copies of a book and leases them to libraries that might not be able to afford adding the book on a permanent basis.

McNaughton books also help fill demand. A library may have taken three copies of something, but their customers are creating wait lists to read it; the library can "borrow" extra copies of the book from the plan. Then, after a specified period, the books are returned to Brodart and show up on remainder or sale tables as *ex-lib* copies.

Mass market titles are sold to the direct accounts and the chains and the distributors just as hardcovers are, and are sold to rack jobbers (or wholesalers) as well, for non-traditional accounts: K-mart, news stands, supermarkets, airport gift shops, all those places where you find books alongside L'eggs, chewing gum, and the platoon-size box of Cheerios. The paperback houses use their orders to estimate print runs, as well: the major accounts represent a certain percentage of total sales, and a wholesaler's figure can be multiplied to arrive at a number.

The business is based on magazine distribution; most of the rack jobbers also sell magazines, and the places the books are finally displayed have no say in what's being put on the racks and spinners and shelves; that's the wholesaler's job. And that's also where it starts getting tricky.

While it's not a stated policy, most rack jobbers allocate the pockets (since the accounts they service invariably use pockets rather than shelving) they control according to the percentage of business each mass market house represents. In short, if Power House represents 10% of the wholesaler's business, and there are a hundred pockets, ten of them will have PowerHouse product. That has several ramifications.

If a book is very thick, fewer copies fit in each pocket. Will PowerHouse lose pockets because two or three have to be given over to the massive volume? Not always. The publisher will offer a special incentive, force the extra space so that the two or three pockets that might be lost are kept and a smaller publisher will lose space. The next month, PowerHouse makes a case for keeping those extra pockets (because the blockbuster busted out) and the landgrab is complete . . . until another publisher comes along with something special. In cases like that the dimensions are not the only factor, and it's one of the reasons some reprints command prices in auction that might not otherwise make sense—if the book is deemed marketable enough, "important" enough in terms of potential sale, the wholesaler has to give it the display space. After all, it'll sell more copies, making the return on the space investment more lucrative.

It's at that point that mass market publishing, especially, becomes a game of Monopoly: it's about controlling as much real estate as possible.

The rack jobbers control things in another way; they create bestseller lists. You've noticed displays (in the non-traditional out-lets) that have the paperbacks displayed according to position on a list. What we generally aren't aware of is that the positioning appears at the same time as the books do; how can it be a bestseller if it hasn't had a chance to sell? By fiat and decree.

The wholesaler has taken what are called "bestseller" numbers, quantities of a title that demand the buying public pay attention (if it's a bestseller you're going to buy it, right? Well, that's the theory); it's a bestseller because someone says so. (The displays based on national bestseller lists are more straightforward; the books are put out according to the list in the *Times*, or *USA Today*, or *Publishers Weekly*. Those lists are, by the way, honest; with the advent of computerized figures, it's easy to know exactly what is selling and in what quantities.)

Why has the wholesaler done this? Sometimes it's because the ranking is a given: Mary Higgins Clark is going to be a bestseller and there's no reason not to support the title. Sometimes it's because of hype: we've paid a fortune for this book, we're really going to get behind it, it's going to be a hardcover bestseller first—and if you take a gazillion copies, we'll give you a billion free. (Those free books may eventually be displayed and sold; they may also sit in the warehouse and be returned. The only risk a bookseller of any kind takes in ordering a large number of copies is in having to find the place to store them. Books are sold on consignment and fully returnable, either as full copy hardcover returns or as paperback "stripped" covers, with the books themselves recycled. When you buy paperbacks being sold for a quarter, without covers, you are an accessory after the fact in a robbery. The publishers have had the book stolen from them, the author has lost royalties.)

The displays of the books, if not being dictated by the wholesaler servicing a rack, are the work of one of the most important people in the field of paperback distribution: a truck driver, the person who loads up a truck in the morning, drives around to accounts, and takes some books away and puts new ones out. If she doesn't like a cover, if his wife liked a book, if you've gone out to the warehouse at five in the morning with a box of doughnuts and coffee for the drivers, or if the boss has said, "that one" . . . whatever it is, it has little to do with anything but numbers and profit and someone's taste or someone owing someone else.

That also affects returns, the infamous short shelf life of paperback books. How long should a book be displayed? (And that includes hardcovers.) How long do you take up space that might be used by something that's selling better, or could if it were displayed? Shelf space has to pay for itself; if it isn't turning a profit, something else has to go there.

The truck drivers calling on accounts know how many books were put in a pocket; when they come back the next day or the next week, whatever the route timing is, if something hasn't moved, but something else has, the deadwood will go back onto the truck and copies of what is selling will come off.

Your publisher can do very little, if anything at all, about it.

And they can't do anything about the on-line booksellers; we don't "sell" to amazon.com or Barnes&Noble.com or Borders or any of the other cyberspace bookstores.

These operations are, essentially, mail order catalogues with unlimited pages and infinite shelf space. A hardcopy catalogue can sell only what the issuing company knows it can sell; pages cost money. For the on-line operations, the volume exists because it can and they don't have to have something in stock; special orders are their business.

Their databases, the available titles, are simple enough to construct: they just take *Books in Print* and list every title that every publisher still has in stock; each season they add the titles from the new catalogues, and you have access to just about everything between covers.

They don't have serious warehousing problems, either: while they stock current and major backlist bestsellers, if you order something they don't have, they put in a call to Ingram or some other distributor (getting a high discount because they're ordering lots of books and simplifying accounting because they have only one bill), get the book the next day, and ship it out to the consumer. There are other sales outlets, not as well-known: school and other book fairs and price club operations. Some of them are serviced by reps (some of whom specialize in book fairs), others order directly from the publisher. The majority of the publishers have telephone sales departments; while they will service single-copy consumer orders (something they'd just as soon not do because of the expense, but no one's going to turn down a sale), they're in place to take orders from any account that needs books. Some fill orders, some "sell": they'll call accounts to make sure there are enough copies of a fast moving title in stock or, when someone orders, will ask about stock on other titles. The depth of that department, and how they approach the job—as sales reps or order takers—depends on the publisher's needs. Some houses won't deal with anyone when it comes to orders; every call or query is directed to a distributor, and they concentrate their efforts (and their money) only on acquisition and production of new titles.

Those are the markets; here's what happens when a rep calls on one.

Armed with information about the books, authors, and the store's sales history, the rep arrives and hopes that the buyer is available, and that there'll be a quiet place in which to talk. Unfortunately, that isn't always the case: if someone's out sick or if the store is very small, the presentation may be made at the checkout counter while the buyer is also fielding calls from, or ringing up sales to a customer.

If you remember the sales conference, you'll remember the emphasis that was placed on a keynote line and facts about the author (and previous books). That's all the bookseller wants to know.

So, the rep shows the buyer the cover, mentions that the author lives around the corner and down the block or that the book's set in the park across town, acknowledges the kind of book it may be, mentions sales history, and gets the order. For most of the books on the list, the rep has about thirty seconds to make the pitch. (And Lee is going to try to keep control of the display book in which the covers are stacked; if the buyer gets his hands on it, the pages may turn even more quickly.)

It isn't as much of a disaster as you might think: if the buyer knows his job, he'll have already gone through the catalogue, read galleys, and thus will have an idea of what he wants to do.

While the direct (independent) account knows his customers, and what sells in the store, the buyer for the chains and distributors also have sales information, based on corporate figures. Using those, the buyer knows how many copies may be needed nationally and also what each outlet or warehouse might need. They'll listen to special pitches or pleas and, if they've worked in the past, be amenable to new ones. But if they've gone high on something that didn't work yesterday, they're not going to listen too seriously the next time.

What all the accounts want to know is: "What deal are you giving me?" Can titles be mixed for discount, is there co-op money available, will the author be available for a signing? Getting the answers, the order is placed . . . and at the independents, the request for a return label is made.

While bookseller returns are a part of the business, they can't be made on a whim; the book has to have (in hardcover) resale value; certain titles or quantities may be restricted—again, this varies from publisher to publisher. The given is that books will come back. The returns label indicates to the publisher that what's in the box was approved by a sales rep. (Another incentive: paperback reps have been known to have extra copies of a cover that they'll leave with a bookseller; an accepted cost of doing business.) The returns are credited to the bookseller's account, deducted from your royalty statement (or the reserve against returns), and the order is transmitted to the home office.

A good rep might, at that time (or earlier, while waiting for the buyer's attention) check stock—on the shelves, in the warehouse or storeroom, may even "dress the racks," turning his product face out, or moving books around so that they're better displayed.

Then it's back into the car and off to the next call. If a bookseller has imparted useful information (just can't sell that these days) we'll hear about it; if he says that something or someone is doing particularly (and surprisingly) well, we'll hear about that. A good sales rep knows how to listen to what the customer is saying. And the editors hear about it; that's one of the reasons the question so often posed to editors—"What are you looking for?"—is so difficult to answer. It can change overnight.

For the moment, however, what we're looking for is your book to do well; the sell trip over, the orders in, the print figure set (and by now we also have the prepub reviews—they usually appear three months before publication date—and have some idea of what reaction to the book is going to be out in the world), the process is coming toward its end.

Pub Date
and Beyond

finished the material you're going to submit for your next work yet? Good; at least it's kept your mind off everything else that's been going on. But with that material in your agent's or editor's hands, it's time to start paying attention again.

Publication dates are pretty much arbitrary, at least in terms of the exact date. It makes a difference when the big books are hitting: they'll arrive in a carton that says DO NOT SELL BEFORE X/X/X. The idea is to give everyone an equal chance and since books travel across country by plane, train and automobile, they're not going to arrive on the same day everywhere; by fixing the on-sale date, it guarantees that no store will have a jump on another; that's a rule that's pretty strictly enforced.

For the rest of the books, though, the ones where demand isn't going to be quite as high, it doesn't matter quite as much and the books go on the shelves . . . well, not necessarily the day they arrive.

When the finished book comes off-press, copies are sent to the publisher's offices, where they are checked and "released." Not every copy is examined; that would be impossible. And that means that sometimes copies with missing or repeated signatures get into the stores; there's nothing that can be done about that, unfortunately, but any bookstore or publisher will replace damaged copies. It's also possible that the book will come off press and only then will we realize that there's a typo on the title page, or a name's been misspelled on the cover—it's not a perfect system and all you can (or should) do when you find problems like those is let your editor know; if there are subsequent printings, we'll take care of them at that time.

Once the books are printed, they're shipped from the plant to our warehouse, from the warehouse to the distributor's or chain's warehouse, and from there to each account. Direct orders ship directly from us to the bookseller. None of which guarantees that the book will be on the shelf when you walk in on pub date, ready to point the copies out to friends and neighbors. Books can, and do, sit on loading docks and storerooms until someone has time to check the order, process it, and move the books out onto the floor. If there's transshipping involved, the delay can be that much longer. Don't panic; most stores can tell you if something has, at least, arrived, if it's on order, some idea of the status of the shipment.

Another word of warning, another aspect of the dark side of the business: you (or your friends) will be looking for your book and a store will say they don't have it, or they've never heard of it, or they can't get it. Before you call out the minions of hell upon the heads of everyone at your publisher, just call your editor and tell her the name of the store, the date you were there, what was said, and by whom. We can't do anything without that information.

I've mentioned stores that may be on hold because they haven't paid: that could be why they don't have the book but they're not going to tell you that. It may be on order but they're waiting for the book to come from a distributor and a clerk may be unaware of that. The idea that they can't get a book is absurd; credit record aside, no publisher is going to refuse to make a sale. If they're one of the houses that don't do any order fulfillment, they'll give the store owner the name of the distributor who carries their line and, too, orders can be placed with any of the national or regional distributors. The book is available; the store hasn't done its job.

It's also possible that the owner decided not to buy your book, for any number of reasons; as you've seen, copies can't be forced into the market. A good bookseller will, though, special order for you, combining that one copy with his next order to the distributor. If they won't do that, do you want to do business with them?

So, make a note: when they say they don't have the book, don't know the book, or can't get the book, get the pertinent information and your editor will follow up.

If you've done as I suggested and cultivated a local bookseller, now's the time to start planning a signing at her store—now, once the books are there. Scheduling something before they arrive can be frustrating and since shipping is an iffy proposition, you want to make sure that anything you plan takes that into consideration. If you've jumped the gun, and books aren't there, call your editor. We may not be able to tell you when the books are going to arrive, but we can arrange to drop ship from the warehouse (if timing's that crucial) or see to it that copies are rushed to the bookseller. You don't want to do that often, but in emergency cases, someone is going to take care of you.

A signing at your local store can be an enormous success; signings on the road can be a disaster. I've sat in major bookstores with bestselling writers and waited and waited and waited. Stephen Greenleaf tells a story about a signing that was done at a local department store. After two hours, the author signed one copy of his book . . . and it was stolen. Keep in mind, then, that the primary importance of a signing is to establish relationships with booksellers so that they'll get behind you.

Authors are resorting to lots of gimmicks to promote themselves; many of them have learned the tricks from a booklet prepared by Sisters in Crime. While they've done a lot to increase writers' awareness of what can be done in the way of brazen self-promotion,

I think the jury's still out on the overall effectiveness of the attempts. There are a number of books available today with suggested promotion and publicity approaches; it can't hurt to look at them and see what might work for you.

If you're going to try to do something, however, do check in with your publicist. There are some companies that don't seem to be very supportive of authors' efforts; I don't know why, I don't pretend to understand it. It's just the way it is. Other companies, though, will offer you some kind of support: mailings, art, covers, whatever they can do. If they know what you're planning, they will also be in a position to make suggestions and to coordinate certain efforts. The publisher may know of a bookstore in a town you're planning to visit and can help set something up there and see to it that books are available. We may have a local media contact. The possibilities are endless, but if you go charging off on your own, I can guarantee that we won't be able to do anything for you. At Walker, when one of my writers shows up in town, the publicist arranges to spend the afternoon with him, taking him to the local mystery specialty shops, arranging for him to sign stock, meet the bookseller, touch all the bases.

And use common sense: Don't "drop in" on a wholesaler or distributor and don't call them, trying to push your book. Everyone resents it and it can, ultimately, backfire. If you do want to do a morning coffee with the drivers, talk to your editor and let her work with the sales department to make it happen. Keep in mind that the distributors and wholesalers and jobbers are middlemen, filling orders on demand. They are not sales organizations, though some will, if the publisher pays them enough, direct the people taking orders to mention your book. (If the book's selling well enough on its own, they'll do that anyway.) What you do when you call on these people without your publisher's support is step on toes.

With the bound books in stock, the publicity department begins the second round of review submissions. By the time the book gets in the hands of the reviewer, it should be approaching the shelves; we try to get the books off press at least a month before the announced pub date. Certain papers won't be timely; others will: the review will be based on the uncorrected galley and the finished copy allows the reviewer to check the review against the finished book.

As reviews come in, they'll be forwarded to you; if you don't want to see the bad ones, let your editor know. I think you should see the negatives: it's always possible that what's said is something you (and the editor) needs to hear. I read them all; if certain complaints crop up again and again, it means that I have to be on the lookout for that problem in the next book . . . if I agree; there are times when, as a writer and an editor, I'd rather try something new rather than publish by rote. But it's always good to know what's on the minds of the people judging us, even if we don't agree.

With reviews and bound books, the sub rights director makes a renewed effort to sell whatever rights remain to be sold. Reprint editors are often far too cautious, waiting for the world to tell them what they should think. If they'd moved early, they might've gotten the book for less; with good reviews and that dynamite jacket, the price goes up. It's to our advantage.

Sometimes the rights don't sell. We'll stop making the effort after a while, but when your next book comes along, we have proof of your existence as an ongoing author, we have your sales history, and we can make a case for a two book deal. That's nice, too.

Sometimes the rights don't sell. All we can do, then—both of us together—is keep on keepin' on.

Your book isn't the only one the company's publishing and it's unreasonable to expect everything to come to a halt so that we can concentrate on you. Your editor, however, font of all wisdom, your best friend in court, is always there for you. Never hesitate to call or write; don't whine too much or too loudly (and keep in mind that the editor has a lot invested in your book, too; she wants it to work, she does care), but if there are problems or questions, don't hesitate for a moment to ask.

One of the questions you're probably going to ask at some point is, "You've sold out the first printing. Why won't you go back to press?"

We will, if there are sufficient orders and if there are no copies in the field. Just because we don't have any in the warehouse doesn't mean the book's ceased to exist. Just because a book has been shipped it doesn't mean it's been sold. There are copies in the warehouses of the distributors, there are copies in the stores, and we don't know, at this point, whether they're coming back or how many will, or when. It isn't unheard of for a publisher to call one distributor, with a big stock and no discernible order activity, and ask for copies back so that they can be used to fulfill other orders.

Reprints are viable but only at certain levels; we can't afford, usually, to print the minimum 1,500 copies if the orders are dribbling in at two a week; all too often reprints are nothing more than instant remainders.

The sales department tracks orders and returns on a daily basis; if something is happening, if orders are coming in furiously and there are no returns and the distributors' stocks are dwindling, a reprint is in order. If we can sell more, we want to; if we can make you a favorite of all those people who sell books—meaning they'll want more of you next time—we'll do everything we reasonably can to ensure that it happens.

Reprints, like everything else in the publishing economy, are a matter of supply and demand; two people not being able to find a book isn't demand. And as with the bookseller who told you he couldn't get your book initially, don't blindly accept their word that the book's gone o.p. and they can't get it. (Actually, they may have returned it yesterday. Another fact of life: at the end of the month, with the bills coming in, bookstore owners will look at the shelves, figure out to whom they owe the most and which publisher is over-represented on their shelves, and make returns on that basis. If something's overstocked it means that it didn't sell according to expectations and the manager is comfortable return-ing it to the publisher.)

We want your book out there; that's why we bought it.

You should also follow up on your pre-pub publicity efforts, all those mailings and postings you did; now you let everyone know the book is available, remind them of who the publisher is. Go to con-ventions and conferences that might provide more networking opportunities. Be a presence, but not a nuisance. One writer with whom I've avoided working made such a pest of himself at book-stores (and reprinters offices!) trying to push his book that he was literally banned from entering many of them ever again. Funny, I haven't received many letters from readers or booksellers asking when his next book was coming out.

There comes a time when everything that can be done, every-thing that can be accomplished, has been (unless you've written a runaway bestseller; I just think it's better to keep calm and stay real. Most books don't do that); concentration will turn toward the next book being released. We're still tracking your sales, paying attention to what's going on, but, well, it's time to move on.

And you've moved on: your next book is delivered and the process is beginning again. We've got a leg up this time: you have a history, the world knows who you are and things are a little easier. In fact, everything's easier except this: you've got another book to write; all of a sudden, this little foray into the world of letters has turned into a career.

You may be courted by other publishers now, or your agent may decide it's time to move you up, try to get you more money (salary increases always seem to be connected with changing jobs; this is the same thing); that's all part of the process. No editor likes to lose a writer we've nurtured, a career we've started or support-ed, but it's something we live with. Just as you may have to live with the nightmare of your editor calling one day and saying, "Sorry, no more."

We don't like doing that either, both because of our relationships with the writers and because it means we were wrong.

That doesn't mean we were wrong about you, only that we were wrong about what we thought we could do with you. It's nothing personal and it isn't a comment about you or your work, only about our ability to make things happen the way we wanted to.

If you're a writer, you'll keep writing. If you're a good writer—good by any standard of measurement from literary light to commercial blaze—if you are telling stories people care about, you'll keep at it and keep your place secure.

Repeating something said earlier; the final words on the matter:

Stay confident and never say your work is good enough.

Keep the beginner's mind, always ready to learn, always welcoming the new—so that you can grow.

Keep the faith, keep writing; don't give up.

You are a writer; know thyself.

You are a writer; to thine own self be true.

New books are published every day; this one is yours.

There are literally hundreds of books, magazines, conferences, groups, and peer group organizations available to writers, and there are books, like Eileen Malone's *The Complete Guide to Writers Groups, Conferences, and Workshops* (Wiley) and *The AWP Official Guide to Writing Programs* (AWP & Dustbooks), not to mention all the information available online, to help you find your way.

Still, there are those resources I particularly enjoy, like, respect, admire and/or use, as well as the conferences and workshops in which I participate with some regularity and, therefore, feel comfortable recommending. That doesn't mean that any of the others are in any way less suitable to your needs, just that I don't know them well enough to speak with confidence about them; certainly, if there are those you've found useful, tell your friends about them . . . that's part of the networking that drives everything we do.

In this section, then, you'll find titles, names, and addresses (some of which might have changed since we went to press); as with any tool you're going to use, make sure what is being offered is what you need: look through the books, get in touch with organizers or group spokespeople and find out what they're doing and that you will be getting your money's worth: you're the only one who can make that judgment.

Books

These are the books I use most often, the ones that have taught me most of the valuable lessons I've needed; they're not all about writing, per se, but they all offer the insights any "young writer," as John Gardner called them, should have. Among the other books available are those that are genre specific, that deal with a particular aspect of writing (dialogue, setting, etc.), or that approach the subject from a philosophical standpoint. You'll choose the ones that suit your needs.

The Art of Fiction: Notes on Craft for Young Writers, John Gardner
  (Alfred A. Knopf)
On Becoming a Novelist, John Gardner (Perennial Library)
Mastering Fiction Writing, Kit Reed (Writer's Digest Books)
Story-crafting, Paul Darcy Boles (Writer's Digest Books)
Writing the Novel From Plot to Print, Lawrence Block (Writer's
  Digest Books)
Bird by Bird: Some Instructions on Writing and Life, Anne Lamott
  (Anchor Books)
Living by Fiction, Annie Dillard (Perennial Library)
A Dangerous Profession: A Book About the Writing Life,
  Frederick Busch (St. Martin's Press)
A History of Reading, Alberto Manguel (Viking)

Groups

Some of the groups listed here have eligibility requirements, others are open to all; if one of them seems right for you, get in touch and obtain the membership information. You may not be eligible today, but if you sell your book tomorrow, the situation may change.

American Crime Writers League
219 Tuxedo
San Antonio, TX 78209

American Society of Journalists
and Authors
1501 Broadway, Suite 1907
New York, New York 10036
(212) 997-0947

Associated Writing Programs
Old Dominion University
Norfolk, VA 23529-0079
(804) 683-3839

Authors Guild
330 West 42nd Street
New York, NY 10036
(212) 563-5904
email: authors@pipeline.com

International Association of
    Crime Writers, Inc. North
    American Branch,
JAF Box 1500
New York, NY 10116

Mystery Writers of America
17 East 47th Street (6th Floor)
New York, NY 10017
(212) 888-8171

National Writers Club, Inc.
1450 South Havana, Suite 620
Aurora, CO 80012
(303) 751-7844

National Writers Union, UAW,
    AFL-CIO
873 Broadway #203
New York, NY 10003
(212) 254-0279

Novelists, Inc.
Box 1166
Mission, KS 66222

Poets and Writers, Inc.
72 Spring Street
New York, NY 10012
(212) 226-3586

Private Eye Writers of America
4343 Forest DeVille Drive (H)
St. Louis, MO 63129

Romance Writers of America
13700 Veterans Memorial Drive,
Suite 315
Houston, TX 77014
(713) 440-6885

Science Fiction and Fantasy
Writers of America, Inc.
Five Winding Brook Drive, #1B
Guilderland, NY 12084
(518) 869-5361

Society of Children's Book Writers
22736 Vanowen Street, Suite 106
West Hills, CA 91307
(818) 888-8760

Western Writers of America
416 Bedford Road
El Paso, TX 79922-1204
(915) 584-1001

In addition to these groups, there are local writer's organizations every-where in the country. All offer support and critique, some sponsor confer-ences and workshops—and there are well over three hundred of those every year in the United States and Canada. Information about organizations in your area can generally be found at a public library or school, or in the two volumes I mentioned above.

Conferences and Workshops

By now you know that I think conferences and workshops should be part of every writer's schedule; picking the right one can be difficult until you've experienced one or two and begin to get a feel of how they work and what they offer. *Writer's Digest* magazine usually lists upcoming conferences in its May issue, and most sponsors announce their events in group newsletters and other publications that writers might be turning to for information. The list that follows is (relatively) small: I can't recommend conferences I haven't attended . . . or that I haven't enjoyed. That also means the list is highly per-sonal. It does not mean that other conferences are not worth your time or money, only that I can't speak about them. With that understood, then:

GREEN RIVER WRITERS NOVELS-IN-PROGRESS WORKSHOP is held in Louisville, Kentucky every March. Those interested in attending must sub-mit 60 pages of a novel in progress. People begin arriving on Sunday evening; classes begin on Monday and run for an entire week. Writers workshop and hone their sample with their teacher (always a published author) and can audit other sessions. Evenings are spent reading, critiquing or talking; there may also be exercises and other programs. On Saturday, a group of editors and agents are in attendance; there is a panel in the morning and after lunch writers have the opportunity to pitch the material they've been working on to the professionals.

For information: Green River Writers, 11906 Locust Road, Middle-town, KY 40243   (502) 245-4902

STONECOAST WRITERS CONFERENCE, mid- to late July in Brunswick, Maine, and run by the University of Southern Maine. This is another week-long workshop, and can be taken for college credit. Classes begin Saturday morning and run through the following Sunday; Wednesday is "intersession." Workshops are offered in the novel, short story, poetry, creative non-fiction, and genre fiction; samples must be submitted with your application. The classes are held only in the morning; after lunch there may be readings by faculty or guest authors, panels on publishing or writing matters, or free time. (There is an afternoon set aside for all interested attendees to read from their work.) Students often form their own critique groups that meet when and as they can. In the evenings, there are more readings by the faculty, and then time to write, rewrite, or hang out and talk.

For information: Stonecoast Writers Conference, University of Southern Maine, 96 Falmouth Street, Portland, ME 04103   (207) 780-4291

The following conferences are less workshop oriented; generally two or three days long (over a weekend), they consist of panels on a variety of topics and presentations on some aspect of writing or publishing. One of the features—and a major selling point—is the accessibility to editors and agents, most of them dealing with popular, mass market fiction. Appointments are often arranged for you before the conference begins, and the professionals expect you to present a book or concept (but there's nothing wrong with simply taking your few minutes to talk about anything you think the editor might be able to help you with). Most conferences advise writers not to bring manuscripts with them to the meeting; my recommendation is a bit different: Bring it, but don't offer it unless asked. (A chapter is usually enough; rarely will someone will take a manuscript with them but during the course of a conversation, we might want to get an idea of your writing.) Conferences are most often held in the spring and fall, but there's rarely a weekend during which nothing at all is happening. The list that follows is alphabetical, rather than by region, because, well, that's the way my address book is arranged.

Austin Writers' League, 1501 West Fifth Street, Suite E-2,
    Austin, TX 78703. Fall.
Craft of Writing, University of Texas, P.O. Box 830688,
    Richardson, TX 75083. Fall.
Detroit Women Writers Annual Writers Conference,
    Oakland University, Continuing Education,
    Rochester, MI 48309-4401. Fall.
Golden Triangle Writers Guild, 4245 Calder, Beaumont, TX 77706. Fall.
Jackson Hole Writing Workshops, Box 3972, University Station,
    WY 83001. July.
Oklahoma Writer's Federation, OWFI Conference, c/o Gordon
    Greenem 109 W. Kerr Drive, OKC, OK 73110-4529
    Please enclose an SASE. Spring.
Pennwriters Conference, 122 Westward Ho Drive,
    Pittsburgh, PA 15235. Spring.
Philadelphia Writers Conference, 28 Home Road,
    Hatboro, PA 19040-2026. Late spring.
Pike's Peak Writers Conference, 5550 North Union Avenue,
    Colorado Springs, CO 80918.
    Website: www.poboxes.com/ppwc email: ppwc@poboxes.com Spring.

Professional Writers Conference, University of Oklahoma, 1704
   Asp Avenue, Norman, OK 73037 Late spring.
Rocky Mountain Fiction Writers "Colorado Gold" Conference,
   P. O. Box 260244, Denver, CO 80226-0244 Fall.
Southwest Writers Workshop, P.O. Box 14632,
   Albuquerque, NM 87191 Fall.
Tennessee Mountain Writers Conference, P.O. Box 4895,
   Oak Ridge, TN 37831 (423) 482-6567
   email: tnmtnwrite@aol.com Spring.
The Writer's Club, Ltd., 405 N. Washington Street (#104),
   Falls Church, VA 22046 1-888-SCRIBES
   Website: www.writersclub.com An outgrowth of the web-based The
   Writer's Club, the group schedules conferences in various locations
   around the country and may conduct more than one a year.

Magazines and Markets

There are dozens of magazines devoted to writing and writers; the two most familiar are *Writer's Digest* and *The Writer*, both widely available at newsstands and libraries. As suggested previously, *Publishers Weekly*, is the one magazine all writers should read, but the subscription rates may be prohibitive for individuals. It's at all libraries, however, and is in the magazine racks at major bookstore chains. The address, for those interested, is 245 West 17th Street, New York, NY 10011.

Finally, marketing information. While the best source of information is the publication itself (and if you're writing something of interest to a particular magazine or publisher you're probably reading them regularly), researching markets is always worthwhile. There are more publications out there than we usually imagine and finding a less well-known but nonetheless suitable market is rewarding. *Writer's Digest* and *The Writer* both devote a section to listings in every issue; the *Writer's Digest* website (www.writersdigest.com) keeps a current list and offers a "market of the day." It's worth stopping by, just in case. Both magazines also publish annual market guides; unfortunately, especially when one is looking for magazines, those listings can become obsolete quickly, so it's always a good idea to check with the magazine or book publisher.

One of my favorites is *The Gila Queen's Guide to Markets* (P.O. Box 97, Newton, New Jersey 07860-0097; a website at www.pacifier.com/~alecwest/gila/). Published every six weeks, editor and publisher Kathryn Ptacek offers up-to-date information about markets, received not only from the publishers, but from a devoted readership as well.

A forty-year veteran of the publishing wars, MICHAEL SEIDMAN has been on the editorial side of the desk since 1970. Currently responsible for the mystery publishing program at Walker & Company, he has worked at various publishing houses and was the Editor-in-Chief of Mysterious Press and Editorial Director of Zebra/Pinnacle (now Kensington), and served for ten years as the editor of *The Armchair Detective*.

He's the author of two previous publishing books: *From Printout to Published* and *Living the Dream*; as well as countless articles for magazines like *Writer's Digest*, *The Writer*, *Bylines*, *Bookman's Weekly*, etc. A frequent guest lecturer at conferences and workshops, he also does a column for The Writer's Club, which appears on their website and on AOL, where he also monitors a board called *TalkBack—Ask the Editor*. (It is the most frequently posted to board in the writer's section.) He's been honored for his work as an editor, winning the 1987 American Mystery Award as best book editor (and was nominated two years later for his work as a horror editor); he was also named Editor of the Year by the Southwest Mystery and Suspense Convention. His fiction has appeared in a number of magazines and anthologies, including *Twilight Zone*, *Stalkers*, *The Black Lizard Anthology of Mystery* and *Crime Fiction*, and others.

Mr. Seidman lives in New York City with his wife and family.